GREAT COOKING
IN MINUTES

HOMECHEF® COOKING SCHOOLS

GREAT COOKING IN MINUTES

JUDITH ETS-HOKIN

CELESTIALARTS

Berkeley, California

Celestial Arts Publishing
P.O. Box 7123
Berkeley, California 94707

Jacket photos by Joshua Ets-Hokin
Cover and text design by David Charlsen
Page composition by Jeff Brandenburg/ImageComp

Printed in the United States of America

Library of Congress Cataloging-in-Publication Data

Ets-Hokin, Judith.
    Great cooking in minutes / by Judith Ets-Hokin.
       p.   cm.
    Includes index.
    ISBN 0-89087-746-7
    1. Quick and easy cookery. 2. Cookery, International. I. Title.
TX833.5.E87   1995
641.5′55—dc20   95-25222
                                                         CIP

First Printing, 1995

1 2 3 4 5 / 99 98 97 96 95

TABLE OF CONTENTS

ACKNOWLEDGMENTS

I am grateful first of all to the HomeChef students, past and present, for whom these recipes were originally created.

And, in more or less chronological order, to David Charlsen, my dear friend and designer of this book; David Hinds, my publisher, who has been so supportive throughout the years; Jackie Wan, my editor, who is the most "picky" person I know; Kelly Miller, who diligently went through hundreds of recipe files to find "the best"; Rebecca Ets-Hokin, my daughter and Director of the HomeChef Cooking School, who contributed many of her own wonderful recipes; Susan Weymouth, who would drop everything at a moment's notice to test a recipe here and there; and to my family and friends who have been so encouraging and tolerant. Without them, this book would not exist.

INTRODUCTION

When I started the HomeChef Cooking School, many years ago, I had no idea, no plan, no sense of where it might take me. I started giving cooking lessons in my kitchen because I needed a way to support my three young children and myself, and home cooking and entertaining was the only skill I had developed. A friend had told me how much she admired and loved my cooking and the relaxed way I could give a dinner party. She said she'd be happy to gather a group of her friends together if I would be willing to give a few lessons.

So there I was, with eight or ten young married women gathered around my kitchen table, watching me prepare a dinner party for six or eight people. Because we all had young children, I provided a baby sitter for them in an adjacent room for the two hours it took me to give the class. Still, the children interrupted us frequently, and there were always a few problems to solve. I didn't realize it at the time, of course, but that experience was the real inspiration for this cookbook. Whatever I presented in those classes, I *had* to be able to prepare it in minutes. The children made that imperative!

In those days, housewives were looking for more sophisticated, more complicated recipes than were generally available to them. The typical cookbook of the time was full of boring and simplistic recipes — two or three cans of creamed soup combined with a few boxes of frozen anything, perked up with some fresh ingredients to make the latest party fare. Sophisticated food preparation was confined to restaurants, where all the chefs were men.

After achieving some success teaching in my home, I went to a local professional cooking school to discuss the possibility of my teaching a course especially for the home cook. They laughed at my request. A male chef who sampled some of my cooking told me that it was good, but not great, because "women don't have the developed taste buds men have, and that's the reason there are no famous women chefs." Well that made me mad, and I became determined to prove him wrong. (He was, by the way.)

I had traveled extensively in Europe and Asia and acquired a taste for fine food, and the desire to create it on my own. I learned to cook by reading everything I could find on the art of cooking, taking classes, and practicing and practicing in my own kitchen. When I started teaching, it added another dimension to my cooking. For one thing, as I said earlier, I realized that I had to speed things up. So I learned to go to the essence of every recipe, to simplify the steps and ingredients without sacrificing quality. The more I cooked, and the more I taught, the less intimidated I was by the complicated recipes of the gourmet chefs. Soon I could honestly say that I could teach anyone to cook the classic dishes, with one major difference. I could show them how to do it quickly and easily.

My classes grew, and I published my first book, *The San Francisco Dinner Party Cookbook,* in 1975. About that time, I moved the cooking school to a commercial location in San Francisco because my classes had outgrown my kitchen by then.

As each new session of classes began, I noticed that the same questions and concerns would come up over and over again. Basically, my students wanted to be able to duplicate the dishes that were being served in the fancier restaurants. I began to concentrate on taking professional cooking techniques and adapting them to the home kitchen. It took ten years! The result was the HomeChef Basic Cooking Series which was an instant success, and remains the most popular course at our school.

Out of this course came my second book, *The HomeChef: Fine Cooking Made Simple* in which I attempted to cover everything the home cook needs to know in order to become a great home chef. It includes information on equipment, ingredients, food terms, and basic cooking methods and techniques. It has lots of recipes in it, but the emphasis is on *how* and *why* things work.

Great Cooking in Minutes is a sequel to *The HomeChef,* and is, in essence, a compendium of our students' favorite recipes. Most are my own adaptations of classic recipes, but a few were contributed by friends or other teachers at our school. All have been used in our classes, over and over again. Most recipes average about thirty minutes, none takes more than sixty minutes of preparation time, excluding time for unsupervised cooking, resting, or chilling. *Great Cooking in Minutes* doesn't go into detail on techniques. If you want to learn about a method in depth, I confidently refer you to *The HomeChef.*

I have always loved cooking for many reasons. One of them is the solitary pleasure of preparing food and the process of making something with your hands. Another is the excitement and fun of bringing a dish to the table for family and friends, and watching their enjoyment as they savor each bite. I have always felt, too, that the sensual aspect of cooking — the aroma, feel, and taste of ingredients — connects me to the natural world in a way that is invigorating and healing. For me, cooking is an antidote to the technical, split-second pace of our world. I hope that this book will enable you to experience the same pleasure and delight I feel every time I make and serve another great dish!

YOUR KITCHEN

People are always telling me, apologetically, that they can't cook very well because their kitchen is too small. Actually, a small kitchen is much easier to work in than a large kitchen where everything is all spread out. If you have to walk eight feet from the refrigerator to the sink to wash vegetables, then eight feet to the cook top, and cross back and forth a few more times to find a knife, or a cutting board, or the olive oil, you're wasting time and effort. The ideal is to have approximately three feet from any work center to any other work center.

Of course, most of us have to live with the physical layout of our kitchens, but there is a lot that can be done to make any kitchen more efficient. The key is *organization*. Just think of your kitchen in terms of a factory assembly line — analyze the tasks you perform most frequently, and store the tools you need for each task above or below the work space in which you would perform that task, keeping like things together, and removing the tools you don't need.

So, when you set up your kitchen, put all your knives together in a knife holder on top of the counter or in a drawer next to your cutting board, all your small tools should be together hanging on the backsplash behind your work area or in a drawer below, baking equipment (cake pans, bread pans, baking sheets, cookie cutters, etc.), together in a cabinet or drawer, next to all the mixing equipment (bowls, electric mixer, etc.), next to all the measuring equipment. Keep frequently used pieces of equipment, like your electric mixer and food processor, out on the counter or easily accessible. If you have to pull a piece of equipment out of a remote closet each time you need to use it, you will be less inclined to do so.

Probably the most important area to organize is the food preparation center. If you have to bend over or climb up on a stool to retrieve your cutting board, then haul it to the sink for cleaning when you finish, then hunt around for a peeler, a knife, and a garlic press, you may never get started. For your preparation area, a built in 18- by 36-inch chopping board is ideal. If that's not possible, get a portable board that size and leave it out on top of the counter all the time.

If you organize your kitchen in a logical, uncomplicated fashion, I think you will find that simple tasks such as peeling, slicing, and chopping will become a pleasurable experience.

BASIC EQUIPMENT

Following is a list of equipment you need to prepare the recipes in this book, with the exception of a few specialized items that are explained in individual recipes. For a comprehensive discussion on kitchen equipment, refer to *The Home Chef* cookbook where you will find a whole chapter devoted to the basic kitchen, with photographs of tools and equipment, and details on materials and construction.

POTS AND PANS

Saucepans   1½-quart, 2½-quart, 4½-quart, and 6-quart saucepans with covers. A 1-quart double boiler is also recommended, and remember that each part can be used separately.

Steamer basket   to fit one of your saucepans — the size depends upon the amount of food you usually steam.

Soup or stockpot   an 8-, 10-, or 12-quart pot with cover.

Skillets   8-, 10-, and 12-inch skillets. Covers can be purchased separately if you want them.

Saute pans   10- or 12-inch with cover. Similar to skillets except they are straight-sided.

Roasting pans 10×14 and 17×12 inches, and a roasting rack (one rack will do for both).

Casseroles   a 2½-quart and a 6-quart casserole, oval, round, or rectangular, both with covers.

Baking sheets 11×15-inch flat; 11×15-inch with sides (a jelly-roll pan).

Cake pans   8-, 9- and 10-inch round pans; 9×9-inch square, and 9×13-inch rectangular pans.

Pie plates   9-inch, 10-inch.

Tart pans   a 9-inch, with removable-bottom.

KNIVES

Chopping knife   8 to 12 inches long, with sturdy angled blade and a raised handle to allow clearance for knuckles. You will use it for all kinds of chopping.

Carving knife   8 to 10 inches long, with narrow blade, for slicing boneless meats.

Paring knife   2 to 3½ inches long, with a sharp, tapered, or blunt point. You will use this versatile knife so much for paring vegetables and fruits, etc., that you might as well buy two.

Serrated bread knife   also good for cutting tomatoes and cakes.

Curved serrated knife   sometimes called a grapefruit knife, used for hollowing out fruits and vegetables that are to be stuffed, and for separating the segments of citrus fruits.

Sharpening steel   Use to maintain the edge on all straight-edged knives. It is a good idea to have your knives professionally sharpened once a year or so.

SMALL TOOLS AND ACCESSORIES

baster (basting bulb)
cheesecloth
cherry and olive pitter
citrus zester
colanders
corers (apple, tomato)
flour sifter
garlic press
grater
ladles
measuring cups
measuring spoons
meat pounder
melon baller
nutmeg grater
oyster/clam knife
parchment paper
pastry blender

pastry brushes
peeler
pepper grinder
potato masher
rolling pin
salad spinner
scissors, kitchen
shrimp deveiner
sieves, fine and coarse
skimmer
spatulas
spoons, wooden and metal, for mixing
thermometer, "instant read" for meats
thermometer, candy-deep-fry
tongs, spring-action
wire whisks, 8-inch sauce and 12-inch balloon
wooden skewers, in 2 lengths

OTHER EQUIPMENT

Mixing bowls   A graduated set of four or five bowls—glass, stoneware, or metal.
Cutting board   At least 18 × 24-inch.
Electric food processor   Highly recommended. Use it to chop, mix, slice, grate, and *purée*. If you own a heavy duty food processor, a blender is not necessary.
Electric mixer   Highly recommended. A heavy-duty 5-quart bowl capacity mixer is best.
Electric blender
Food mill
Spice grinder or mortar and pestle
Kitchen scale   For really accurate measurements of dry ingredients, a scale marked for both grams and ounces is recommended.
Baker's stone   Sometimes referred to as pizza stones or pizza bricks. Flat, stoneware bricks that you place inside your oven. Bread and pizza can be baked directly on them. I leave one on the lowest rack of the oven all the time because it keeps the oven temperature more constant, and everything cooks more evenly.
Copper beating bowl   A 10-inch unlined copper bowl. Not absolutely essential, but excellent for whisking egg whites — they expand more quickly, gain greater volume, and are more stable.

Your Pantry

The meals I have the most fun preparing are the ones I can make from start to finish *without* going to the grocery store. Sometimes I leave work late, too tired to stop off at the grocery store, or sometimes after a relaxing day at home, shopping is the last thing I want to do. On those days, it's a relief to be able to go to my refrigerator, freezer, or pantry and find everything I need to put together a really delicious meal. Having a well-stocked pantry, I think, is one of the keys to *Great Cooking in Minutes*. I tell my classes to think of their pantry like their wardrobes — keep a selection of foods on hand as you would keep clothing in the closet, waiting for the right occasion.

IN THE REFRIGERATOR

Dairy products   Milk, eggs, and cheese — Parmigiano-Reggiano, Gruyère, a blue cheese such as Roquefort or gorgonzola, and an extra sharp cheddar.
Produce   Green onions, flat-leaf parsley, salad greens, carrots *with* their tops intact, celery, and fresh ginger.
Salad dressings   Homemade vinaigrette (p. 103), at least a week's supply.
Mustards   Keep a Dijon mustard, a hot and sweet mustard, and a dill mustard on hand at a minimum. Mustards can be added to spur of the moment sauces, salad dressings, and simply used on their own to spice up cold meats or fish. Mustard can also be added to mayonnaise on a one-to-one basis for a very quick and delicious dipping sauce for vegetables.
Mayonnaise   Even though I like to make my own, I also keep a jar of good-quality commercially made mayonnaise on hand to be used as a base for other sauces, such as horseradish or mustard sauce.

IN THE FREEZER

Beef, Veal, Chicken or Vegetable Stock   Whether you make it yourself or not, never be without it. There is no substitute! Freeze it in quantities that are most useful for you. If you mostly use it in smaller quantities, freeze it in ice cube trays and pop the cubes out into plastic bags for storage. Stock is used as the basis for soups, stews, and many sauces.
Butter   Always use unsalted butter. Salt is a preservative, and since unsalted butter contains none, it must be stored in the freezer.
Breads   Wrapped well, French and Italian breads with a lot of crust will last several weeks in the freezer. To serve, dampen the outside of the loaf with a little water and place in a 300° oven, for approximately 15 minutes.
Filled pasta   Ravioli, tortellini, agnolotti, preferably from Italy. Available in fancy food markets. An excellent meal in about 1 minute.
Meats   Bacon, pancetta, sausages, and ground meat.
Vegetables   Tiny peas, corn, and spinach: the only frozen vegetables I would consider using. Not a substitute for fresh, but good to have on hand in a pinch. Great for adding to soups, chiles, stews, and bean or rice dishes. They do not need to be cooked for the time recommended on the box — just a minute or two will do.
Tomato sauce   Homemade, of course. Can be heated and tossed with pasta for an almost instant meal
Frozen fruit   Cherries, raspberries, blueberries, frozen without syrup.
Applesauce   Homemade, of course. Can be warmed and served with chocolate sauce for a fabulous quick dessert.
Nuts   Hazelnuts, walnuts, and almonds. Storing them in the freezer keeps them from going rancid. They are great in salads, or to garnish vegetables, and of course in cakes and other desserts. You can freshen them up by toasting them in a low oven for 5 to 10 minutes before using.

Pastry dough   Wrapped well, plain pastries, or puff pastry you make yourself, store well in the freezer. There are also some very good frozen commercial doughs available in gourmet food markets. Frozen doughs defrost very quickly.

Whole wheat flour   Since it still contains the germ, whole wheat flour turns rancid after a couple of months on the shelf, and should be stored in the freezer.

Bread crumbs   Always good to have on hand, since all kinds of leftovers can be made into croquettes with bread crumbs as a binder.

Bones   Keep a large plastic bag in the freezer, where you can store bones as you acquire them until you have enough to make stock.

IN THE PANTRY

Flour   Unbleached white flour
Baking powder
Baking soda
Cornstarch
Sweeteners   Granulated sugar, brown sugar, confectioners' sugar, superfine sugar, honey.

Oils   Extra-virgin olive oil — for salad dressings and to cook with. Hazelnut and walnut oil, unprocessed, unfiltered — for salad dressings, to marinate and cook meats, fish, and poultry; or to use sparingly to dress cooked green vegetables. Rice bran, avocado, and grape seed oils are excellent when you want an oil that is tasteless and has a high smoking point. All oils should be kept in a cool dark place, rather than in the refrigerator.

Vinegars   Balsamic vinegar — from Italy, this special aged vinegar is fabulous in salad dressings, sauces, on strawberries, or in marinades for meats and fish. Buy the oldest one you can afford. In addition, you should have on hand sherry vinegar, imported from Spain, and red and white wine vinegars. Make sure you are buying pure vinegars, not the watered down variety. The label should indicate at least 6% acidity.

Spices, herbs, and seasonings   Fine and coarse sea salt, white, black, and green peppercorns, whole nutmeg, chile powder, curry powder, cumin, turmeric, Hungarian paprika, saffron threads, cinnamon sticks, ground cinnamon, coriander seeds, dried oregano, dried tarragon, sesame seeds, bay leaves, cloves, juniper berries, dry mustard, Tabasco sauce.

Flavorings   vanilla extract or powder, almond extract or powder, powdered espresso, unsweetened cocoa, and a vanilla bean buried in sugar.

Chocolate   Bittersweet, semisweet, unsweetened, and white chocolate. Kept in a cool dark place, fine-quality cooking chocolate actually improves with age.

Tomatoes   Vacuum-packed vine-ripened tomatoes from Italy are an essential staple in my pantry. They come chopped and puréed: keep several boxes of each. They can be substituted for fresh tomatoes in almost all the recipes in this book. Once opened, store any leftovers in the refrigerator.

Tomato paste   I use tomato paste in tubes, imported from Italy. Tomato paste is usually used in small quantities, so opening up a can always seemed so wasteful. Once opened, store in the refrigerator.

Beans and lentils   Keep black beans, pinto beans, lentils, and small white beans on hand for soups, chiles, and casseroles.

Dried pastas   Keep a variety of pastas on hand such as penne, spaghetti, linguine, and fettuccine. I like the pasta imported from Italy.

Rice   All rice keeps very well on the shelf. Keep on hand: Arborio rice, to make risottos and paella; long-grained white and brown rice and wild rice.

Cornmeal or Polenta   Stores very well and can be cooked quickly as an accompaniment to vegetables, meats and sausage (page 123).

Couscous   Purchased in boxes, it keeps very well, and can be cooked quickly and eaten alone or served with meat or vegetable stews.

Pickles   A jar of tiny sweet gherkins or French *cornichons*. Can be served with pâtés, chopped up in potato, egg, or ham salads, or used in sauces for meats and fish.

Dried mushrooms   My favorite are porcini imported from Italy (domestic porcini do not have the flavor). Also useful are dried morels, chanterelles, and shiitakes. Keep one or two ounces of each on hand, ready to be reconstituted and added to a quick pasta dish, a stew or sauce.

Sun-dried tomatoes. Packed in oil.

Raisins   And other dried fruits, such as apricots, currants, etc.

Soy sauce   Even if you do not prepare Oriental dishes, soy sauce can be added in small amounts (a teaspoon or less) to salad dressings, soups, sautéed vegetables, especially mushrooms, and stews.

Tabasco sauce

Spirits   White wine, red wine, Marsala, sherry, Madeira, vermouth, Grand Marnier (or other orange-flavored liqueur).

Vegetable and fruit bin   Lemons, onions, garlic, shallots, baking potatoes, boiling potatoes.

GROWING YOUR OWN

Herbs   Most herbs actually thrive on neglect, so you don't need a green thumb. If you don't have a garden, you can grow herbs in containers on a balcony or on a sunny window sill. A few easy-to-grow herbs that I consider essential are flat-leaf parsley, tarragon, oregano, mint, rosemary.

Lemons   Dwarf lemon trees do well in containers, so even if you're limited to a deck garden, you can grow your own lemons. Freshly picked lemons are incomparable. As a bonus, the leaves can be used for garnish, and the blossoms will create a fantasy of fragrance for you every spring.

Salad greens   This requires a little more time and work, but is well worth it. Try buying flats of two or three varieties of lettuces and planting them out in your garden. My special trick is to pick lettuce the same afternoon it is to be served, rinse it, crisp it, and serve it. It's an experience that cannot be duplicated with store-bought varieties.

THE BASICS

I've gathered some of the recipes and methods I consider "basic," and put them all here in one short chapter. I have started with Stocks, probably the most often used basic in cooking. There is no substitute for a good home made stock, and I suggest you keep a supply on hand; make it up in large amounts, and freeze it in convenient quantities. Next, there is a Basic Tomato Sauce with a lot of versatility, and a recipe for créme fraîche for those who are unable to find it at the market. If you want to "Make It Light," there are exact instructions for making Yogurt Cheese, a substitute for rich cream products. There are two methods for making croutons, instructions for toasting spices and nuts, and how to make clarified butter. Finally, I have explained the method for reconstituting dried mushrooms. I think that you'll use these recipes so often that, after a short time, you will probably not have to refer to this chapter at all. You will know your basics by heart!

If you want your stock to be flavored by chicken only, use all chicken bones, or for a stronger beef flavor, use all beef bones. The more veal bones you use, the more gelatinous the stock will be. You can also use the carcass and cooked scraps of a roasted chicken, turkey, or duck.

BEEF, VEAL, OR CHICKEN STOCK

Makes about 1 to 2 quarts

6 pounds bones (beef shanks or neck bones, veal shanks or neck bones, chicken necks and/or backs)
1 onion, peeled, and stuck with 6 cloves
2 carrots, cleaned and cut into 4 pieces

2 stalks of celery, cleaned and cut into 4 pieces
¼ bunch parsley, chopped coarsely, stems included
a bouquet garni

1. Place all the ingredients into a large stock or soup pot and add enough cold water to cover. Bring very slowly to the boil, and skim off the surface foam. Turn the heat down as low as possible, cover partially and simmer 3 to 4 hours, depending upon how strong you want the stock.
2. Strain the stock through a coarse sieve, then through a fine sieve or cheesecloth, and chill at least 8 hours.
3. Remove the congealed fat formed on top of the stock. Store the stock in the refrigerator for 3 or 4 days, or in the freezer for up to 6 months.

BROWN STOCK

Follow the directions for making stock above, but first roast the bones and vegetables on a baking sheet in a 350° oven until browned.

CONCENTRATED STOCK

Follow the directions for making stock above, strain, chill, and remove all the congealed fat. Simmer the stock over a medium-low heat, and reduce slowly to approximately ⅓ or less of its original volume. Pour into containers, label, and store in the refrigerator or freezer.

You can use any vegetables to make your stock, but be aware that some — cabbage, broccoli, and Brussels sprouts, for instance — are very strong-flavored, and should be used in small amounts, or they may overpower the stock.

VEGETABLE STOCK OR BROTH
Makes about 2 quarts

3 leeks, cleaned and thinly sliced
3 stalks celery, cleaned and cut into
  3 pieces each
3 onions, thinly sliced
6 carrots, cleaned and cut into
  3 pieces each
1 bunch Swiss chard, cleaned and
  coarsely chopped

1 head lettuce, cleaned and coarsely
  chopped
½ bunch parsley with stems, coarsely
  chopped
  a bouquet garni
1 bay leaf

1. Place all the ingredients into a large stock or soup pot with enough water to cover Bring slowly to a boil, skim, lower the heat, cover partially, and simmer for 1 hour.
2. Strain the stock through a very fine strainer or cheesecloth, without pressing any of the vegetables through the strainer. Store in the refrigerator for up to 3 days, or in the freezer for up to 3 months.

Fish Stock can be used as the base for sauces and many fish soups and as a poaching medium for fish. The fish used to make the stock should be compatible with the dish in which the stock is to be used.

FISH STOCK
Makes about 1 to 1½ quarts

2 pounds white fish heads and bones,
  rinsed in cold water
1 onion, peeled and left whole
1 shallot, peeled and left whole
1 carrot, cleaned and cut into 3 pieces

  a handful of celery tops, cleaned
  a bouquet garni
1 cup dry white table wine
  cold water to cover

1. Place the fish parts, onion, shallot, carrot, celery tops, bouquet garni, and wine in a large stock or soup pot. Add enough water to cover, and bring very slowly to the boil. Skim off the surface foam, turn the heat down as low as possible, partially cover and simmer 30 minutes.
2. Strain through a coarse sieve, then through a fine sieve or cheesecloth. Store in the refrigerator for up to 2 days, or in the freezer for up to 2 months.

This sauce goes well with pasta, rice, boiled meats, hamburgers, and meat loaf. Herbs, garlic, onions, or wine may be added when desired. When tomatoes are not in season, substitute with vacuum-packed Italian tomatoes.

TOMATO SAUCE

Makes about 2 cups

2 tablespoons extra virgin olive oil
1 stalk celery, coarsely chopped
1 carrot, coarsely chopped
2 shallots, peeled and coarsely chopped
2½ pounds ripe tomatoes, coarsely chopped

2 tablespoons tomato paste
1 cup Beef or Brown Stock (page 12)
1 teaspoon each fine sea salt, pepper, and sugar

Heat the oil in a saucepan, and sauté the celery, carrot, and shallots over medium heat for 5 minutes. Add the tomatoes, tomato paste, and stock, and simmer gently until thickened, about 35 to 40 minutes. Season with salt, pepper, and sugar. For a smooth sauce, pass it through a coarse sieve or food mill. Store in the refrigerator or freezer.

CRÈME FRAÎCHE

I love the taste of crème fraîche, and use it a lot in my cooking, in place of sour cream or heavy cream. It is particularly good in soups and sauces because it does not curdle when boiled. It is slightly tart, somewhere between whipped cream and sour cream, but with a unique taste of its own. It is available in specialty markets and gourmet food stores. If you cannot find it anywhere and would like to make your own, the following is fairly close to the real thing.

To prepare Crème Fraîche: Combine 1 cup whipping cream and ½ cup buttermilk or sour cream in a jar, cover, and let stand in a warm place for 12 hours, then refrigerate. If you have a yogurt maker, proceed as though you were making yogurt. It will keep about 10 days in the refrigerator.

YOGURT CHEESE

Many of the "Make It Light" suggestions throughout this book are based on substituting Yogurt Cheese for sour cream, crème fraîche, or whipping cream. Yogurt Cheese is very simple to make, all you need is a yogurt strainer (widely available in kitchen stores) and some yogurt. Yogurt Cheese made from plain yogurt is mildly tart. You can add ½ teaspoon of maple syrup to each cup of Yogurt Cheese to offset this natural tartness. Another option is to make the Yogurt Cheese with vanilla-flavored yogurt. The result will be a slightly sweet product that makes a good substitute for cream cheese. You can use regular, low-fat or nonfat yogurt. Just check the label to be sure the yogurt contains no gelatin or thickeners.

To prepare Yogurt Cheese: Place the yogurt strainer over a container to catch the whey that will drain out of the yogurt. Put yogurt with **no gelatin or thickeners added** into the yogurt strainer, and refrigerate for 24 hours until reduced by approximately half. For a firmer, thicker result, drain yogurt for 3 days. Transfer the Yogurt Cheese to a covered container and store in the refrigerator. The whey that drains from the yogurt can be used in any recipe calling for milk.

Croutons are toasted or sautéed cubes or slices of bread and are a standard garnish for soups and salads. Raw garlic is sometimes rubbed over the bread before it is toasted or sautéed. Depending on the soup or salad they are to accompany, you can use all butter or all olive oil to prepare them rather than a combination. If a recipe does not specify, you can choose your own options. For best results, use day-old bread.

CROUTONS

4 slices day-old French or Italian bread   4 ounces unsalted butter, melted
2 or 3 cloves garlic (optional)   ¼ cup olive oil

Rub the bread with garlic, if desired; cut into ¼-inch cubes or leave the slices whole. Combine the melted butter and olive oil. To toast, place the bread on a baking sheet, brush with the butter and oil, and toast in a preheated 375° oven until pale brown, about 5 to 7 minutes. To sauté, heat the butter and oil over medium heat in a large skillet, and sauté the bread until pale brown (slices should be turned once, cubes need to be stirred to brown evenly).

TOASTED NUTS AND SPICES

Spread the nuts or spices on a baking sheet or jelly-roll pan. Roast in a preheated 300° oven for 5 to 10 minutes. Watch carefully to prevent burning.

CLARIFIED BUTTER

Clarified butter is butter which has the milk solids removed, leaving only the pure butterfat. It is used for sautéing foods because it has a higher smoking point than unclarified butter. Properly stored, it will keep for months.

To prepare Clarified Butter: Melt unsalted butter slowly over low heat, allow to stand 5 minutes, and carefully skim off the foam floating on top. Strain through a fine sieve. Store in the refrigerator or freezer.

WILD MUSHROOMS

Dried wild mushrooms are more intensely flavored than fresh. Once reconstituted, they may be combined with cultivated mushrooms to simulate fresh wild mushrooms. Use about 1 ounce dried combined with 12 ounces fresh cultivated mushrooms to simulate 1 pound fresh wild mushrooms. To reconstitute dried mushrooms, soak in warm water for 1 hour. Rinse to remove any sand. The soaking water is often used, as it has a lot of flavor. It should be strained before using.

NOTES TO THE READER

Please read over each recipe before you get started to see if you have all ingredients on hand, and to see if you need to allow time for soaking, marinating, chilling, etc. More important though, there is a "Make It Light" section at the end of most recipes which give options for reducing the fat content of the dish, and a "Make It Ahead" section, too, to help you plan your time. You need to consider all this beforehand.

There are a few ingredients that I call for repeatedly that you may have a little difficulty finding, especially if you do not live in a large city. I urge you to make every effort to obtain those ingredients, but if they are not available to you, here are some easily found substitutes:

extra virgin olive oil	virgin or pure olive oil
Parmigiano-Reggiano	domestic Parmesan cheese
pancetta	bacon
crème fraîche	heavy cream
sea salt	ordinary table salt

In general, it is not necessary to be absolutely precise in measuring ingredients. In fact, this is where the creativity comes in. The exception is in baking, where exact measurements can be critical. Where accuracy is important, ingredients are given by weight first, followed by the volume measure (in cups or teaspoons). If you do not have a kitchen scale, use the cup measure.

Because so many of the recipes can be either first courses, side dishes, or main courses, the serving sizes are approximate.

Finally, if there is a term or ingredient with which you are not familiar, look for it in the glossary.

APPETIZERS AND FIRST COURSES

To me, an appetizer is like the overture before a musical or an opera — it sets the stage for what is to come, creating a little excitement, and stimulating the appetite, rather than satisfying it. The appetizer can be a single dish that is served at the table before the main course, a "first" course, but more often than not, appetizers are an assortment of tidbits or finger foods that are served more informally before your guests come to the table. Sometimes, the entire menu at a party is made up of nothing but appetizers, and guests "graze" all evening, eating small amounts here and there when they feel like it.

In this chapter you will find dishes that would make imaginative first courses for more formal dining, some delicious tidbits meant for more casual occasions, as well as some recipes that could fill either role.

PÂTÉS AND TERRINES

Nowadays the words *pâté* and *terrine* are used interchangeably to indicate any molded, loaf-shaped preparation that is dense enough to be sliced. Originally, *terrine* was defined as a deep, straight-sided earthenware casserole with a lid. The meaning gradually stretched to include the ground meat concoctions that are typically baked in a terrine. The word *pâté*, is thought to come from the French word for pastry, and strictly speaking refers to a pastry-wrapped meat loaf. A meat loaf, then, is a terrine, and meat pie is a pâté, but only from an academic point of view. Call them what you wish, pâtés and terrines are served cold as appetizers, first courses, or as light luncheons or suppers. They are often accompanied by tiny gherkins called *cornichons* and crusty French bread and butter. Ready-made pâtés and terrines can be purchased in fancy food markets and gourmet delicatessens, but at HomeChef our students like to make their own.

To make the following pâtés and terrines, you can use any shape 6- or 8-cup terrine with cover, although oblong or oval shapes are classic. If the terrine is to be baked, don't overfill the mold, as the terrine will swell a little as it bakes. Bake the terrine in a water bath (that is, set it in a larger container that is half-filled with water). The water diffuses the direct heat around the bottom of the mold. The final step is to place a weight on top of it. As the terrine cools, this weight compresses it, giving it its characteristic dense texture and making it easy to slice.

If possible, have the butcher grind all the meats for this pâté. Otherwise put them through a meat grinder or chop in your food processor. They should have the texture of coarse raw hamburger.

HOMECHEF'S FAVORITE PÂTÉ

Serves 12 to 15 as a first course; 24 to 30 as an appetizer

1 tablespoon clarified butter
1 pound pork loin, cut into 1-inch cubes
½ teaspoon each coarse sea salt, freshly ground pepper, and dried thyme
4 ounces chicken livers
¼ cup Madeira
3 shallots, finely chopped
1 pound coarsely ground pork

1 pound coarsely ground veal
1 tablespoon coarse sea salt, or to taste
½ teaspoon each freshly ground pepper, dried thyme, and allspice
3 tablespoons chopped fresh flat-leaf parsley
3 tablespoons crème fraîche
2 eggs, lightly beaten

1. Heat the butter in a skillet over high heat and brown the pork cubes. Season with salt, pepper, and thyme, and remove from the skillet. Add the chicken livers and sauté for 1 minute; add the Madeira and shallots, cook 2 minutes more, and remove from the heat.
2. In a large mixing bowl, combine the ground pork, veal, seasonings, parsley, crème fraîche, and eggs. Mix well. Add the sautéed mixture from step 1 and thoroughly combine. Sauté 2 tablespoons of the pâté in order to taste for seasonings. Correct accordingly.
3. Pack into a 6- or 8-cup oval or rectangular casserole and cover; place in a water bath, and bake in a 350° preheated oven for 2 hours or until the fat and juices which will have risen to the top are clear yellow. Remove the terrine from the oven, uncover, and allow to cool 30 minutes.
4. Loosely cover the mold with foil and place a weight on top (a foil-covered brick works well). Refrigerate at least 1 day with the weight. If you wish, remove any white fat that may have accumulated on top of the pâté. Unmold, cut into ¼-inch-thick slices, and serve with crusty bread and *cornichons*.

Make It Light: Substitute ground turkey for the ground pork, and use only 1 egg.

Make It Ahead: A minimum of 1 day, and up to 3 days.

This recipe calls for the tender pale rabbit meat to be marinated to intensify its special flavor. Then the terrine is mixed together and assembled in the mold with the two tenderloins buried in the middle. You will not know until you slice and serve this marvelous traditional terrine what an artistic effect you have created. The spectacular results will be your reward! If possible, have the butcher grind all the meats. Otherwise put them through a meat grinder or process in your food processor. They should have the texture of coarse raw hamburger.

RABBIT TERRINE

Serves 8 as a first course; 16 as an appetizer

1 rabbit	1 cup cognac
8 ounces ground pork	2 eggs, lightly beaten
12 to 14 slices bacon, blanched 1 minute	2 teaspoons coarse sea salt, or more to taste
1 teaspoon dried thyme	1 bay leaf
3 tablespoons chopped parsley	
freshly ground pepper to taste	

1. Ask the butcher to leave the rabbit tenderloins whole, and to grind up 1 pound of the remaining rabbit meat with the rabbit liver (the bones and remaining meat can be used to make an excellent stock). Put the ground meats in a bowl, along with the tenderloins, blanched bacon, thyme, parsley, and pepper. Pour the cognac over all, and marinate overnight.

2. Lift the bacon slices out of the bowl, and line a 5- or 6-cup oval or rectangular terrine with the marinated bacon strips, leaving the ends hanging over the sides to be folded over the top. Remove the tenderloins and set aside. Add the eggs and salt to the ground meats and cognac and mix well. Sauté 2 tablespoons of the mixture in order to test seasonings; taste and adjust accordingly. Fill about half the mold with ground meat, lay the 2 tenderloins on top, then cover the tenderloins with the remainder of the ground meat. Place the bay leaf on top, fold the bacon over it and cover.

3. Set the covered mold in a water bath and bake in a preheated 350° oven for 1½ hours, or until the juices run clear. Remove the terrine from the oven, uncover, and allow to cool 30 minutes.

4. Loosely cover the mold with foil and place a weight on top (a foil-covered brick works well). Refrigerate at least 1 day with the weight to develop the flavor. Remove any white fat that may have accumulated on top of the pâté. Unmold, cut into ¼-inch-thick slices, and serve with crusty bread and *cornichons*.

Make It Light: Substitute ground turkey for the ground pork, and use 1 egg only.

Make It Ahead: A minimum of 1 day, and up to 3 days.

I developed the following terrine to accommodate HomeChef students who requested a lighter, meatless terrine. This one would make a lovely, elegant, beginning for any meal. (Please note that this is one of the few terrines that is *not* weighted down when it is chilled.) When you unmold this terrine, discard excess juices that accumulate as the terrine chills.

SEAFOOD AND VEGETABLE TERRINE
WITH TOMATO SAUCE

Serves 8 as a first course

1½ pounds cod, halibut, or snapper, puréed in a food processor or blender
1 teaspoon fine sea salt, or to taste
1½ teaspoons freshly ground white pepper, or to taste
¼ cup vermouth
2 eggs, lightly beaten
1 cup crème fraîche

½ bunch watercress, stems removed, leaves blanched and patted dry
3 large artichoke bottoms, cooked until soft
8 ounces fresh green beans, cooked until soft
Tomato Sauce (p. 14)

1. Combine the puréed fish, salt, pepper, and vermouth, and mix well; add the eggs and crème fraîche, a little at a time, whisking after each addition until the mixture is light and fluffy. Place one-third of the puréed fish mixture and the watercress in the bowl of a food processor or blender and process until well combined and pale green in color, with tiny bits of watercress remaining. Reserve remaining two thirds of purée.
2. Lightly butter the sides of a 6-cup terrine, and line the bottom with parchment. Spread a layer of the green fish purée over the bottom. Place the artichoke bottoms in a row on top of the fish mixture, then spread a layer of white fish purée over the artichokes, using about half of it. Follow this with a layer of green beans, and a final layer of fish purée smoothed on over all.
3. Cover the terrine, place in a water bath, and bake in a preheated 375° oven for 30 minutes. Allow terrine to cool, chill overnight, unmold, and discard the accumulated juices. To serve, spoon a little Tomato Sauce on each serving plate, and lay two overlapping slices of the terrine on top of the sauce.

Make It Light: Substitute ½ cup Yogurt Cheese (p. 14) for ½ cup of the crème fraîche.

Make It Ahead: Needs to made **the day before to allow for thorough chilling.**

This terrine is very light and quite simple to make (unlike most other terrines, this one has very few ingredients, and it is not baked). It is the perfect first course of a very rich meal.

LEEK TERRINE WITH RASPBERRY WALNUT VINAIGRETTE

Serves 8 as a first course

12 leeks (about 4 pounds)

about 1 cup Raspberry Walnut Vinaigrette sauce (p. 103)

1. Clean and trim the leeks, leaving them whole so they will stay intact while cooking. Cook the leeks in enough salted boiling water to cover for about 10 minutes, until barely tender. Drain well.

2. Line the bottom of a rectangular 1½-quart terrine with parchment paper. Arrange a layer of leeks in the casserole with the white portions at one end. Arrange a second layer, with the white portions at the opposite end. Continue to fill the terrine in this manner—you will have about 4 layers. Cover with parchment, then weight the terrine (a foil-covered brick works well), and refrigerate overnight.

3. Before unmolding the terrine, drain away the accumulated juices. Unmold the terrine onto a serving dish. Trim the ends if necessary, and cut into thick slices. Spoon the vinaigrette over the slices to serve.

Make It Ahead: You can make this up to 2 days in advance.

DIPS AND SPREADS

The dips and spreads that follow could all be served with your favorite crackers or chips, or with raw vegetables, but for a nice party atmosphere, try serving them on rounds of raw cucumber or zucchini, roasted potatoes, or toasted French baguette. Cooked artichoke leaves are good, too. You'll find directions for all these on pages 25–30.

Vegetables for Dips and Spreads

Any or all of the following are suitable: mushrooms, bell peppers, broccoli florets, celery, carrots, radishes, asparagus, zucchini, turnips, scallions, radicchio, Belgian endive, and all lettuces. Small vegetables can be served whole, large ones cut to bite-size. Select vegetables that are absolutely fresh and unblemished. They may be prepared in advance and kept refrigerated several hours before serving. Once cut, the vegetables look very attractive reassembled and arranged on platters or in baskets. A full, abundant arrangement always looks best, and may be displayed on attractive serving platters, or in rustic wooden bowls or baskets.

Make It Ahead: Vegetables can be prepared up to 6 hours in advance; put them in plastic bags and refrigerate.

Cucumber and Zucchini Rounds

Select the seedless (English) cucumbers if possible. Peel off one strip of skin in a lengthwise direction, turn the cucumber, and peel off another strip, leaving about a ¼-inch strip of skin intact between each peeled-off strip. Continue all the way around. This will leave an attractive pattern of light and dark green after you cut the cucumber into rounds. Cut the cucumber into ¼- to ½-inch-thick rounds. Prepare zucchini in the same manner.

Make It Ahead: You can make these up to 1 day in advance; cover and refrigerate.

Artichoke Leaves

Cook a large artichoke (p. 219), cool it, and strip off the leaves. Put a little of the dip or spread on the meaty part of each leaf, and arrange in a circular pattern on a round platter. If you do not have another use for the bottom, it can be sliced, and arranged in the center of the leaves.

Make It Ahead: Can be made up to 1 day in advance. Cover tightly and refrigerate.

Roasted Potato Rounds

Scrub a baking potato well, and cut ¼-inch-thick rounds (discard the ends, or save them for another use). Place on a well-oiled baking sheet, brush both sides generously with olive oil, and roast in a preheated 400° oven approximately 8 minutes each side, or until golden. Cool before using. An 8-ounce potato will make about 12 rounds.

Make It Ahead: Can be made up to 4 hours in advance.

Baguette Toast Rounds

Slice a day-old French baguette into ¼-inch-thick slices. Place on a well-oiled baking sheet and brush each slice on both sides with melted unsalted butter or good-quality olive oil. Bake in a preheated 350° oven until light brown around the edges, about 5 minutes. One baguette will yield about 32 rounds. You can add a little minced garlic to the butter or oil if you want a garlicky flavor.

Make It Ahead: You can make these up to 1 day in advance, but hide them. They are very tempting.

SUN-DRIED TOMATO, ROASTED RED PEPPER, AND CILANTRO DIP

Makes about 2 cups

8 sun-dried tomatoes packed in oil, drained, oil reserved
2 red bell peppers, roasted, peeled, seeded, and chopped
1 jalapeño chile, roasted, peeled, seeded, and chopped
2 tablespoons chopped fresh cilantro

2 cloves garlic, chopped
2 scallions, cleaned and chopped
1 teaspoon each ground cumin and fresh lemon juice
4 ounces cream cheese
fine sea salt to taste
tortilla chips and raw vegetables

1. In a food processor or blender, process the sun-dried tomatoes, bell peppers, jalapeño, cilantro, garlic, scallions, cumin, and lemon juice, until the mixture is smooth.
2. Add the cream cheese and salt to taste, and blend, adding enough of the reserved oil from the sun-dried tomatoes to thin the dip to the desired consistency. Transfer to a serving bowl and chill until ready to serve. Serve with tortilla chips and raw vegetables.

Make It Light: Substitute Yogurt Cheese (p. 14) for the cream cheese

Make It Ahead: You can make the dip 4 hours ahead, place in a serving bowl, and refrigerate until ready to serve. Prepare the vegetables, and refrigerate in plastic bags up to 4 hours in advance.

CHICKEN LIVER SPREAD

Enough for about 36 appetizers

8 tablespoons unsalted butter (4 ounces)
8 ounces chicken livers
2 shallots, finely chopped
fine sea salt and freshly ground pepper to taste
¼ teaspoon each dried thyme and dried oregano

2 tablespoons Marsala
2 tablespoons crème fraîche
3 tablespoons chopped fresh flat-leaf parsley
Cucumber, Zucchini, or Baguette Toast Rounds (p. 25)

1. Melt 2 tablespoons of the butter in a skillet and sauté the livers and shallots for 5 minutes. Season with salt, pepper, and the herbs. Remove from the heat and stir in the Marsala, scraping up all the juices stuck to the bottom of the pan. Allow to cool, then transfer to a blender or food processor.
2. Purée the livers. Add the remaining butter, crème fraîche, and parsley and blend in. Taste and correct the seasoning. Transfer to a small serving bowl, and chill at least 1 hour before serving. To serve, spread on cucumber, zucchini or toast rounds, and arrange on a platter.

Make It Light: Reduce the butter to 4 tablespoons (2 ounces), and substitute Yogurt Cheese (p. 14) for the crème fraîche.

Make It Ahead: The spread can be made up to a day in advance and chilled.

JALAPEÑO CHICKEN APPETIZERS

Makes 64 appetizers

1 whole chicken breast, poached, skinned, boned, and diced
12 ounces cream cheese (1½ cups)
2 jalapeño chiles, roasted, skinned, seeded, and finely chopped
2 cloves garlic, finely chopped
1 teaspoon each ground cumin and chile powder

6 ounces Cheddar cheese, grated (about 1½ cups)
fine sea salt and freshly ground black pepper, to taste
64 Baguette Toast Rounds (p. 25)

Combine all the ingredients in a bowl, except the toasts, and mix well. Mound each toast with the chicken mixture, and place on a baking sheet. Just before serving, bake in a preheated 375° oven 7 minutes, or until puffed and bubbling. Serve hot.

Make It Light: Substitute Yogurt Cheese (p. 14) for the cream cheese, and Parmesan cheese for the Cheddar cheese.

Make It Ahead: You can spread the filling on toasts up to 1 hour in advance of baking.

PORCINI AND OLIVE SPREAD

Makes about 24 appetizers

1 ounce dried porcini mushrooms, soaked in warm water for 1 hour
2 tablespoons extra virgin olive oil
6 tablespoons finely chopped olives

fine sea salt and freshly ground pepper to taste
24 Baguette Toast Rounds (p. 25)

Drain the mushrooms and rinse well; heat the olive oil in a small skillet, and sauté the mushrooms 4 minutes over very low heat. Remove the mushrooms from the skillet and chop finely. Combine with the olives, and add salt and pepper to taste. Spread on prepared toasts to serve.

Make It Ahead: You can spread the toasts up to 30 minutes before serving.

ROASTED GARLIC AND GOAT CHEESE SPREAD

Makes 24 appetizers

2 large heads Roasted Garlic (p. 220)
7 ounces fresh goat cheese (about 1 cup)

24 Baguette Toast or Roasted Potato Rounds (p. 25)

Arrange the garlic and the goat cheese on a serving plate surrounded by the toasts. To serve, turn the head of garlic upside down and squeeze the pulp out of the cloves. Either you or your guests can spread the toasts with garlic, and then with cheese.

Make It Ahead: Garlic can be roasted up to 2 hours in advance. You can have the platter completely prepared and ready up to 30 minutes before serving.

ROQUEFORT SPREAD
Makes about 60 appetizers

1 pound ricotta cheese
8 ounces Roquefort cheese
1 clove garlic, finely chopped
2 ounces walnuts (about ½ cup),
   toasted and coarsely chopped
2 tablespoons each chopped fresh
   chives, chopped fresh oregano, and
   chopped fresh flat-leaf parsley

fine sea salt and freshly ground white
   pepper, to taste
Baguette Toast, Cucumber, Zucchini,
   or Roasted Potato Rounds (p. 25)

In a bowl, combine the ricotta, Roquefort, and garlic. Add the walnuts and herbs and mix well. Taste for seasoning and add salt and pepper to taste. Cover and chill before serving. Spread on the toasts or other rounds and arrange on a platter or tray.

Make It Light: Substitute nonfat Yogurt Cheese (p. 14) for the ricotta, and reduce the Roquefort to 4 ounces.

Make It Ahead: The spread can be made up to 8 hours in advance. You can spread it on the toasts or other rounds up to 30 minutes before serving.

SMOKED SALMON SPREAD
Makes about 24 appetizers

4 ounces smoked salmon
4 ounces cream cheese
4 tablespoons unsalted butter (2 ounces)
2 hard-cooked eggs
3 tablespoons chopped fresh dill
   fine sea salt and freshly ground
   white pepper to taste

24 Cucumber, Roasted Potato, or
   Baguette Toast Rounds (p. 25)

Put all ingredients except cucumber, roasted potato or toast rounds in a food processor or blender, and purée. Check seasoning and add salt and pepper to taste. Put in a small serving bowl, cover, and chill. Serve on an attractive platter, surrounded by toasts or other rounds.

Make It Light: Substitute Yogurt Cheese (p. 14) for the cream cheese Reduce the butter to 1 tablespoon.

Make It Ahead: You can make the spread up to 3 hours in advance. Cover and refrigerate.

This is Steak Tartare's seafood cousin, and like anything made with salmon, is very popular. It makes a great first course or appetizer. It can also be made with other raw fish, such as tuna or halibut.

SALMON TARTARE

Serves 8 as a first course; makes about 36 appetizers

1½ **pounds skinless salmon fillets, coarsely chopped**
½ **medium red onion, finely chopped**
2 **medium scallions, cleaned and finely chopped**
3 **tablespoons each drained capers and finely chopped fresh flat-leaf parsley**
1 **tablespoon finely chopped mint**

3 **tablespoons each aquavit and extra virgin olive oil**
2 **tablespoons freshly squeezed lime juice**
salt and freshly ground pepper to taste
buttered black bread or Cucumber Rounds (p. 25)

1. In a medium-sized bowl, combine everything except the bread or Cucumber Rounds. Chill at least 1 hour.

2. For individual appetizers, form the mixture into 1-inch patties using a generous tablespoon of tartare for each patty, and arrange the patties on a tray with the buttered black bread and Cucumber Rounds. As a first course, divide the mixture into 8 equal portions, form patties, and arrange on individual plates. Pass the black bread and Cucumber Rounds.

Make It Ahead: You can make the tartare up to 2 hours ahead of serving, and refrigerate.

Bagna Caôda, which comes from the Piedmont region of Italy, is similar to a Swiss meat fondue, except that it features vegetables instead of beef, and the cooking oil is flavored with garlic and anchovies. You need a small flameproof dish or fondue pot, and a table-top burner for this. It's a do-it-yourself event, with everyone choosing what they want to eat, and warming it in the dip, using their fingers or long wooden skewers. They can dip the bread in the sauce, too, or use the bread to catch the drippings from the vegetables as they come out of the dip. It is easier to estimate vegetable quantities while the vegetables are whole. I take a handful and judge what would be a single serving. Bagna Caôda is traditionally served in winter, but I think your guests will welcome this wonderful dish all year round.

BAGNA CAÔDA

Serves 8 to 10

4 tablespoons unsalted butter (2 ounces)
1 tablespoon finely chopped garlic
10 anchovy fillets, finely chopped
1 cup extra virgin olive oil, preferably Italian

salt to taste
raw vegetables (spinach, mushrooms, bell peppers, celery, carrots, radishes, asparagus, zucchini, scallions, lettuces, etc.)
Italian bread, cut into ½-inch-thick slices

1. Clean the vegetables and prepare them as needed (trim, peel, cut into bite-sized pieces, etc.). The leafy greens should be washed and dried. Arrange them attractively on platters or in baskets or rustic wooden bowls.
2. Place the flameproof dish on top of the burner. Light the burner and add the butter. Add the garlic and chopped anchovies and heat, stirring frequently with a wooden spoon, until the anchovies dissolve into a paste, about 3 or 4 minutes. Add the olive oil, and salt to taste.

Make It Light: Reduce the butter to 1 tablespoon and supply a plate lined with several paper towels so that guests may drain excess sauce.

Make It Ahead: Prepare the vegetables and arrange them for serving up to 2 hours ahead. Cover with plastic and refrigerate. Have all ingredients ready next to the burner on the table. And don't forget the matches to light the burner.

PASTRIES AND TARTS

These delicious rich little pastries are wonderful served as an accompaniment to salads and soups as well as on their own as an appetizer.

PARMESAN CRISPS

Makes about 40 appetizers

2 ounces Parmigiano-Reggiano, grated (about ½ cup)
5 ounces unbleached white flour (about 1 cup)

6 tablespoons unsalted butter (3 ounces), cut into 6 pieces
½ teaspoon baking powder
⅛ teaspoon freshly ground white pepper

1. In a mixer or food processor, combine the Parmigiano, flour, butter, baking powder, and pepper. Mix just until the dough forms a ball, about 1 minute. Wrap in plastic and chill for 1 hour.
2. Roll the dough out on a lightly floured surface to a thickness of about ⅓ inch. Cut out 1-inch rounds, and place them on a lightly oiled baking sheet. Gather the scraps and pat them into a ball; roll out, and cut out more rounds.
3. Bake in a preheated 400° oven for about 8 minutes, until golden. Serve hot or at room temperature.

Make It Ahead: These will keep 2 or 3 days in an airtight container.

STILTON, BACON, AND SCALLION PUFFS

Makes about 36 appetizers

½ cup water
2 ounces unsalted butter (4 tablespoons)
2½ ounces unbleached white flour (about ½ cup)
2 large eggs

4 ounces Stilton cheese, crumbled (about 1 cup)
4 slices bacon, cooked and crumbled
3 tablespoons minced scallions
fine sea salt and freshly ground pepper to taste

1. In a small heavy saucepan combine the water and butter and bring to a boil over high heat. Reduce the heat, add the flour all at once, and stir until the dough pulls away from the sides of the pan.
2. Remove the pan from the heat, add the eggs, one at a time, beating well after each addition, and stir in the Stilton, bacon, scallions, and salt and pepper to taste.
3. Drop rounded teaspoons of the batter 2 inches apart onto a parchment-lined baking sheet and bake the puffs in a preheated 425° oven for 15 to 20 minutes, or until golden. Allow to cool 10 minutes before serving.

Make It Ahead: You can bake these 1 hour in advance and serve at room temperature or reheat them in a 300° oven for 5 minutes.

To serve this as finger food, make the tart in a rectangular or square tart pan and cut into small squares. Otherwise, it makes a lovely first course baked in a round tart pan and served in wedges at the table. This is one of the many recipes in this book that were created by our talented cooking school director, Rebecca Ets-Hokin. It is her version of the classic French *pissaladière*.

ONION, ANCHOVY, AND OLIVE TART

Serves 8 as a first course, 12 to 16 as an appetizer

2 tablespoons extra virgin olive oil

2 pounds yellow onions, peeled, cut in half and thinly sliced

1 teaspoon each fine sea salt, sugar, and freshly ground pepper

an 11-inch unbaked pie or tart shell

2 ounces anchovy fillets, soaked in milk to cover for 20 minutes

20 oil-cured black olives, pitted

1. Heat the olive oil in a large sauté pan or skillet, add the sliced onions, the sugar and salt, and toss well. Cook over low heat, covered, for about 45 minutes, or until the onions are very soft. Add the pepper and allow to cool.

2. Fill the pie or tart shell with the cooked onions. Drain the anchovy fillets, and lay them and the pitted olives in a symmetrical design over the onions.

3. Bake in a preheated 375° oven for 45 minutes, or until the tart is lightly browned. Unmold and let cool on a rack. Serve warm or at room temperature.

Make It Ahead: This stands beautifully for 2 or 3 hours before serving at room temperature.

This is such a beautiful dish, that you will want to include it in a buffet, setting it out on the table and slicing it at the last minute. If you are serving it as a first course, bring it to the table on a little cutting board, so that everyone can see it before you cut and serve it. You can purchase these larger sausages at a French or an Italian delicatessen.

SAUSAGE BAKED IN PASTRY

Serves 6 or 8 as a first course, 12 to 14 as an appetizer

a 1 to 1½ pound uncooked French or Italian sausage
1 recipe HomeChef's Basic Pastry Dough (p. 251)

1 egg, beaten with 1 tablespoon water

1. Prick the sausage in 5 or 6 places to prevent the skin from bursting. Place in a saucepan and add enough cold water to cover. Bring to a boil, lower the heat, and simmer covered, for about 30 minutes. Drain and cool the sausage on paper towels, then split the skin with a sharp knife and peel it off.
2. Roll the pastry dough into a 14 × 20-inch rectangle about ⅛ inch thick. Cut off the corners of the dough. Place cooked and cooled sausage in the center of the dough, and gently lift the long sides of the pastry up over the sausage. The pastry should overlap by about an inch; trim off anything more. Brush the edges with the egg wash. Brush the ends of the roll with the egg wash, fold them back, and neatly seal.
3. Turn the wrapped sausage seam side down on a lightly greased baking sheet and decorate the top with scraps of pastry dough cut into various shapes like hearts, diamonds, or half-moons. Brush well with the egg wash and bake at 375° for 40 to 45 minutes until golden. Allow to cool 15 minutes before serving. Slice and serve with prepared hot mustard.

Make It Ahead: You can make the sausage in pastry up to 4 hours in advance, place it on the baking sheet, cover with plastic wrap, and refrigerate until you are ready to bake it.

NUTS AND OLIVES

I first tasted this rustic dish in Italy, at a farm in the Tuscan countryside. It is unusual as well as delicious, and is so light that it won't interfere with the rest of the meal, no matter what it is you're planning to serve.

BAKED OLIVES
Serves 8 as a first course

24 large black Italian olives
 3 cloves garlic, lightly crushed
 ¼ cup extra virgin olive oil

½ cup dry white wine
Italian bread, optional

Place olives and garlic cloves in a baking dish. Add the olive oil and toss. Pour the wine over all, cover, and bake in a preheated 350° oven for about 15 minutes, or until the olives plump up. Serve warm, directly from the baking dish, with thick slices of crusty bread, if desired.

Make It Ahead: You can have the olives in the baking dish all ready to go into the oven up to 2 hours in advance.

Once you sample these nuts, store-bought will never be good enough again. An important tip — once they are made, keep them out of sight until you want to serve them. They are so good, that once you start eating them — well . . . you know.

CURRIED NUTS
Makes 2 pounds

1 tablespoon each dried hot chile
  peppers, cumin seed, coriander seed
2 teaspoons each dried oregano,
  black peppercorns, pink peppercorns,
  and Hungarian paprika
2 cloves garlic

½ teaspoon turmeric
1 tablespoon fine sea salt
8 tablespoons unsalted butter
  (4 ounces)
2 pounds assorted raw nuts (almonds,
  cashews, pecans, etc.)

1. Grind everything except the butter and nuts in a mortar or spice grinder.
2. Melt the butter in a small saucepan, add the ground seasonings, and mix well.
3. In a large bowl, toss the nuts and spiced butter until well mixed.
4. Place the nuts on baking sheets and roast in a preheated 350° oven for 15 minutes. Allow to cool and serve at room temperature.

Make It Light: Reduce the butter to 2 tablespoons.

Make It Ahead: Can be made up to 1 week in advance. Store them in an airtight container.

MEAT AND CHICKEN

I always serve the following two appetizers at parties where the entire menu consists of nothing but finger food. Each is substantial enough to qualify as a light supper. No matter how many other appetizers you are serving, plan on at least two or three of each of these per person.

ROASTED CHICKEN WINGS AFRICANA

Makes 48 appetizers

4 cloves garlic, peeled and mashed
2 shallots, peeled and mashed
2 teaspoons each fine sea salt and
   Hungarian paprika
1 tablespoon Chinese five-spice powder
   (available in Asian markets)

1 teaspoon Tabasco sauce
2 tablespoons vegetable oil
24 chicken wings, tips cut off, each
   wing cut into two at the joint
   Peanut Sauce (see recipe below)

1. Combine all ingredients, stirring to coat the wings well with the marinade. Marinate overnight in the refrigerator.
2. Arrange the wings in an open roasting dish, and roast them in a preheated 400° oven for 20 to 25 minutes, or until they are golden brown. Serve warm or at room temperature with Peanut Sauce.

Make It Light: Substitute wedges of lime for the Peanut Sauce

Make It Ahead: The wings need to marinate about 8 hours. After that, if you wish, you may arrange them in the baking dish hours ahead, cover, and return to the refrigerator. Roast shortly before serving.

PEANUT SAUCE

½ cup peanut butter
½ cup coconut milk
½ cup water
2 cloves garlic, chopped

½ red bell pepper, chopped
½ teaspoon Tabasco sauce
1 teaspoon soy sauce

In the bowl of a food processor or blender combine all ingredients and process until smooth.

Make It Ahead: The sauce may be made several days in advance and stored covered in the refrigerator. Bring to room temperature before serving.

HONEY-GLAZED PORK RIBLETS

Makes about 50 appetizers

4 pounds baby back ribs, halved crosswise and cut into individual ribs

⅓ cup honey

⅓ cup hoisin sauce (available where Asian foods are sold)

¼ cup soy sauce

2 cloves garlic, squeezed through a press

¼ teaspoon each salt and freshly ground pepper to taste

½ teaspoon hot dry mustard

¼ cup white wine vinegar

1. Drop the riblets into boiling water, cover, lower the heat, and simmer gently 10 minutes. Drain and pat dry.

2. In a large bowl, whisk together the honey, hoisin sauce, soy sauce, garlic, salt, pepper, dry mustard, and vinegar. Add the ribs and stir to thoroughly coat. Marinate overnight in the refrigerator.

3. Remove the ribs from the marinade, arrange in a single layer on a baking sheet, and broil under a preheated broiler about 4 inches from the heat for 2 or 3 minutes. Turn, brush with marinade, and broil 2 or 3 minutes more, or until the ribs are browned well and beautifully glazed.

Make It Ahead: The ribs may be broiled 2 to 3 hours in advance, and rewarmed in a 300° oven for 5 minutes before serving.

SEAFOOD

This is a classic dish, rich and elegant. Use small natural bay scallop shells when serving this dish as an appetizer; use larger sea shells from the sea scallop or individual gratin dishes to serve it at the table as a first course. Natural scallop shells are available in gourmet kitchen stores.

SHRIMP AND SCALLOPS MORNAY

Serves 6 as a first course, 16 as an appetizer

2 tablespoons unsalted butter
2 tablespoons flour
½ cup Fish, Vegetable, or Chicken Stock (pp. 12–13)
¾ cup milk
2 ounces Parmigiano-Reggiano, grated (about ½ cup)
¼ cup crème fraîche

fine sea salt and freshly ground pepper to taste
8 ounces shrimp, peeled, deveined, cut into 3 pieces each, then poached for 30 seconds
8 ounces scallops, each cut into 4, and poached for 30 seconds
coarse salt

1. In a saucepan, melt the butter over medium heat and blend in the flour. Gradually stir in the stock and milk. Bring to a boil, stirring. Reduce the heat, add all but 4 tablespoons of the grated Parmigiano cheese, and stir until it melts. Add the crème fraîche, and season to taste with salt and pepper. Remove from the heat.

2. Spread a layer of coarse salt about ½-inch deep on a baking sheet, and place the shells on the salt. (The salt will keep the shells level. If you are using gratin dishes, this step is unnecessary, as the dishes can go directly onto the oven rack.). Divide the shrimp and scallops among the shells (or gratin dishes). Spoon the sauce over the seafood, and sprinkle with remaining Parmigiano.

3. Just before serving, place the baking sheet or gratin dishes under a preheated broiler, 4 inches from the heat, and broil until lightly browned, about 3 minutes.

Make It Light: Substitute nonfat milk for both the milk and crème fraîche.

Make It Ahead: The dish can be prepared through step 2 up to 2 hours before serving. Place the whole baking sheet, covered in plastic, in the refrigerator. Just before serving, broil as directed above, allowing an additional minute, if necessary, to heat through.

SKEWERED MUSTARD-GINGER SHRIMP

Makes about 50 appetizers

1 cup red wine vinegar
¾ cup walnut oil
2 tablespoons sugar
2 tablespoons grated fresh ginger
1 tablespoon prepared mustard
1 teaspoon fine sea salt, or to taste
½ teaspoon freshly ground pepper, or to taste

2 pounds medium shrimp, peeled and deveined (about 50)
1 red and 1 green bell pepper, seeded and cut into ½-inch squares
2 bunches fresh cilantro for garnish

1. In a saucepan, whisk together the vinegar, oil, sugar, ginger, mustard, salt, and pepper. Bring the mixture to a boil, and simmer for 2 minutes. Add the shrimp and stir over the heat 1 minute; cover and let stand off the heat for 2 minutes.

2. Transfer the mixture to a bowl, add the bell peppers, tossing well, and refrigerate 2 hours.

3. Drain the shrimp and bell peppers and discard the liquid. Thread on wooden toothpicks — a piece of bell pepper, a shrimp, and another piece of bell pepper on each. Arrange the skewered shrimp attractively on a bed of cilantro.

Make It Ahead: You can make this dish completely up to 2 hours before serving. Arrange the serving platter and refrigerate.

Gravlax is a special type of cured salmon that originated in Scandinavia. Thinly sliced, arranged with its delicious mustard sauce, it is always the first of all the dishes on a buffet to disappear. It will only take a few minutes of your time to prepare, but 48 hours to cure, so be sure to plan ahead. Gravlax should be consumed within two days after it has been cured.

GRAVLAX WITH TRIG'S MUSTARD SAUCE

Serves 8 as a first course, 16 as an appetizer

1½ pounds fresh center-cut salmon fillet, skin left on, halved lengthwise	1 tablespoon white wine vinegar
	lemon wedges
½ bunch fresh dill	thinly sliced black bread,
3 tablespoons coarse sea salt	lightly buttered
2 tablespoons sugar	Trig's Mustard Sauce
1 tablespoon crushed peppercorns	(see recipe below)

1. Place half the fish skin side down, in a deep nonmetal container. Scatter the dill over the fish. Sprinkle the salt, sugar, peppercorns, and vinegar over the dill, and cover with the other half of fish, skin side up.

2. Cover with foil and place a weight on top (a foil-covered brick works well). Refrigerate 2 days, turning the fish every 12 hours, basting with the liquid that accumulates.

3. Remove from the marinade, rinse, and pat dry. Place the separated halves skin side down, and slice the salmon very thinly on the diagonal. Arrange slices on individual plates or on a platter with lemon wedges, black bread, and Trig's Mustard Sauce.

My Swedish friend Trig contributed the recipe for this sauce. It's meant to accompany the gravlax, but it's equally good with cracked crab, or combine it with 1 cup of mayonnaise to make a dipping sauce for vegetables.

TRIG'S MUSTARD SAUCE

3 tablespoons sugar	1 teaspoon dry mustard
2 tablespoons red or white wine vinegar	½ cup extra virgin olive oil
6 tablespoons Dijon mustard	2 tablespoons chopped fresh dill

Have all ingredients at room temperature. In a small deep bowl, combine the sugar and vinegar, stir until sugar is dissolved, then stir in mustards. Slowly add the oil, whisking constantly, until it thickens and forms a sauce. Stir in the chopped dill.

Make It Ahead: Prepare the sauce a day in advance, cover, chill. Bring to room temperature and stir well before serving.

Everyone loves these crab cakes, not only because they taste delicious, but because they are baked instead of fried, which make them much lighter. It makes the preparation easier, too.

BAKED CRAB CAKES WITH PEACH SALSA

Serves 8 as a first course; makes 16 appetizers

2 tablespoons unsalted butter	⅓ cup mayonnaise
½ medium onion, finely chopped	pinch of cayenne pepper
2 large stalks celery, finely chopped	¼ teaspoon freshly ground pepper
1 clove garlic, minced	1 tablespoon hot and sweet
4 scallions, green parts only,	prepared mustard
finely chopped	1 teaspoon each baking soda and
2 tablespoons fresh flat-leaf parsley,	fine sea salt
finely chopped	1½ cups crushed saltine crackers
1 pound cooked crabmeat	Peach Salsa (see recipe below)

1. Melt the butter in a skillet over medium heat, and sauté the onion, celery, garlic, and scallion greens 3 minutes. Transfer to a bowl, cool slightly, and combine with the parsley and crabmeat.

2. In a small bowl, combine the mayonnaise, cayenne pepper, mustard, soda, and salt, and stir into the crabmeat mixture. Add ⅓ cup of the cracker crumbs, and mix well. Form the crab mixture into 8 large patties or 16 small ones and coat with the remaining crumbs.

3. Place the crab cakes on a greased baking sheet and bake in a preheated 400° oven about 10 minutes each side, until very lightly browned. Serve with Peach Salsa.

Make It Light: As crab cakes go, these are light, since they are baked instead of fried.

Make It Ahead: You can make the crab cakes up to 6 hours in advance through step 2; cover and refrigerate. When you are ready, proceed with step 3.

PEACH SALSA

1 pound fresh peaches (about 3),	1 tablespoon each chopped jalapeño
peeled and coarsely chopped	chiles and chopped fresh cilantro,
2 ripe medium tomatoes, peeled and	or to taste
coarsely chopped	8 tablespoons extra virgin olive oil
1 tablespoon fresh lemon juice	6 tablespoons sherry vinegar
6 scallions, cleaned and chopped	2 tablespoons honey

Combine the peaches and tomatoes. Add the lemon juice, scallions, jalapeños, and cilantro and mix well. Whisk together the oil, vinegar, and honey. Pour over the peach mixture and mix gently.

Make It Ahead: The salsa can be prepared up to a day in advance and refrigerated. Bring to room temperature before serving.

Clams Casino are a revival from the thirties. Try serving it in the living room as an appetizer, accompanied by a pitcher of martinis to complete the mood.

CLAMS CASINO
Serves 6 to 8

6 slices thick-sliced bacon
8 ounces coarse salt
4 dozen cherrystone clams, scrubbed, shucked, and left on the half shell
  juice of 2 lemons

6 tablespoons unsalted butter (3 ounces)
1 green and 1 red bell pepper, seeded and finely chopped
1 tablespoon finely chopped garlic

1. Blanch the bacon for 40 seconds and drain. Coarsely chop and set aside.
2. Spread a layer of coarse salt on a baking pan. Place the clams in the shell on top of the salt, and sprinkle each with a little lemon juice.
3. Melt the butter in a saucepan, and cook the bell pepper and garlic over low heat for 5 minutes. Spoon a little of the mixture over each clam and sprinkle with a little chopped bacon.
4. Bake in a preheated 425° oven for 6 minutes. Serve hot, arranging the clams on individual plates.

Make It Light: Reduce butter to 2 tablespoons, and reduce bacon to 4 slices.

Make It Ahead: You can make this through step 3 up to 1 hour in advance. Bake the clams just before serving (step 4).

The New Orleans chef who invented this classic dish of the thirties named it after the oil tycoon, John D. Rockefeller. It's not really so rich in the calorie sense, but it is certainly rich in flavor! You can lighten it, if you wish, by following the Make It Light suggestion below. Either way, the oysters should be baked in the larger half of their shells, right on the serving plates (the coarse salt serves to keep the shells from tipping over: if you have special oyster plates, you won't need the coarse salt). These are usually served as a first course, but could be a whole meal for oyster lovers. And one more suggestion — have the market shuck the oysters for you. I always do.

OYSTERS ROCKEFELLER

Serves 8 to 10 as a first course

48 oysters scrubbed and shucked,
   on the half-shell
1 pound coarse salt
6 tablespoons unsalted butter
   (3 ounces)
8 slices bacon, cooked until crisp,
   drained, and chopped

1 pound spinach, cleaned, stems
   removed, and leaves finely chopped
3 tablespoons each chopped fresh
   flat-leaf parsley and chopped scallions
½ cup dry bread crumbs
   fine sea salt and cayenne to taste
¼ cup Pernod

1. Arrange the oysters in their half-shells, on a bed of coarse salt on individual oven-proof serving plates, or on oyster plates.
2. Melt the butter in a skillet or sauté pan, and add the bacon, spinach, parsley, scallions, and bread crumbs. Sauté the mixture 7 or 8 minutes over low heat, stirring occasionally, until it holds together. Season to taste with salt and cayenne pepper. Sprinkle the bacon and spinach mixture over the oysters and spoon a little Pernod on each.
3. Place the plates in a preheated 425° oven until oysters are hot and bubbling, about 5 minutes.

Make It Light: Reduce the bacon to 4 slices, and the butter to 4 tablespoons.

Make It Ahead: You can make the oysters through step 2 up to 1 hour before serving. When you are ready, proceed with step 3.

VEGETABLES

GRILLED OR BROILED MUSHROOMS
Serves 8 as a first course

¼ cup extra virgin olive oil
¼ cup balsamic vinegar
1 teaspoon each fine sea salt and
   freshly ground black pepper
1 clove garlic, crushed

1 tablespoon each chopped fresh basil
   and chopped fresh flat-leaf parsley
16 large fresh mushrooms, cleaned and
   stems trimmed

In a large bowl, mix together the olive oil, vinegar, salt, pepper, garlic, basil, and parsley. Toss the mushrooms in the marinade and allow to marinate overnight in the refrigerator. Remove from the marinade and grill or broil the mushrooms on a preheated grill or broiler until soft, about 10 minutes.

Make It Ahead: These may be finished several hours ahead and served at room temperature or reheat them in a 300° oven for 5 minutes.

I never discard baked potato skins any more. Instead, I use them to make this appetizer, even if I have no one else to serve them to but myself! They're so easy to make, and they taste so good: they make great finger food at a large cocktail party.

TWICE-BAKED POTATO SKINS
Makes about 64 appetizers

4 large baking potatoes, scrubbed
   (about 2 pounds)
2 tablespoons vegetable oil
8 drops Tabasco sauce

8 tablespoons unsalted butter
   (4 ounces), melted
   salt and freshly ground black pepper

1. Rub the unpeeled potatoes with the oil, prick with a fork 2 or 3 times and bake in a preheated 375° oven for about 45 minutes, until tender.
2. Allow the potatoes to cool, cut in half lengthwise, and with a spoon remove all but a very thin layer of the pulp. (The potato pulp may be used for another dish, such as Garlic Mashed Potatoes [p. 210].)
  With kitchen scissors cut each half potato skin into 4 pieces lengthwise, then cut in half crosswise. Spread them on oiled baking sheets. Combine the Tabasco sauce with the melted butter and brush evenly over the skins. Season lightly with salt and freshly ground black pepper. Bake in a preheated 350° oven for 5 to 8 minutes, until crisp. Serve warm or at room temperature.

Make It Light: Reduce the butter to 2 tablespoons

Make It Ahead: These may be made several hours ahead and reheated for 5 minutes in a 300° oven.

If you wish, each round sandwich may be cut into four and served as finger food at a cocktail party.

EGGPLANT AND MOZZARELLA SANDWICHES

Serves 8 as a first course; 12 to 16 as an appetizer

1 medium eggplant (about 1 pound)
coarse sea salt
about ½ cup extra virgin olive oil
½ pound fresh mozzarella, cut into
8 slices

16 fresh basil leaves, chopped
2 tablespoons chopped fresh
flat-leaf parsley
1 teaspoon each green, white, and
black peppercorns, ground

1. Slice the eggplant into 16 rounds, each about ¼ inch thick. Sprinkle with coarse salt and let stand for 1 hour. Rinse and pat dry with paper towels. Brush a baking sheet with olive oil, place the eggplant slices on the sheet, and brush with oil. Bake in a preheated 375° oven until soft to the touch, about 30 minutes.
2. Place a slice of mozzarella on 8 of the eggplant rounds, sprinkle with basil and ground pepper, and top with another eggplant.
3. Reduce the heat to 350° and bake 5 minutes, or until the cheese melts. Transfer to a serving platter.

Make It Light: Reduce the olive oil to 2 tablespoons.

Make It Ahead: Assemble the sandwiches up to 3 hours in advance and bake just before serving.

Don't let the richness of this dish dissuade you. You can always "make it light." It is best served as a first course, or as a light luncheon or supper with a green salad.

EGGPLANT PIE

Serves 8 as a first course

1 medium eggplant, about 1 pound
  coarse sea salt
  about ½ cup extra virgin olive oil
½ teaspoon each fine sea salt,
  freshly ground pepper, sugar, and
  dried thyme, or to taste
5 tablespoons finely chopped fresh
  flat-leaf parsley

4 medium tomatoes, sliced
1 medium onion, finely chopped
1 green bell pepper, finely chopped
8 ounces fresh mozzarella
  cheese, sliced
3 egg yolks
1½ cups crème fraîche

1. Cut the eggplant into 16 rounds about ¼ inch thick. Sprinkle with coarse salt and let stand for 1 hour. Rinse and pat dry with paper towels. Brush a baking sheet with olive oil, place the eggplant slices on the sheet, brush the eggplant with oil, and bake in a preheated 375° oven until soft to the touch, about 30 minutes.
2. In a small bowl, combine the fine sea salt, pepper, sugar, thyme and parsley. Place the eggplant slices in a 12-inch baking dish, and sprinkle the seasonings, chopped onion, and bell pepper over the eggplant. Cover with sliced tomatoes, then top with the mozzarella over all.
3. Combine the egg yolks and crème fraîche, and pour this over the cheese. Bake in a preheated 325° oven about 40 minutes, until the custard is set and lightly browned. Allow to stand 30 minutes before cutting and serving.

Make It Light: Substitute nonfat milk for the crème fraîche and 2 whole eggs plus 1 egg white for the 3 egg yolks.

Make It Ahead: This stands beautifully for 2 to 3 hours before serving at room temperature, or you may prepare it up to a day ahead through step 2. Cover and refrigerate; about an hour before serving, proceed with step 3.

California's close proximity to Mexico has given us the opportunity to adopt many Mexican dishes. These quesadillas have been a longtime favorite at HomeChef.

CORN AND CHEESE QUESADILLAS

Serves 4 as a first course, 8 as an appetizer

8 10-inch flour tortillas
3 tablespoons unsalted butter, melted
8 ounces Monterey Jack cheese, grated
   (about 2 cups)
1 cup cooked corn kernels

2 jalapeño chiles (or to taste), seeded
   and finely chopped
   Guacamole (see recipe below)
   Fresh Tomato Salsa (see recipe below)

1. Arrange 4 tortillas on a baking sheet and brush them lightly with butter. Turn and sprinkle with cheese, corn, and chiles, dividing everything evenly among the tortillas. Top each with a second tortilla, and brush lightly with butter.
2. Bake about 6 minutes in a preheated 375° oven, until the cheese is melted. Cut the quesadillas into wedges and serve with Guacamole and Fresh Tomato Salsa.

Make It Ahead: You can assemble the quesadillas up to 3 hours in advance. Cover and refrigerate; bake just before serving.

GUACAMOLE

2 ripe avocados, peeled, pitted,
   and mashed with a fork
1 small onion, finely chopped
1 clove garlic, squeezed through a press
½ teaspoon fine sea salt
1 tablespoon fresh lime juice, or to taste

2 tablespoons vegetable oil
1 jalapeño chile, seeded and
   finely chopped
3 tablespoons each chopped
   fresh cilantro and chopped fresh
   flat-leaf parsley

Combine all ingredients in a bowl. Stick the avocado pits in the guacamole, cover and refrigerate until serving. (The pits keep the guacamole from turning dark; discard them before serving.)

Make It Ahead: Can be made up to 4 hours in advance. Cover and refrigerate.

FRESH TOMATO SALSA

1 pound tomatoes, chopped
1 small onion, finely chopped
1 jalapeño chile, seeded and
   finely chopped
1 tablespoon fresh lime juice
1 teaspoon sugar

   fine sea salt to taste
2 tablespoons each chopped
   fresh cilantro
   and chopped fresh flat-leaf parsley
2 tablespoons extra virgin olive oil

Combine all ingredients in a bowl and mix well. Cover and refrigerate until serving.

Make It Ahead: Can be made up to 4 hours in advance. Cover and refrigerate.

SOUPS

The word soup has such comforting implications — hot soup on a cold winter night, chicken soup to make you feel better, a sweet iced soup to cool you down when it's hot. Throughout the year we have steady requests from our students for soup recipes, and we actually have a complete class where we cook nothing but soups. Everybody seems to love soup!

I love to *make* soups because they allow me more creativity than any other phase of cooking. Unlike pastries or cakes, ingredients for soups do not have to be measured exactly, and beans, grains, pastas, and vegetables can all be substituted for one another, allowing great freedom to invent limitless combinations and flavors.

Making soup is not the time-consuming task most people envision. Once the initial preparations are completed, most soups can simmer untended until done. And since most freeze well, they can actually be time-savers. I can come home tired at the end of a day, and simply "heat up some soup."

And finally, soups are the perfect answer for people who are interested in eating lighter. Just add a salad and some crusty French bread for a nourishing and satisfying meal. Of course, soups also make an ideal first course. In that case, though, the servings should be kept rather small. Following are some of HomeChef's favorite and best soups!

Here is a classic soup I have adapted for today's needs by streamlining the preparation and cutting back on the amount of meat (the original recipe called for 3 pounds of beef!). It is still a hearty soup that could be the main course at a light supper.

UKRAINIAN BORSCHT

Serves 8

2 pounds beef shanks
8 cups water
2 onions
1 bay leaf
  coarse sea salt and freshly ground
  pepper, to taste
1 pound large white new potatoes,
  scrubbed and cut into ½-inch dice
½ green cabbage, core removed, and
  coarsely chopped

2 cloves garlic, finely chopped
3 large beets, peeled and grated
1 teaspoon sugar
1 tablespoon red wine vinegar
2 cups Beef Stock
4 tablespoons chopped fresh dill
¾ cup crème fraîche or sour cream

1. Put the beef shanks into a large pot with the water, onions, bay leaf, salt, and pepper to taste. Bring to a boil, skim off the surface foam and partially cover the pot. Reduce the heat to low and simmer until meat is tender, about 1½ hours. Strain and defat the stock, and pull the meat off the bones.
2. Return the stock to the pot. Add the potatoes, cabbage, garlic, beets, sugar, vinegar, additional Beef Stock, and meat. Simmer for 1 hour partially covered.
3. Taste and adjust seasonings. Combine the dill and crème fraîche or sour cream and garnish each serving with the herbed cream.

Make It Light: Reduce butter to 1 tablespoon and omit the cream garnish.

Make It Ahead: You can make this up to a day in advance, refrigerate, and when you are ready, reheat to serve.

A simple country soup. With only half of it puréed, the texture is both smooth and chunky at once.

TOMATO SOUP, COUNTRY STYLE

Serves 8

10 slices bacon, minced
2 medium onions, chopped
2 leeks, white parts only, cleaned and chopped
2½ pounds tomatoes, chopped
1 cup light sauterne
1½ cups Chicken Stock
1 small savoy cabbage, heart only, finely chopped

1 tablespoon chopped fresh basil leaves
1 teaspoon dried thyme
1 tablespoon sugar
1 cup cooked long grain rice
2 cloves garlic, crushed
2 teaspoons fine sea salt, or to taste
½ teaspoon freshly ground pepper, or to taste

1. Sauté the bacon in a large soup pot over low heat, for 5 minutes. Discard all but 1 tablespoon of the fat and add the onions and leeks. Sauté gently for 5 minutes. Add the tomatoes, half the sauterne, and all the stock, and bring to a boil. Add the cabbage, basil, thyme, and sugar, and simmer gently, partially covered, for about 40 minutes. Add the rice and garlic, and combine well.
2. Allow the soup to cool slightly, and purée half the soup in batches, in a blender or food processor, until smooth. Return the puréed portion of the soup to the pot, add the remainder of the sauterne and simmer gently, covered, for 30 minutes. Taste and adjust seasoning. (If soup is not thick enough, simmer uncovered until it is reduced.)

Make It Light: Omit the bacon, and substitute 1 tablespoon of vegetable oil for the 1 tablespoon of bacon fat.

Make It Ahead: You can make this up to a day in advance. Refrigerate it, then reheat to serve.

Put this soup on the menu when the weather turns hot. There's no cooking involved in its preparation, and it's meant to be served chilled.

FRESH TOMATO SOUP WITH DILL

Serves 6

3 pounds ripe summer tomatoes,
   peeled and seeded
½ teaspoon each fine sea salt and
   paprika, or to taste
1 tablespoon coarsely chopped fresh
   dill leaves

1 small clove garlic
1 tablespoon sugar
   freshly ground pepper to taste
6 tiny sprigs of dill

Purée the tomatoes in a food processor with the salt, paprika, dill, garlic, and sugar. Chill. Add pepper to taste, and additional salt if needed. Serve garnished with tiny sprigs of dill.

Make It Ahead: You can make this soup up to 6 hours in advance. Refrigerate until you are ready to serve.

Eggplant is so popular at HomeChef, we actually had eight eggplant soups under consideration. In the end, we narrowed it down to the next two outstanding soups. The Spicy Eggplant Soup is delicious served hot or at room temperature.

SPICY EGGPLANT SOUP WITH ANCHO CHILE SAUCE
Serves 8

2 eggplants (about 1 pound each), cut in half
coarse sea salt
4 tablespoons olive oil
2 yellow onions, coarsely chopped
1 jalapeño chile, coarsely chopped
5 cloves garlic, chopped
½ teaspoon ground cardamom
2 teaspoons ground cumin
2 pounds tomatoes, chopped
4 tablespoons tomato paste
10 cups Vegetable Stock
1 tablespoon soy sauce
¼ cup dry sherry
2 tablespoons sherry vinegar
fine sea salt and freshly ground pepper to taste
Ancho Chile Sauce (see recipe below)

1. Sprinkle the eggplant with coarse salt and let stand for 1 hour. Rinse and pat dry with paper towels and brush the cut sides with a little olive oil. Place cut side down on a baking sheet, and bake in a preheated 425° oven until softened, about 25 minutes. Cool, scoop out the eggplant pulp, and reserve.
2. Heat the remaining olive oil in a large soup pot, and sauté the onions, jalapeño, garlic, and ground spices for 3 minutes. Stir in the chopped tomatoes and tomato paste, increase the heat, and cook over high heat for 2 minutes. Add the eggplant pulp, stock, and remaining ingredients, except for the Ancho Chile Sauce, lower the heat and cook for 10 minutes. Remove from the heat and cool slightly.
3. Purée in a blender or food processor in batches until smooth. Return to the soup pot; taste, and adjust seasoning. Reheat and, if the soup is too thick, thin with a little stock or water. Garnish each serving with Ancho Chile Sauce, swirling it around in a simple design.

ANCHO CHILE SAUCE

3 dried ancho chiles, soaked in water 2 hours and drained, stems, and seeds discarded
1 red bell pepper, roasted, peeled, and seeded
2 cloves garlic
½ teaspoon each sugar and balsamic vinegar
fine sea salt, to taste

In a food processor or blender, purée the chiles, bell pepper, garlic, sugar, and balsamic vinegar. Thin with a little water if necessary. Taste and adjust for salt.

Make It Ahead: You can make both the soup and the sauce up to a day in advance, and refrigerate. Reheat soup before serving. Allow the Ancho Chile Sauce to stand at room temperature 1 hour before serving.

ITALIAN ROASTED EGGPLANT SOUP

Serves 8

3 eggplants, (about 1 pound each)
  tops cut off, quartered
  coarse sea salt
¼ cup olive oil
8 cloves garlic, peeled
2 shallots, peeled
6 cups Beef Stock
2 teaspoons finely chopped fresh basil

1 teaspoon sugar
  fine sea salt and freshly ground
  pepper to taste
2 small red bell peppers, roasted,
  peeled, seeded, and puréed
4 tablespoons mascarpone or
  crème fraîche

1. Sprinkle the eggplant with coarse salt and allow to stand for 1 hour. Wipe with paper towels, place on an oiled baking sheet, brush with oil, and roast in a preheated 375° oven for 20 minutes, or until soft. Add the garlic and shallots to the pan, and continue to roast for an additional 25 minutes until everything is a rich brown color.
2. Purée the eggplant, garlic, and shallots in a food processor or blender. In a large soup pot, bring the stock to a boil, and stir in the eggplant purée. Stir in the basil, sugar, salt, and pepper, and simmer gently for 5 minutes.
3. Combine the puréed bell peppers and mascarpone or crème fraîche, and use as a garnish with each serving of soup.

Make It Light: Substitute Yogurt Cheese (p. 14) for the mascarpone or crème fraîche.

Make It Ahead: You can make the soup up to a day ahead and refrigerate. Reheat to serve. The garnish can be prepared up to 2 hours in advance and kept refrigerated.

You can't make a really good onion soup in a hurry, because the onions have to cook very slowly and gently to develop their full flavor. I think you will agree, though, that the end result is well worth it. Besides, your actual preparation time only amounts to about 15 minutes; the rest of the time the onions can cook unattended.

CLASSIC FRENCH ONION SOUP

Serves 6

2 tablespoons unsalted butter
1½ pounds white onions, quartered
   and thinly sliced
1 tablespoon sugar
½ teaspoon coarse sea salt
1 cup dry white table wine

6 cups Brown Stock
6 thick slices day-old French bread
3 ounces Parmigiano-Reggiano,
   grated (about ¾ cup)
3 ounces French or Swiss Gruyère,
   grated (about ¾ cup)

1. Melt the butter in a large skillet. Add the onions, sugar, and salt, and sauté over a moderate heat until onions are very soft , about 40 minutes. Add the wine, and reduce by half.

2. Heat the stock to boiling. Place 6 deep ovenproof soup bowls on a baking sheet. Distribute the onions among the bowls, and pour the hot stock over the onions. Float a slice of bread on top of each serving, and sprinkle with the grated cheeses.

3. Place the soup bowls under a hot broiler, and broil until cheese is brown and bubbly. Serve immediately.

Make It Light: Reduce the butter to 1 tablespoon, and reduce the cheese by half.

Make It Ahead: Complete the recipe through step 1. Have everything else ready to finish the soup (the onions in the bowls, the stock on the stove ready to be heated, the bread sliced, and the cheese grated), and complete steps 2 and 3 just before serving.

The news that broccoli is such a healthy vegetable has created a demand for more broccoli recipes among our students. Since broccoli has always been very popular in Italy, and we give lots of Italian classes, we happen to have a bunch of recipes — and they are all wonderful. It was hard to choose, but here are two that are especially good.

BROCCOLI AND MACARONI SOUP

Serves 6

2 **thin slices pancetta, finely chopped**
1 **tablespoon extra virgin olive oil**
1 **clove garlic, finely chopped**
3 **tablespoons tomato paste**
6 **cups Chicken, Beef, or Vegetable Stock**
1 **teaspoon each fine sea salt and sugar**
  freshly ground pepper, to taste

1 **pound broccoli, stems discarded,**
  cut into small florets
6 **ounces short macaroni**
  (about 2 cups)
2 **ounces freshly grated**
  Parmigiano-Reggiano (½ cup)

1. Brown the pancetta in a large soup pot; add the oil, garlic, tomato paste, stock, and seasonings; bring to a boil and simmer over low heat 20 minutes.
2. Add the broccoli, cover and cook 5 minutes. Stir in the macaroni and simmer 10 minutes longer. Serve in wide soup bowls, and pass the Parmigiano.

Make It Light: Eliminate the pancetta.

Make It Ahead: You can make it up to 2 hours in advance; when you are ready, reheat to serve.

Certain combinations of fruits and vegetables make really unusual, delicately flavored soups. This soup is a good example. Serve it as a first course, in very small portions.

BROCCOLI AND APPLE SOUP

Serves 8

4 tablespoons unsalted butter (2 ounces)
1 small onion, sliced
2 large apples, cored and coarsely chopped (do not peel)
1½ pounds broccoli, cleaned, trimmed, and coarsely chopped

5 cups Chicken Stock
1 teaspoon each coarse sea salt and sugar
½ teaspoon freshly ground pepper
½ cup crème fraîche
3 tablespoons chopped chives

1. Melt the butter in a large soup pot. Stir in the onion and apple, cover, and cook over very low heat for 10 minutes. Add the broccoli, stock, salt, sugar, and pepper. Bring to a boil and simmer, covered, over medium heat for 30 minutes.

2. Allow the soup to cool slightly, and purée in batches, in a blender or food processor, until smooth. Taste for seasoning and adjust, if necessary. Return soup to the pot and reheat gently before serving. Spoon the soup into warm bowls, garnish with a dollop of crème fraîche, and sprinkle with chives.

Make It Light: Reduce butter to 2 tablespoons and omit crème fraîche.

Make It Ahead: You can make this soup up to 1 day in advance and refrigerate. Reheat to serve.

We make this soup in our basic cooking series; it gets people started with unexpected combinations of fruits and vegetables. Aside from all that, it is a truly delicious soup, perfect served in small portions as a first course. It is especially good served as a prelude to Sautéed Calves Liver with Port Wine Sauce (p. 138).

ROASTED BUTTERNUT SQUASH AND PEAR SOUP
Serves 8

2 medium butternut squash, peeled, seeded, and cut into 1-inch cubes
fine sea salt and freshly ground pepper to taste
3 tablespoons unsalted butter
1 onion, chopped
6 fresh sage leaves

4 pears, peeled, cored, and chopped
4 cups Chicken Stock
1 ounce Roquefort cheese (2 tablespoons)
¾ cup crème fraîche
2 ounces hazelnuts (about ½ cup), toasted and chopped

1. Place squash in a lightly oiled baking dish, season with salt and pepper; cover, and bake in a preheated 350° oven until tender, about 45 minutes.
2. Melt the butter in a large soup pot, and sauté the onion and sage 5 minutes over medium heat. Add the pears, roasted squash, and Chicken Stock, and simmer for 20 minutes. Cool slightly, and purée in a blender or food processor. Return the soup to the pot, and reheat gently before serving.
3. Mix the Roquefort and crème fraîche together (it should not be too smooth). Serve the soup in warmed bowls, with a dollop of Roquefort cream in the center of each serving, and hazelnuts sprinkled over the top.

Make It Light: Reduce the butter to 1 tablespoon, reduce the Roquefort cheese to 1 tablespoon, and reduce the crème fraîche to ½ cup, or eliminate them altogether. Another option is to substitute Yogurt Cheese (p. 14) for the crème fraîche.

Make It Ahead: You can make the soup up to a day in advance, and refrigerate. Reheat before serving.

Chervil is a delicate herb with a subtle licorice flavor. Since it is the "secret" ingredient that makes this recipe outstanding, be sure to include it in this soup. This soup is delicious served hot or cold.

CUCUMBER SOUP WITH CHERVIL AND DILL
Serves 4 to 6

1 tablespoon light vegetable oil
1 leek, whites only, cleaned
  and chopped
¼ medium onion, chopped
4 cucumbers, peeled, seeded,
  and chopped
4 cups Chicken Stock

½ cup crème fraîche
1 tablespoon each chopped fresh dill
  and chopped fresh chervil, plus
  extra sprigs for garnish
  fine sea salt and freshly ground
  white pepper to taste

1. In a large soup pot, heat the oil over medium heat, add the leek, onion, and cucumber, and sauté for 2 minutes. Add the stock and bring to a boil. Reduce the heat and simmer uncovered for 20 minutes.
2. Allow the soup to cool slightly, and purée in batches, in a blender or food processor.
3. Stir in the crème fraîche and chopped herbs, and season to taste with salt and pepper. Depending on whether you wish to serve the soup hot or cold, you can return it to the pot and reheat it, or put it in the refrigerator to chill. Garnish each serving with a sprig of chervil or dill.

Make It Light: Substitute Yogurt Cheese (p. 14) for the crème fraîche.

Make It Ahead: You can make this soup up to a day in advance, and refrigerate. Reheat before serving if serving hot.

Make this in the summer when peas are tiny and sweet.

MINTED GREEN PEA SOUP
Serves 8

2 **pounds fresh young peas, shelled**
  and boiled or steamed until soft,
  about 5 minutes
½ **ounce fresh mint leaves**
  (about ½ cup)
6½ **cups Vegetable Stock**

1 **cup dry white table wine**
1 **tablespoon fresh lemon juice**
  fine sea salt and freshly ground
  white pepper, to taste
½ **cup crème fraîche**

1. Purée the peas and mint leaves in a blender or food processor until coarsely chopped, then add ½ cup stock and continue blending until smooth and creamy.
2. Combine the purée, remaining stock, wine, and lemon juice in a soup pot and bring to a boil. Simmer gently, uncovered, for 10 minutes. Season to taste with salt and pepper.
3. Garnish each serving with a dollop of crème fraîche.

Make It Light: Eliminate the crème fraîche.

Make It Ahead: You can make this up to 1 day in advance, and refrigerate. Reheat to serve.

This is an unusually tasty carrot soup, rich and sweet.

CARROT AND LEEK BISQUE

Serves 6

5 cups Chicken Stock
6 carrots, peeled and cut into
  4 pieces each
4 leeks, whites only, cleaned and
  cut into 1-inch pieces
½ teaspoon each coarse sea salt and
  freshly ground pepper, or to taste

½ cup fresh flat-leaf parsley, coarsely
  chopped, plus 3 tablespoons
  finely chopped for garnish
3 egg yolks
3 tablespoons crème fraîche

1. Bring the stock to a boil in a large soup pot, add the carrots, leeks, salt, and pepper. Reduce the heat, cover partially, and simmer for about 1 hour, or until the vegetables are very soft.
2. Allow the soup to cool slightly, and purée in batches in a blender or food processor, until it is thick and smooth. Add the ½ cup parsley, and process again until smooth. Return the soup to the pot.
3. Just before serving, combine the egg yolks and crème fraîche in a small bowl. Bring the soup to a boil, remove from the heat, and stir in the egg yolk mixture, continuing to stir until smooth. Serve garnished with finely chopped parsley.

Make It Light: Omit egg yolks and crème fraîche.

Make It Ahead: You can make this soup through step 2 up to 4 hours in advance. When you are ready, proceed with step 3.

This is a hearty soup that makes a satisfying meal. Serve it with thick slices of crusty French or Italian bread. If it is a first course, serve small portions and follow it with a simple main course like Emily's Grilled Turkey Breast (p. 173) or Grilled Herbed Salmon (p. 178).

LEEK, POTATO, AND CABBAGE SOUP

Serves 6

4 tablespoons unsalted butter (2 ounces)

4 leeks, whites only, cleaned, and finely chopped

6 thin slices prosciutto, finely chopped

4 medium new white potatoes, scrubbed and cut into ¼-inch dice

½ medium cabbage, cored, rinsed, and coarsely grated

6 cups Chicken Stock or Vegetable Stock

½ cup crème fraîche

fine sea salt and freshly ground pepper to taste

1. Melt the butter in a soup pot, and sauté the leeks and prosciutto until softened, about 5 minutes. Add the potatoes, cabbage, and stock. Bring to a boil, lower the heat, and simmer gently until tender, about 20 to 25 minutes.

2. Off the heat, add the crème fraîche and stir until well mixed. Season to taste with salt and pepper, and serve.

Make It Light: Reduce butter to 2 tablespoons, and eliminate crème fraîche.

Make It Ahead: You can make this soup up to a day in advance, refrigerate, and reheat to serve.

Dried wild mushrooms, once reconstituted, have a very intense, earthy flavor. In this soup they are combined with fresh mushrooms and orzo, a tiny rice-shaped pasta, to make a rich tasting, satisfying main dish soup. I like to serve it either before or after a Caesar Salad (p. 80).

MUSHROOM SOUP WITH ORZO
Serves 8

4 ounces dried mixed wild mushrooms, soaked in warm water for 1 hour
4 tablespoons unsalted butter (2 ounces)
2 tablespoons extra virgin olive oil
2 large onions, finely chopped
6 cloves garlic, finely chopped
1 pound fresh domestic mushrooms, sliced medium thick
½ cup red table wine

2 tablespoons soy sauce
½ teaspoon each dry thyme and dry sage
1 cup port
2½ quarts Vegetable, Chicken, or Beef stock
4 ounces orzo (about ½ cup)
salt and pepper, to taste

1. Place the wild mushrooms and their soaking liquid in a medium-sized saucepan; simmer covered, over low heat, for 20 minutes. Cool slightly; strain the liquid into another saucepan, squeezing the juices from the mushrooms. Rinse any sand from the mushrooms and chop. Reduce the mushroom liquid by half, then strain and reserve.
2. Heat the butter and olive oil in a large soup pot. Sauté the onions, garlic, and fresh and dried mushrooms for 5 minutes. Add the wine, soy, thyme, sage, port, reduced mushroom liquid, and stock; bring to a boil, lower the heat, and simmer gently, partially covered, for 20 minutes. Add the orzo and simmer until pasta is soft, about 5 minutes. Season with salt and freshly ground pepper to taste.

Make It Light: Eliminate the butter.

Make It Ahead: You can make this soup up to a day in advance and refrigerate. When you are ready, reheat to serve.

LENTIL SOUP
Serves 8 to 10

10½ ounces lentils (about 1½ cups)
½ lemon
1 pound thick sliced bacon
4 tablespoons plus 1 teaspoon unsalted butter
2 onions, 1 finely chopped, the other peeled, left whole, and stuck with 6 cloves
2 cloves garlic, finely chopped
4 cups Chicken Stock

¼ cup each white table wine and Madeira
1 bay leaf
4 ounces cooked ham, cut into ½-inch dice
2 egg yolks
2 tablespoons cognac
1 cup crème fraîche
4 ounces sorrel, stems removed, finely shredded

1. Put the lentils and lemon in a pot; add water to cover, and soak 1 hour.

2. Cook the bacon in a large sauté pan until lightly brown. Drain off the fat and chop or crumble the bacon. Drain the lentils, discarding the lemon.

3. In a large soup pot, melt 4 tablespoons of butter and sauté the onion and garlic over low heat for 3 minutes. Add the lentils, bacon, stock, wines, bay leaf, and onion stuck with cloves; bring to a boil, lower the heat, cover, and simmer gently for about 45 minutes, or until the lentils are soft, adding more liquid if necessary.

4. Allow the soup to cool slightly, and discard the salt pork , bay leaf, and onion stuck with cloves. Pass the soup through a food mill, or purée in a blender. Return the puréed soup to the pot, and add the ham.

5. In a small bowl, combine the egg yolks, cognac, and crème fraîche, and stir into the soup. Sauté the sorrel in remaining teaspoon of butter for about 30 seconds. Stir in the sorrel and reheat the soup to serve.

Make It Light: Reduce the butter to a tablespoon, and omit the egg yolks and crème fraîche.

Make It Ahead: You can make this soup through step 4. When you are ready, reheat the soup, and proceed with step 5.

For a really hearty meal, serve this with a platter of sliced Emily's Grilled Turkey Breast (p. 173) and crusty French or Italian bread.

BLACK BEAN SOUP
WITH MADEIRA AND ORANGE JUICE
Serves 6

1 cup black beans, soaked overnight
1 medium onion, chopped
4 cups Chicken or Vegetable Stock
1 carrot, chopped
1 stalk celery, chopped
3 cloves garlic, chopped
2 medium ripe tomatoes, seeded and chopped or ½ cup canned chopped tomatoes
1 jalapeño chile, seeded and chopped
12 sprigs cilantro, chopped, plus extra whole sprigs for garnish
2 bay leaves
1 teaspoon chopped fresh thyme
1 teaspoon each coriander seeds and cumin seeds, toasted and ground
¼ cup Madeira
½ cup fresh orange juice
1 tablespoon each sherry vinegar and sugar
sea salt and freshly ground pepper to taste
½ cup crème fraîche for garnish

1. Drain the beans, and put them in a pot with fresh water to cover. Bring to a boil, reduce to a simmer, cover partially, and cook until the beans are done, about 1½ to 2 hours. They should be tender but not mushy.
2. Place the onion in a soup pot with ½ cup of stock and bring to a boil. Lower the heat, partially cover the pot, and simmer until the onion is tender, about 15 minutes. Stir in the carrot, celery, and garlic, and cook 5 minutes over medium heat. Add the cooked black beans, remaining stock, tomatoes, jalapeño, chopped cilantro, bay leaves, thyme, coriander, and cumin, and simmer for 20 minutes. Add the Madeira, orange juice, vinegar, sugar, salt, and pepper to taste, and cook 5 minutes longer.
3. Allow the soup to cool slightly, remove the bay leaves and purée 2 cups of the soup in a blender or food processor. Combine the purée with the rest of the soup; taste and adjust the seasoning. Serve hot with a garnish of cilantro sprigs and a dollop of crème fraîche.

Make It Light: Substitute ½ cup plain yogurt for the crème fraîche garnish.

Make It Ahead: You need to soak and cook the beans first before making the soup, so allow time for that. The soup can then be made up to a day in advance and refrigerated. When you are ready, reheat before serving. Since the beans absorb liquid as they stand, it may be necessary to add more stock before reheating.

TUSCAN WHITE BEAN SOUP WITH GARLIC CROUTONS

Serves 6 to 8

¾ pound small white beans (1½ cups), soaked overnight

2 bay leaves

8 cups Chicken Stock

¼ cup extra virgin olive oil

1 large leek, whites only, cleaned and sliced

1 carrot, peeled and coarsely chopped

1 fennel bulb, coarsely chopped (p. 180)

2 stalks celery, coarsely chopped

10 cloves garlic, chopped

1 red bell pepper, roasted, peeled, and chopped

2 tablespoons finely chopped mixed fresh herbs (rosemary, flat-leaf parsley, marjoram, sage)

1 teaspoon each coarse sea salt and freshly ground black pepper, or to taste

Croutons, made with slices of bread rubbed with garlic (p. 15)

1. Drain and rinse the soaked beans, place them in a soup pot with the bay leaves, pour the stock over the beans, and bring to a boil. Reduce the heat, cover partially, and allow to simmer gently for 1½ hours, or until the beans are tender, adding more water or stock if necessary. Discard the bay leaves.

2. Heat the olive oil in a skillet and sauté the leeks, carrot, fennel, and celery over low heat until tender, about 10 minutes. Remove from the heat, combine with the garlic and bell pepper, and add the vegetables to the beans, along with the chopped herbs, salt, and pepper. Simmer about 10 to 15 minutes more, until vegetables are tender, adding more stock or water if necessary. To serve, place 2 or 3 Croutons in each soup bowl and spoon the soup over them.

Make It Light: Omit the olive oil and steam the vegetables instead of sautéing them.

Make It Ahead: You can make this soup up to 1 day in advance, refrigerate, and reheat to serve. You may need to add additional stock because, as the soup stands, the beans absorb liquid.

This is our Rebecca's version of a classic bean-and-vegetable soup that comes from the Provençal region of France. The *pistou* itself is an uncooked sauce made of tomatoes, garlic, basil, and Parmesan cheese that is stirred into the soup at the last minute, and it's just as good on pasta as it is in this soup. She has reduced the oil and cheese from the classic version.

PISTOU SOUP

Serves 8

¼ cup extra virgin olive oil
1 onion, 1 carrot, and 1 white turnip, chopped
6 cups Chicken Stock
2 large red or white new potatoes, scrubbed and cut into ½-inch dice
1 large leek, white and light green parts only, cleaned and chopped
1 small zucchini, cut into small dice
8 ounces fresh green beans, cut in 1-inch pieces
2 large tomatoes, seeded and chopped

3 tablespoons each chopped fresh basil, chopped garlic, and chopped flat-leaf parsley,
1 ounce grated Parmigiano-Reggiano (about ¼ cup)
½ cup cooked small white beans (p. 66) a handful (about 3 ounces) thin spaghetti, broken into thirds
1 teaspoon each sugar and coarse sea salt, or to taste
freshly ground white pepper to taste

1. Heat 1 tablespoon olive oil in a large soup pot over medium heat. Add the onion, carrot, and turnip, and cook 3 minutes. Stir in the Chicken Stock, and bring to a boil. Reduce to a simmer, partially cover the pot, and cook 10 minutes. Add the potatoes, leek, zucchini, and green beans. Simmer for 20 minutes more.
2. For the *pistou*, combine the tomatoes, basil, garlic, parsley, remaining olive oil, and grated Parmigiano in a small bowl. Set aside.
3. Stir the white beans and spaghetti into the soup and simmer 10 minutes longer. Two minutes before serving, stir the *pistou*, sugar, salt, and pepper into the soup. Serve hot or at room temperature, but not chilled.

Make It Light: You can eliminate the olive oil and cheese from the *pistou*.

Make It Ahead: You can make the soup and the *pistou* up to 1 day in advance, and refrigerate separately. Reheat the soup or bring it to room temperature; stir in the *pistou* just before serving.

This was my grandmother's answer to canned chicken soup. Every time she served it to me, she would say "Now, don't you think this is so much better than the canned ones?" As a child, I really wanted the canned soup so I could be like all my friends, but did not want to hurt her feelings, so I always told her "Oh, yes," and finished every last noodle. Of course I came to love her soup, and now I'm so glad that I learned the difference at an early age!

GRANDMOTHER'S CHICKEN NOODLE SOUP

Serves 8

a 3- or 4-pound chicken
2 onions, each stuck with 3 cloves
4 stalks celery, cut into 1-inch pieces
4 carrots, cut into 1-inch pieces
¼ bunch flat-leaf parsley
3½ quarts water

fine sea salt and freshly ground pepper to taste
8 ounces fettuccine, broken in half
1 pound tiny green peas, cooked
3 tablespoons chopped fresh flat-leaf parsley for garnish

1. Place the chicken in a large soup pot. Add the onions, celery, carrots, parsley, and water. Bring to a boil, then lower the heat, partially cover, and simmer for 2 hours, skimming off any foam that appears on the top of the soup. Remove from the heat, and let the chicken cool in the soup for 2 hours.
2. Remove the chicken from the soup, and remove the skin and bones (best done with your hands). Slice the meat into long strips, saving the scraps for another use. Reserve the meat in the refrigerator.
3. Strain the soup, discarding the vegetables, and return to the pot. Season to taste with salt and pepper. Bring to a boil and cook, uncovered, for 20 minutes, to intensify the flavor.
4. Add the noodles and cook until they are tender, about 5 minutes. Stir in the reserved chicken and the peas. Serve garnished with chopped parsley.

Make It Light: Chill the broth overnight, and skim off the congealed fat.

Make It Ahead: You can make this soup up to 1 day in advance through step 3. When you are ready, bring the soup to a boil and proceed with step 4.

This is a soup we have made year after year in our basic cooking series. It is a simple but elegant-tasting soup, and serves as a perfect illustration of the small bridge between a good stock, which is what our first class is all about, and a great soup. Once your stock is made, this soup will only take you about 10 minutes to make.

ITALIAN EGG-RIBBON SOUP
Serves 6 to 8

3 eggs
1 tablespoon cold water
1 ounce freshly grated
   Parmigiano-Reggiano (¼ cup)
3 tablespoons chopped fresh
   flat-leaf parsley

6 cups Chicken Stock
   fine sea salt and freshly ground
   pepper to taste

Beat the eggs and water in a bowl; stir in the Parmigiano and parsley. Just before serving, bring the stock to a boil and slowly pour the egg mixture into the soup, stirring steadily with a fork until the eggs are set. Taste, adjust seasonings and serve immediately.

Make It Light: Substitute 2 eggs and 2 tablespoons Parmigiano-Reggiano for amounts called for in recipe.

Make It Ahead: You can assemble all your ingredients up to 2 hours in advance. Follow recipe for final instructions.

Here's another recipe we have borrowed from our neighbors south of the border.

MEXICAN RANCH SOUP

Serves 8

6 cups Chicken Stock
2 whole chicken breasts, boned,
 skinned, and julienned
1 cup cooked white rice
 a bouquet garni
2 jalapeño chiles, seeded, stemmed,
 and chopped
2 medium tomatoes, seeded
 and chopped

½ onion, chopped
1 medium-sized ripe avocado, peeled,
 seeded, and chopped
3 tablespoons chopped fresh cilantro
 sea salt and freshly ground pepper
 to taste
4 limes

1. In a soup pot, bring the Chicken Stock to a boil, reduce the heat, add the chicken, rice, and bouquet garni, and simmer over low heat for 10 minutes.
2. Add the jalapeños, tomatoes, onion, avocado, and cilantro, bring to a boil, stir, and cook for 1 minute. Remove the bouquet garni and season with salt and pepper to taste. Ladle the hot soup into 8 bowls, and squeeze the juice of ½ lime into each bowl.

Make It Ahead: You can make this soup up to 1 day in advance, and refrigerate. When you are ready, reheat to serve.

When asparagus is in season, this is my favorite way to begin a "company" dinner.

ICED ASPARAGUS SOUP WITH CRAB AND SHRIMP
Serves 8

2 pounds asparagus, tips cut off and reserved; stalks cut into 2-inch pieces
1 cup water
1 bunch green onions, cleaned and coarsely chopped
¼ teaspoon each dry thyme, fine sea salt, and freshly ground white pepper
3 tablespoons unsalted butter

5 tablespoons flour
2 cups Chicken Stock
1 cup crème fraîche
fine sea salt and freshly ground white pepper
4 ounces each tiny cooked shrimp and crabmeat

1. Blanch the tips of the asparagus in boiling water for 2 minutes, drain, and chill.
2. In a saucepan, bring the cup of water to a boil, add the asparagus stalks, green onions, thyme, salt, and pepper, cover, and simmer slowly until tender, about 20 minutes. Cool slightly; transfer to a food processor or blender, and purée until smooth.
3. Melt the butter in a large soup pot, add the flour, and cook, stirring continuously, for 2 minutes. Add the stock and bring to a boil, stirring constantly. Add the puréed asparagus and crème fraîche; taste and correct seasoning. Chill well and serve cold, garnished with the reserved asparagus tips and shrimp or crabmeat.

Make It Light: Substitute nonfat milk for the crème fraîche.

Make It Ahead: You can make this soup up to 1 day in advance.

Bisques are thick, creamy soups, sometimes made with vegetables, but usually with shellfish. In this case, it's a combination of shrimp and oysters.

SHRIMP AND OYSTER BISQUE

Serves 8

2 cups shucked oysters, coarsely chopped, liquor reserved
8 ounces shrimp, shelled, deveined, and chopped
4 cups milk
1 cup crème fraîche
1 stalk celery, chopped
3 tablespoons chopped shallots

1 tablespoon chopped fresh flat-leaf parsley
¼ teaspoon each ground mace, fine sea salt, and freshly ground white pepper
2 tablespoons unsalted butter
2 tablespoons flour
2 egg yolks, lightly beaten (optional)

1. Put the oysters, shrimp, and oyster liquor in a soup pot; add the milk, crème fraîche, celery, shallots, parsley, and seasonings. Simmer, partially covered, for 30 minutes. Cool slightly, then purée in a food processor or blender, and return to the soup pot. Check seasoning and adjust.

2. In a small saucepan, melt the butter, sprinkle in the flour, and cook over low heat for 4 minutes, stirring all the while. Stir this roux into the soup, and simmer over low heat 1 minute. Remove from the heat, and stir in the egg yolks for extra richness, if desired. Serve in wide shallow soup bowls.

Make It Light: Substitute milk for crème fraîche, and omit egg yolks.

Make It Ahead: Entire recipe can be prepared up to 3 hours before serving. Reheat gently to serve.

There are many versions of the Greek avgolemono, or egg and lemon soup. Our version is an adaptation of a recipe that was given to us by our Greek cooking instructor.

GREEK EGG AND LEMON SOUP

Serves 8

2 quarts Chicken Stock
4 ounces long-grain rice (about ⅓ cup)
1 teaspoon (or more) coarse sea salt
½ teaspoon (or more) freshly
   ground pepper

4 egg yolks
  juice of 2 large lemons
1 bunch flat-leaf parsley, stems
   discarded, leaves chopped

1. Bring the stock to a boil and add the rice, salt, and pepper; simmer over low heat, covered, until rice is tender, about 15 minutes.
2. Whisk the egg yolks, lemon juice, and parsley together in a bowl; gently whisk in a cup of hot soup, then pour this mixture back into the soup, stirring until the soup thickens. Serve immediately.

Make It Ahead: You can complete step 1 up to 2 hours before serving. Have the remainder of the ingredients and the serving bowls ready; just before serving, reheat the soup and proceed with step 2.

For people who love Roquefort, this is a little like going to heaven!

ROQUEFORT SOUP

Serves 8

4 tablespoons unsalted butter (2 ounces)	4½ cups Chicken Stock or Vegetable Stock
1 onion, chopped	fine sea salt and freshly ground pepper to taste
1 stalk celery, chopped	
1 carrot, scrubbed and chopped	2 ounces Roquefort cheese (4 tablespoons)
1 clove garlic, chopped	
3 tablespoons flour	4 tablespoons crème fraîche
¾ cup milk	8 slices French bread, lightly toasted

1. Melt the butter in a large soup pot, stir in the onion, celery, and carrot, cover, and sauté over very low heat for 10 minutes. Add the flour and cook 3 minutes more over low heat, stirring all the while. Add the milk, stock, and salt and pepper to taste; bring to a boil, reduce heat to low, and simmer 10 minutes more.

2. Mash the cheese with a fork and mix with the crème fraîche. Remove the soup from the heat, and whisk in the cheese mixture. Taste and adjust the seasoning. Place the toasted bread in individual warmed soup bowls and pour the soup over the toasts. Serve at once.

Make It Light: Reduce the butter to 2 tablespoons and the flour to 1 tablespoon; substitute 4 tablespoons nonfat milk for the crème fraîche.

Make It Ahead: You can make this soup up to 3 hours ahead through step 1. Have the rest of the ingredients assembled, including the warmed soup bowls. When you are ready, reheat the soup and proceed with step 2.

Stanley Eichelbaum was the film and theater critic of the *San Francisco Examiner* for many years prior to embarking on a second career as a chef and food writer. We have been very fortunate to have Stanley as a guest instructor at HomeChef and really had a hard time selecting a single favorite recipe of his. It took a while to decide, but here it is, a marvelous soup that can be a first course or a dessert. He says, "Here is a refreshing summertime soup made with ripe peaches and your choice of berries. The recipe calls for blueberries and raspberries, but pick the kind you like. And if you want a zestier soup, stir in some chilled champagne at the end."

CHILLED PEACH AND BERRY SOUP
Serves 8 to 10

10 medium-sized ripe peaches,
7 ounces sugar (about 1 cup)
1 cup water
1 cinnamon stick
2 whole cloves

1 cup white table wine
¼ cup brandy
1 cup each blueberries and raspberries
1 cup chilled champagne (optional)
   julienned mint leaves for garnish

1. Blanch the peaches in boiling water for 2 minutes and remove from the pot. Allow to cool, slip off the skins, cut in half, and remove the pits.
2. In a heavy-bottomed saucepan, bring the sugar and water to a boil over medium heat. Break the cinnamon stick in half and add to the saucepan along with the cloves, white wine, and brandy. Simmer 10 minutes over low heat. Remove from the heat, discard the cinnamon stick and cloves, add the peaches to the hot syrup, and let steep 3 hours.
3. Purée the peaches and syrup in batches in a blender or food processor. Transfer to a glass or porcelain serving bowl, cover, and refrigerate for 3 or 4 hours, until chilled. If you wish, stir in the optional champagne. Serve in shallow soup bowls with berries floating on the chilled soup. Garnish with julienned mint leaves.

Make It Ahead: You can make this up to 1 day in advance.

SALADS

Salads and desserts are the two most popular food categories with our students at HomeChef. For me, salads win out over desserts. Rarely does a day go by that I don't have some kind of salad as part of a meal, or sometimes as the meal itself.

To help you with menu planning, I have arranged the salads in groups. Generally, the leafy green salads are best served before or after the main course. The vegetable and fruit combinations are definitely first courses, and are not usually served after the main course. Seafood, poultry, grain, bean, and pasta salads, in very small portions, can be served as a first course, but in larger portions, could be the main dish of a light meal. If you're entertaining a large crowd, you can arrange a variety of salads on a buffet table for an all-salad meal.

I have specified 1 to 1½ pounds of greens for eight people, but this is a "more-or-less" amount that you will need to adjust, based on what else you will be serving. I have also specified salad dressing amounts (usually about ½ cup for a salad that will serve six to eight people), but you should use your own judgment here, too. Each salad has its recommended dressing, but feel free to experiment. For instance, Pasta, Peach, and Chicken Breast Salad with Jalapeño-Lime Mayonnaise becomes a new dish when it is dressed with Chipotle Dressing. The salad dressing recipes are all grouped together at the end of the chapter so that you can see them all at a glance, in case you want to make substitutions.

With salads, there is really only one important rule: Think of how a garden looks and then try to bring a bit of it to the table, always using the freshest, best-quality fruits and vegetables available, and arranging them artfully.

PREPARING GREENS FOR SALADS

All leafy greens, including watercress, chard, and spinach, should be swished briefly in a large basin full of lukewarm water. Shake off the excess water, and dry in a salad spinner (do this in batches, if necessary). To crisp, wrap in paper towels or linen towels (this will take care of any remaining moisture), place in a plastic bag, and store in the vegetable bin of your refrigerator. Greens will stay crisp this way for up to two days. If the greens are to be torn or cut into smaller pieces, this is best done just before the salad is dressed and served.

It is not necessary to separate the leaves of a Belgian endive in order to clean it. First, cut off the root end and, with the tip of your knife, remove the bitter core by cutting it out with a circular motion. Rinse the entire head, wrap each one in a towel, and place in a plastic bag.

Note: Before washing the entire lettuce, check for dirt or sand. Many varieties are only sandy in the outer leaves—the inner ones may not need washing.

LEAFY GREEN SALADS

Making a basic green salad is very simple, especially if you have the greens rinsed and crisped ahead of time, and the dressing prepared as well. Just remember to give the dressing 30 minutes to come to room temperature, then all you need to do is toss everything together at the last minute — the greens, the dressing, and any extras you want to add to the salad (nuts, herbs, crumbled bacon, etc.). If you want to be a little dramatic, you can do this at the table. The salad can be served before or after the main course, it is simply a matter of personal preference.

For eight people, figure on 1 to 1½ pounds of salad greens such as spinach, romaine, butter lettuce, or ruby or red leaf lettuce, and about ½ cup of salad dressing. I have found that a large wooden bowl works best for tossed salads — 16 or 17 inches is ideal. With a bowl this size, you can toss salads for one or two people or as many as eight or ten, and the greens won't spill out.

Here are two light leafy green salads:

WATERCRESS AND ENDIVE
WITH RASPBERRY WALNUT VINAIGRETTE
Serves 8

3 bunches watercress, large stems removed, rinsed and crisped

2 heads Belgian endive, core removed, and leaves thinly sliced

about ½ cup Raspberry Walnut Vinaigrette (p. 103)

Toss everything together in a large salad bowl just before serving.

MIXED LETTUCES WITH TOASTED WALNUTS,
BACON, AND SHERRY WALNUT VINAIGRETTE
Serves 8

1½ pounds mixed lettuces, rinsed and crisped

4 ounces bacon, cooked, drained, and crumbled

1 hard-cooked egg, chopped

2 ounces toasted walnut halves (about ½ cup)

about ½ cup Sherry Walnut Vinaigrette (p. 103)

Toss everything together in a large salad bowl just before serving.

As the story goes, Caesar Cardini invented this classic salad in the early 1920s for the "smart Hollywood set" who frequented his chic restaurant in Tijuana, Mexico. I think the most interesting aspect of this salad is that he used only the romaine lettuce hearts, and left the small leaves whole because he intended for this salad to be eaten with the fingers. If you wish to carry on this tradition, you will probably have to lead the way when the salad is served, because most people won't know how it's supposed to be eaten.

CLASSIC CAESAR SALAD
Serves 6 to 8

1 clove garlic, crushed
6 anchovy fillets, soaked in milk
    5 minutes, drained and patted dry
½ cup extra virgin olive oil
1 teaspoon each fine sea salt and sugar
½ teaspoon each freshly ground black
    pepper and Worcestershire sauce
3 tablespoons fresh lemon juice

2 heads romaine lettuce, 6 of the
    outer leaves discarded, the
    inner leaves rinsed and crisped
2 eggs, coddled for 1 minute
3 ounces Parmigiano-Reggiano,
    freshly grated (about ¾ cup)
    Croutons

Rub the crushed garlic around the inside of the salad bowl, then leave it in the bowl. Add the anchovy fillets, olive oil, sea salt, sugar, pepper, and Worcestershire sauce and mix with a wooden spoon until the anchovies are dissolved and the mixture is smooth. Stir in the lemon juice. Add the romaine (tear it into bite-sized pieces, first, if you don't want whole leaves), and toss well. Break the eggs into the bowl; toss well, and add the grated Parmigiano. Toss one last time and arrange salad on individual plates. Garnish each salad with Croutons.

Make It Light: Omit the egg yolks and reduce the Parmigiano-Reggiano to ⅓ cup.

Make It Ahead: You can have all the salad ingredients and salad plates ready for the final assembly. Toss and serve at the table.

This spinach salad is light because we have substituted slivered almonds and hard-cooked egg whites for the usual bacon and whole hard-cooked eggs. In addition, it features a Roquefort dressing that contains no oil. Our students voted this a "favorite" to be included here, even though I consider it a specialty salad with a smaller audience.

HOMECHEF'S LIGHT SPINACH SALAD

Serves 8

1½ pounds spinach, stems removed, rinsed, and crisped
about ½ cup Light Roquefort Dressing (p. 107)
1 ounce slivered almonds (about 2 tablespoons), toasted

4 hard-cooked eggs, whites chopped, yolks discarded
10 mushrooms, sliced and steamed 1 minute

Tear the spinach into bite-sized pieces, and place in a salad bowl. Toss with ½ cup of dressing, then add more if needed. Garnish each serving with almonds, chopped egg whites, and sliced mushrooms.

Make It Ahead: Several hours in advance, you can have the spinach crisped and torn, the almonds, egg white, mushrooms, and dressing prepared (store the dressing in the refrigerator). Set the dressing out at room temperature for 30 minutes before tossing with the spinach.

BAKED GOAT CHEESE SALAD
WITH RASPBERRY WALNUT VINAIGRETTE

Serves 8

12 ounces goat cheese	Raspberry Walnut Vinaigrette (p. 103)
3 tablespoons walnut oil	¾ pound raspberries (1 small basket)
3 ounces dry bread crumbs (about 1 cup)	3 ounces toasted walnut halves (about ½ cup)
1 pound mixed lettuces, rinsed and crisped	

1. Cut the cheese into 8 pieces. Brush each piece with walnut oil, then roll in bread crumbs. Place in a baking dish and refrigerate at least 2 hours.

2. Bake the cheese in a preheated 475° oven until lightly browned, about 10 minutes.

3. Toss the greens with Raspberry Walnut Vinaigrette, and divide into 8 portions. Place the warm cheese on the greens, and garnish with raspberries and walnuts.

Make It Light: Omit the walnuts and substitute HomeChef's Light Salad Dressing (p. 104) for the Raspberry Walnut Vinaigrette.

Make It Ahead: Prepare and chill the goat cheese up to 4 hours ahead (step 1). When you are ready, proceed with step 2. The greens can be cleaned and chilled up to 2 days in advance. The dressing can also be made up to 2 days ahead: refrigerate it, then allow 30 minutes for it to come to room temperature.

Be sure to use fresh mozzarella in this next salad. You can find fresh mozzarella in cheese shops, packed in liquid. It is very soft and very white and very delicious — bearing very little resemblance to the rubbery, packaged cheese found in markets under the name mozzarella.

MARINATED MOZZARELLA CHEESE, RADICCHIO, AND BELGIAN ENDIVE
Serves 8

6 tablespoons extra virgin olive oil (preferably Italian)

3 tablespoons balsamic vinegar

2 tablespoons finely chopped fresh oregano

½ teaspoon each fine sea salt, freshly ground pepper, and sugar

1 pound fresh mozzarella cheese, cut into ½-inch dice

16 leaves radicchio, rinsed and crisped

6 heads Belgian endive, core removed, and leaves thinly sliced

In a large salad bowl, combine the olive oil, vinegar, oregano, salt, pepper, and sugar. Add the mozzarella, cover, and marinate 4 hours. Shortly before serving, coarsely chop 8 leaves of radicchio. Use the whole leaves to line 8 salad plates. Toss the endive, chopped radicchio, and mozzarella together, and arrange on the whole radicchio leaves.

Make It Light: Substitute ½ cup HomeChef's Light Salad Dressing (p. 104) for the olive oil and vinegar in the recipe.

Make It Ahead: The mozzarella cheese needs to marinate 4 hours. The endive and radicchio can be prepared up to 4 hours ahead. Toss and arrange salad just before serving.

An unusual salad that sparkles with flavor. Romaine lettuce provides a perfect crispness to balance the soft tender figs, toasted pine nuts, and rich feta cheese.

ROMAINE WITH FETA CHEESE, FRESH FIGS, AND PINE NUTS
Serves 8

3 ounces toasted pine nuts
  (about ¾ cup)
½ red onion, thinly sliced
2 medium heads romaine lettuce,
  rinsed, crisped, and torn into
  bite-sized pieces

½ cup Sherry Walnut Vinaigrette (p. 103)
¾ pound feta cheese, crumbled
  (about 1½ cups)
10 black figs, sliced into ¼-inch rounds
  freshly ground black pepper to taste

In a large salad bowl, combine the pine nuts, red onion, and romaine. Sprinkle half the dressing over the salad and toss well. Arrange the salad on 8 plates, and top each salad with feta cheese and sliced figs. Season with freshly ground pepper, and pass the remainder of the dressing at the table.

Make It Light: Substitute HomeChef's Light Salad Dressing (p. 104) for the Sherry Walnut Vinaigrette, and reduce pine nuts to 1 ounce or approximately ¼ cup.

Make It Ahead: You can make the dressing up to 2 days ahead of time. Have all ingredients ready for final assembly up to an hour ahead of serving.

VEGETABLE AND FRUIT SALADS

This classic French salad lends itself to creative arrangement.

SALAD NIÇOISE
Serves 4

1 pound tiny boiling potatoes, cooked until tender, drained, and cut into 4 pieces each

8 ounces fresh green beans, left whole, blanched 3 minutes and drained

1 English cucumber, halved lengthwise, seeded, and cut into ¼-inch slices

3 large tomatoes, peeled, 2 cut into ¼-inch slices, the other into 8 wedges

1 can (7 ounces) imported Italian tuna, drained and flaked

½ cup HomeChef's Basic Vinaigrette made with fresh oregano and thyme

10 anchovy fillets

2 hard-cooked eggs, quartered

15 or 20 Niçoise olives

Arrange the potatoes, beans, half the cucumber slices, tomato slices, and tuna in layers on a serving dish, and sprinkle with the dressing. Arrange the remaining cucumber slices over the top, cover with a lattice of anchovy fillets, and decorate with hard-cooked eggs, Niçoise olives, and tomato wedges.

Make It Light: Substitute HomeChef's Light Salad Dressing (p. 104) for the Basic Vinaigrette.

Make It Ahead: You can make this salad up to 4 hours in advance. Refrigerate it, and allow to stand at room temperature 30 minutes before serving.

This salad is elegant, and quite complex in flavor. The sweet, slightly sour, and toasty flavors will surprise even jaded palates. Because it is simple to prepare and serve, it is a good salad to make if there is a lot of preparation involved in the rest of the meal.

TOMATO, DATE, FRESH FIG, AND FENNEL SALAD
Serves 8

¾ cup pitted and coarsely chopped dates
6 black figs, chopped
   juice of 2 oranges
   juice of 1 lemon
2 tablespoons orange liqueur
2 medium heads butter lettuce, rinsed and crisped
1 large head fennel, stalks removed, strings removed, halved, and thinly sliced

1 medium red onion, halved, and thinly sliced
4 ripe tomatoes, coarsely chopped
5 ounces toasted walnuts (about 1 cup)
2 cloves garlic, finely chopped
2 shallots, peeled and finely chopped
   about 1 cup Raspberry Walnut Vinaigrette (p. 103)

1. Combine dates, figs, citrus juices, and liqueur in a small bowl, and marinate 4 hours.
2. Divide the butter lettuce among 8 salad plates. Arrange the sliced fennel, onions, and tomatoes on the greens; drain the figs and dates, and arrange on top of the fennel. Garnish with toasted walnuts.
3. Stir the chopped garlic and shallots into the dressing; sprinkle each salad with dressing, and pass the remainder at the table.

Make It Light: Substitute HomeChef's Light Salad Dressing (p. 104) for the Raspberry Walnut Vinaigrette.

Make It Ahead: You can assemble the individual salads up to 2 hours in advance through step 2; refrigerate until serving. When you are ready, proceed with step 3.

This colorful salad is a little like a chameleon. It easily changes names, depending on which class we use it in. When it is on a French menu, it is called *Poivrons à la Provençale,* or if it is an Italian menu, it's *Pepperoni alla Piemontese.* When we include it on a holiday menu, we call it Christmas Salad. It's a natural choice for that because of its beautiful reds and greens, but, of course, it is also perfect as a summer salad. After you try it, you may think of several other appropriate titles for this versatile salad.

SLICED TOMATO AND ROASTED BELL PEPPER SALAD

Serves 8 to 12

8 tomatoes, cored, and cut into ¼-inch-thick slices

1 cup Vinaigrette with Herbs and Garlic (p. 103)

8 green bell peppers, roasted, peeled, seeded, and cut into 1-inch strips

6 hard-cooked eggs, cut into ¼-inch slices

12 anchovy fillets

12 small pimento-stuffed olives

1. Place a layer of tomato slices on the bottom of a large oval or square serving dish and sprinkle with a little vinaigrette. Add a layer of peppers, sprinkle with dressing, and continue until all the tomatoes and peppers are layered.

2. Arrange the sliced eggs over the top, make a lattice of anchovies over the eggs, and place an olive in the center of each diamond. Allow to marinate several hours before serving.

Make It Light: Substitute 1¼ cups HomeChef's Light Salad Dressing (p. 104) for the suggested Basic Vinaigrette.

Make It Ahead: This is best made up to 4 hours ahead and allowed to marinate at room temperature.

This is a personal favorite of mine. I love it served as an accompaniment to Bourbon and Honey Marinated Pork Tenderloin (p. 149).

WARM CABBAGE SALAD WITH APPLES, FETA, AND PISTACHIOS

Serves 6

3 tablespoons extra virgin olive oil
1 red onion, halved and thinly sliced
1 clove garlic, finely chopped
½ head red cabbage, thinly sliced
2 tablespoons balsamic vinegar
1 teaspoon sugar
½ teaspoon each coarse sea salt and freshly ground pepper, or to taste

1 tart apple, peeled, cored, and coarsely chopped
2 ounces feta cheese, crumbled (about 4 tablespoons)
1 tablespoon toasted shelled pistachios

1. Heat the olive oil in a large skillet over moderate heat. Add the garlic and onions and sauté 2 minutes. Increase the heat and add the cabbage. Sauté for 2 minutes more, stirring constantly, until the cabbage begins to wilt slightly.
2. Off the heat, add the vinegar, sugar, salt, and pepper, and combine well. Taste and adjust the seasoning. Stir in the apples, feta, and pistachios.
3. Before serving, rewarm over a low heat, tossing constantly, for 1 minute.

Make It Light: Reduce the feta by half.

Make It Ahead: You can make this salad up to an hour in advance through step 2. When you are ready, proceed with step 3.

MARINATED CARROTS

Serves 8

¾ cup Raspberry Walnut Vinaigrette (p. 103)
2 cloves garlic, crushed

2 pounds carrots, peeled and julienned
3 tablespoons chopped fresh flat-leaf parsley

Place the dressing and crushed garlic in a large bowl. Blanch the carrots for 2 minutes, drain, dry on towels, and while still hot drop into the dressing. Allow to marinate at least 1 hour. Discard garlic, and sprinkle with chopped parsley before serving. Can be served at room temperature, or chilled.

Make It Light: Substitute HomeChef's Light Salad Dressing for the Raspberry Walnut Vinaigrette.

Make It Ahead: You can make these carrots up to a day ahead and refrigerate. Leave out at room temperature for 1 hour before serving.

WARM BROCCOLI SESAME SALAD

Serves 4 to 6

2 pounds broccoli, cut into florets, stems peeled and cut into 2-inch pieces
2 tablespoons sesame oil
2 cloves garlic, finely chopped

1 tablespoon rice vinegar
1 tablespoon toasted sesame seeds
4 scallions, finely sliced, whites and greens separated
2 tablespoons soy sauce

1. Blanch the broccoli for 1 minute and drain.

2. Heat the oil in a large wok or skillet over medium heat. Add the garlic, vinegar, sesame seeds, and whites of the scallions; stir and sauté for 30 seconds. Increase the heat to high, add the soy sauce and broccoli and toss about 30 seconds more, until broccoli is well coated with the sauce. Transfer to a serving dish and garnish with scallion greens. Serve warm or at room temperature.

Make It Ahead: You can make this dish up to 2 hours in advance through step 1. Have all the other ingredients prepared, and proceed with step 2 just before serving.

ROASTED RED, GOLDEN, AND PURPLE BELL PEPPER SALAD

Serves 8

¾ cup HomeChef's Basic Vinaigrette (p. 103)
4 cloves garlic, crushed
2 red, 2 golden, and 2 purple bell peppers, roasted, peeled, seeded, and cut into 1-inch strips

3 tablespoons finely chopped fresh flat-leaf parsley

Pour the dressing into a 10- or 12-inch serving dish and add the garlic. Add the peppers, and allow to marinate for at least 4 hours at room temperature. Sprinkle with parsley before serving.

Make It Light: Substitute HomeChef's Light Salad Dressing for the Basic Vinaigrette.

Make It Ahead: You can make this salad up to 1 day in advance, and refrigerate. Allow it to stand at room temperature 1 hour before serving.

I think you will agree that the two potato salads that follow are special. Please note that we do not boil the potatoes but roast and grill them, and that is the secret to their great taste.

ROASTED POTATO SALAD
Serves 8 or 10

3 pounds small boiling potatoes, scrubbed and halved or quartered
2 tablespoons extra virgin olive oil fine sea salt, freshly ground white pepper, and Hungarian paprika to taste

1¼ cups Sun-Dried Tomato Dressing
4 stalks celery, peeled and thinly sliced
½ medium red onion, finely chopped
2 ounces Niçoise olives (about ¼ cup)

1. Toss the potatoes in a baking dish with enough oil to coat them lightly, and season with salt, pepper, and paprika. Roast in a preheated 400° oven until tender, about 25 minutes.
2. Pour the dressing into a serving bowl large enough to hold the potatoes. Remove the potatoes from the oven and while still hot, toss with the dressing. Stir in the celery and onion, taste and adjust seasoning, then add the olives. Allow to stand 2 hours before serving.

Make It Light: Substitute HomeChef's Light Salad Dressing for the Sun-Dried Tomato Dressing.

Make It Ahead: You can make this salad up to 1 day in advance and refrigerate. Allow it to stand at room temperature 1 hour before serving.

To make grilling small foods such as vegetables or shrimp easier, fit a fine wire mesh screen over the barbecue grill or use long handled grill "baskets." They are available in gourmet kitchen stores and hardware stores.

GRILLED POTATO SALAD WITH CHIPOTLE DRESSING

Serves 6

2 pounds boiling potatoes, scrubbed and halved

3 or 4 tablespoons extra virgin olive oil fine sea salt, freshly ground pepper, and Hungarian paprika to taste

1 clove garlic, finely chopped

2 medium red onions cut into 1-inch rings

2 red or yellow bell peppers, cut into 1-inch rings, and seeded

¾ cup Chipotle Dressing (p. 104)

1 tablespoon coarsely chopped fresh cilantro

¾ pound mixed salad greens, rinsed, dried, and crisped

1. Toss the potatoes in a small baking dish with enough oil to coat them lightly, and season with salt and pepper. Roast in a preheated 400° oven until tender, about 20 minutes. Set aside to cool.

2. Combine the garlic and 1 tablespoon olive oil, and brush it over the potatoes, onion rings, and bell pepper strips. Season with salt, pepper, and paprika. Preheat the grill. Place the vegetables on the grill, the cut side of the potatoes down. Turn the onions after 5 minutes, and, move the peppers and potatoes to a cooler part of the grill or remove if they are soft. You do not need to turn the peppers and potatoes.

3. When the onions are tender and browned on both sides, transfer to a bowl and toss with the potatoes, peppers, Chipotle Dressing, and cilantro. Arrange the greens on a platter and spoon potato salad over them.

Make It Light: Substitute HomeChef's Light Salad Dressing for the Chipotle Dressing.

Make It Ahead: You can make the potato salad up to a day in advance and refrigerate. Allow to stand at room temperature 1 hour before serving.

SEAFOOD AND POULTRY SALADS

Served on a bed of mixed greens, this tuna salad makes an ideal light luncheon or dinner salad. It is also excellent on crusty French bread as a cold sandwich, or as an open-faced grilled sandwich.

CURRIED TUNA SALAD

Serves 4 as a first course, 2 as a main course

½ cup HomeChef's Basic
  Mayonnaise (p. 105)
1 teaspoon (or more) curry powder
½ clove garlic, squeezed through a press
1 tuna steak, about 8 ounces, poached,
  cooled, drained, and chopped
½ Granny Smith apple, finely chopped

1 scallion, rinsed and thinly sliced
3 tablespoons toasted slivered almonds
1 stalk celery, peeled and thinly sliced
½ teaspoon each fine sea salt and
  freshly ground pepper
1 tablespoon chutney, chopped

In a small bowl, combine the mayonnaise, curry powder, and garlic; mix well. In a larger bowl, combine all ingredients with a fork; taste and correct seasoning.

Make It Light: Reduce the mayonnaise to 4 tablespoons, or just enough to hold the mixture together. Or, if you prefer use the Light Yogurt "Mayonnaise" (p. 106).

Make It Ahead: You can make this up to 4 hours in advance, and refrigerate. Drain any excess liquids before serving.

The next three salads make excellent light lunch or dinner main courses.

CHINESE CHICKEN SALAD

Serves 4 as a main course

a 3-pound chicken
fine sea salt and freshly ground
pepper to taste
2 tablespoons toasted sesame seeds
3 tablespoons hoisin sauce
(available in Asian markets)
4 tablespoons sesame oil

1 clove garlic, finely chopped
4 scallions, finely sliced
1 teaspoon dry mustard
2 tablespoons each rice vinegar
and soy sauce
3 tablespoons chopped fresh cilantro
1 head iceberg lettuce, shredded

1. Place the chicken in a roasting pan. Season with salt and pepper inside and out. Roast in a preheated 350° oven for 1½ hours. Remove from the oven and allow to cool completely. Using your fingers, take the chicken meat off the bones, discarding the skin. Still using your fingers, shred the meat into bite-sized pieces. Arrange chicken on a platter.
2. In a small bowl, combine the sesame seeds, hoisin sauce, sesame oil, garlic, scallions, mustard, vinegar, soy sauce, and cilantro. Pour the sauce over the chicken, and allow to marinate 30 minutes at room temperature, or up to 2 hours in the refrigerator. Serve on a bed of shredded lettuce.

Make It Light: Reduce the sesame oil to 2 tablespoons.

Make It Ahead: You can roast the chicken up to 1 day in advance and refrigerate until you are ready to take the meat off the bones. Allow 30 minutes to 2 hours for the shredded chicken to marinate. Assemble the salad just before serving.

This is a stunning combination of ingredients and my favorite main dish for lunch. For an all-salad menu, serve it with two other salads, like one of the potato salads, plus one of the vegetable or leafy green salads. Or, if you prefer, cut the recipe in half to serve eight people as a first course.

TARRAGON PECAN CHICKEN SALAD

Serves 8 to 10 as a main course

8 half chicken breasts, boned and skinned
1½ cups crème fraîche
½ cup HomeChef's Basic Mayonnaise (p. 105)
6 stalks celery, peeled and thinly sliced on the diagonal
2 ounces toasted pecan halves (about ½ cup)

2 tablespoons chopped fresh tarragon
1 teaspoon each fine sea salt and freshly ground white pepper
4 tablespoons chopped fresh flat-leaf parsley
16 cherry tomatoes, cut in half

1. Arrange chicken breasts in a single layer in an open roasting dish. Spread 1 cup crème fraîche over the breasts and bake in a preheated 375° oven for 20 minutes. Allow to cool and slice the breasts into 1-inch strips.
2. Combine the remaining ½ cup crème fraîche, mayonnaise, celery, pecans, tarragon, salt, pepper, and parsley in a bowl large enough to hold the chicken.
3. Add the sliced breast meat to the bowl and gently combine. Arrange the chicken attractively on a large platter or on individual serving plates, and garnish with cherry tomatoes.

Make It Light: Substitute Light Yogurt "Mayonnaise" (p. 106) for Basic Mayonnaise.

Make It Ahead: You can make this chicken salad up to 1 day in advance and refrigerate. Remove from refrigerator and allow to stand 1 hour at room temperature before serving.

DUCKLING AND CHICORY SALAD
WITH WALNUTS AND POACHED PEARS

Serves 4 as a main course

1 duckling, about 4 pounds
   fine sea salt and freshly ground pepper
1 cup Sherry Walnut Vinaigrette (p. 103)
1 pound chicory, rinsed, crisped,
   and torn into serving pieces
   Pears Poached in Red Wine Syrup
   (see recipe below)

4 tomatoes, peeled and seeded,
   each cut into 8 wedges
32 toasted walnuts halves

1. Rub the duck inside and out with salt and pepper. Prick the skin on the thighs and breast to allow the fat to drain. Place the duck on a rack in a roasting pan and roast in a preheated 425° oven for 2 hours. Remove from the oven and allow to cool.

2. Cut the duck meat off the bones. (Save the skin, meat scraps, and carcass for stock.) Slice the duck meat into 1-inch strips. Place the duck on a platter and sprinkle with half the vinaigrette. Allow to marinate in the refrigerator for at least 3 hours or up to a day in advance.

3. Just before serving, toss the chicory with the remaining dressing, or to taste, and divide between the serving plates. Arrange slices of duck on top of the chicory, and garnish with pears, tomatoes, and walnuts.

Make It Light: Substitute HomeChef's Light Salad Dressing (p. 104) for the Sherry Walnut Vinaigrette.

Make It Ahead: You can prepare the salad through step 2 up to 1 day in advance. When you are ready proceed with step 3.

PEARS POACHED IN RED WINE SYRUP

1 cup of red table wine
1 cup water
4 ounces sugar (about ½ cup)

4 pears, peeled, cored, and
   quartered lengthwise

Combine the wine, water, and sugar and bring to a boil. Add the pears and simmer gently until soft, 5 to 10 minutes. Remove from the heat and allow pears to cool in the syrup.

Make It Ahead: The pears can be poached up to 1 day in advance.

GRAINS AND BEANS

LENTIL SALAD WITH CUCUMBER DRESSING

Serves 8 as a first course

14 ounces lentils (2 cups), rinsed in
   cold water
1 small yellow onion
1 teaspoon each fine sea salt and
   coarsely ground pepper
1 stalk celery, finely chopped
½ small red onion, finely chopped
1 carrot, finely chopped

½ teaspoon peeled and finely
   chopped fresh ginger
2 tablespoons each fresh lemon juice
   and soy sauce
3 tablespoons extra virgin olive oil
3 large ripe tomatoes, peeled, seeded,
   and finely chopped
   Cucumber Dressing (see recipe below)

1. Place the lentils in a saucepan with water to cover. Bring to a boil, skim off the foam, and add the onion, salt, and pepper. Lower the heat, cover the pot, and simmer until the lentils are tender (but not mushy), about 35 minutes. Drain, remove the onion, and chill.
2. Place the cooked lentils in a mixing bowl. Add the celery, red onion, carrot, ginger, lemon juice, soy sauce, and olive oil, and gently combine. Check the seasoning and add salt and pepper if necessary.
3. Divide the lentil salad among 8 individual plates, and top each with some chopped tomato. Pass the Cucumber Dressing at the table.

CUCUMBER DRESSING

1 English cucumber, seeded
   and chopped
1 tablespoon sherry vinegar
3 tablespoons extra virgin olive oil

1 teaspoon prepared mustard
½ teaspoon each sugar, fine sea salt,
   and freshly ground pepper, or
   to taste

Place all the ingredients in a food processor or blender and process until very smooth.

Make It Ahead: You can make the salad through step 2 up to 3 hours in advance and chill. Bring to room temperature to serve (allow about 30 minutes). The dressing can be made up to 1 day in advance.

CURRIED RICE AND SHRIMP SALAD

Serves 8 as a first course

2 teaspoons each curry powder
and paprika
1 cup Sherry Walnut
Vinaigrette (p. 103)
2½ cups unsalted Chicken Stock (p. 12)
10 ounces basmati rice (1½ cups)
¾ pound cooked shrimp

1 red and 1 yellow bell pepper,
seeded and chopped
1 medium onion, chopped
2 hard-cooked eggs, chopped
4 stalks celery, chopped
4 tablespoons chopped fresh
flat-leaf parsley

1. In a small deep bowl, mix together the curry powder, paprika, and Sherry Walnut Vinaigrette, and set aside.

2. Bring the stock to a boil in a saucepan, stir in the rice, reduce the heat, and simmer partially covered until all the liquid is absorbed and the rice is tender, about 10 minutes. Remove from the heat and let stand covered for an additional 10 minutes. Fluff the rice with a fork, and transfer to a serving bowl to cool.

3. Combine the cooled rice, shrimp, bell peppers, onion, eggs, celery, and parsley. Pour the dressing over all and mix well. Taste, and add more curry or paprika seasoning if needed.

Make It Light: Substitute HomeChef's Light Salad Dressing (p. 104) for the Sherry Walnut Vinaigrette.

Make It Ahead: You can make this salad up to 2 hours in advance of serving, refrigerate or serve at room temperature.

TUSCAN WHITE BEAN SALAD

Serves 8 as a first course

1 pound small dried white beans, soaked overnight
½ cup extra virgin olive oil
2 cloves garlic, finely chopped
3 tablespoons each chopped fresh flat-leaf parsley and chopped fresh basil
2 teaspoons chopped fresh rosemary

2 fresh sage leaves, chopped
2 teaspoons fine sea salt, or more to taste
½ teaspoon each sugar and freshly ground black pepper
4 tablespoons fresh lemon juice
20 black olives, pitted

1. Drain the beans, and put them in a pot with fresh water to cover. Bring to a boil, reduce to a simmer, cover partially, and cook until the beans are done, about 1½ to 2 hours. They should be tender but not mushy.

2. Heat the olive oil in a skillet. Add the garlic, parsley, basil, rosemary, and sage, and cook over low heat 1 minute, without letting the garlic brown. Add the cooked beans, salt, sugar, and pepper, and toss very gently. Allow to cook, covered, over very low heat for 5 minutes. Remove from the heat, transfer to a serving bowl, and stir in the lemon juice and the olives. Serve warm or at room temperature.

Make It Ahead: You can make this up to 1 day in advance, and refrigerate. Rewarm, or allow to stand at room temperature for 1 hour before serving.

PASTA SALADS

Pasta salads leave a lot of freedom for creativity because you can substitute vegetables, dressings, or even the pastas to suit yourself. When it comes to substituting pastas, however, try to stick with those of similar size and shape (macaroni could replace penne, since both are short and tubular, but fettuccine, which is long and flat, would not be a good choice). I like to use the pastas imported from Italy, because they are made with a high proportion of hard wheat, they retain their texture even after they have been cooked and marinated with a sauce or dressing. You can find imported pasta in Italian delicatessens and other specialty markets. Pastas should be cooked in plenty of lightly salted boiling water until just *al dente*, then drained, tossed in a little oil, and allowed to cool.

PASTA SALAD WITH CHICKEN, PEACHES, AND JALAPEÑO-LIME MAYONNAISE

Serves 8 as a first course

1 pound penne (or ziti or macaroni)
1 tablespoon coarse sea salt, for cooking pasta
1 tablespoon extra virgin olive oil
4 half chicken breasts, boned, skinned, poached, and cut into 1-inch cubes
3 ripe peaches, peeled, pitted, and cut into ½-inch dice

3 stalks celery, peeled and chopped
1 small jalapeño chile, seeded and finely chopped
  juice of 1 lime
¾ to 1½ cups Jalapeño-Lime Mayonnaise (p. 105)

Cook the pasta in plenty of lightly salted boiling water until it is al dente; drain, toss with olive oil, and cool. In a large bowl, toss the chicken, peaches, celery, and jalapeño with the lime juice. Add the pasta and toss well. Gently mix in ¾ cup Jalapeño-Lime Mayonnaise and toss all ingredients together. Add more mayonnaise if needed.

Make It Light: Make the Jalapeño-Lime Mayonnaise with HomeChef's Light Yogurt "Mayonnaise" (p. 106).

Make It Ahead: You can make the salad up to 3 hours in advance and refrigerate. Allow to stand at room temperature 30 minutes before serving.

Agnolotti, ravioli, or tortellini can be substituted for the tortelloni in this salad—all are filled pastas, but tortelloni are generally somewhat larger than the others.

TORTELLONI AND VEGETABLE SALAD

Serves 8 to 10 as a first course

1 pound tortelloni
1 tablespoon coarse sea salt,
   for cooking pasta
1 tablespoon extra virgin olive oil
1 cup HomeChef's Basic
   Mayonnaise (p. 105)
2 tablespoons each chopped fresh basil,
   chopped flat-leaf parsley, and
   chopped shallots

3 hard-cooked eggs, chopped
8 radishes, thinly sliced
3 stalks celery, thinly sliced
4 scallions, thinly sliced on
   the diagonal

1. Cook the tortelloni in plenty of lightly salted boiling water; drain, toss with olive oil, and cool.
2. In a small deep mixing bowl, combine the mayonnaise, basil, parsley, and shallots, and mix gently. Set aside.
3. Put the cooled pasta in a large serving bowl, and combine it with the chopped eggs, radishes, and celery. Toss with the mayonnaise, starting with ½ cup, and adding more if needed. Serve chilled or at room temperature. Garnish with slivered scallions.

Make It Light: Substitute Light Yogurt "Mayonnaise" or Medium-Light Mayonnaise (p. 106) for the Basic Mayonnaise, and use only the chopped whites of the eggs.

Make It Ahead: Prepare up to 3 hours in advance and chill. To serve at room temperature, remove it from the refrigerator 30 minutes before serving.

Our students love this dish because it is so flexible. For instance, it can be prepared with half basmati rice and half wild rice or one-third brown rice, one-third white rice, and one-third wild rice, and so on. You can also substitute other vegetables or pastas, if you like. Anyway, I am sure you will think of a combination we have not thought of, and this is what makes cooking so much fun!

WILD RICE AND TORTELLINI SALAD
Serves 8 to 10 as a first course

4 cups Chicken Stock (p. 12) or Vegetable Stock (p. 13)

10 ounces wild rice or combined rices (about 1½ cups)

8 ounces tortellini

1 tablespoon coarse sea salt, for cooking pasta

2 cloves garlic, squeezed through a press

⅔ cup walnut oil

⅔ cup red wine vinegar

1 tablespoon each fine sea salt and sugar

1 teaspoon freshly ground pepper

4 stalks celery, peeled and thinly sliced

1 red and 1 yellow bell pepper, roasted, peeled, seeded, and cut into ½-inch squares

4 scallions, cleaned and sliced

4 tablespoons chopped fresh flat-leaf parsley

1. Bring the stock to a boil in a saucepan, add the rice, and cook covered over very low heat until tender (cooking time will vary according to the kind of rice you are using). While the rice is cooking, cook the tortellini in plenty of lightly salted boiling water, and drain.

2. In a large bowl, combine the garlic, walnut oil, vinegar, salt, sugar, and pepper. Gently mix in the warm tortellini.

3. While still warm, add the rice to the bowl, along with the celery, bell peppers, scallions, and flat-leaf parsley. Combine gently. Taste and adjust seasonings. Allow to stand at least 1 hour before serving if you are serving at room temperature. Refrigerate if serving chilled.

Make It Light: Substitute 1¼ cups HomeChef's Light Salad Dressing (p. 104) for the walnut oil and red wine vinegar.

Make It Ahead: This salad can be prepared up to 4 hours in advance and refrigerated. To serve at room temperature, remove it from the refrigerator 30 minutes before serving.

I have tried a number of different pasta shapes with this salad, but I always come back to penne, it seems the perfect size and shape. This salad can also be made richer by using a regular mayonnaise, but I suggest you try the light version first. It's so good, you probably won't miss the extra calories, just joking of course, we all love less calories these days!

FRESH SALMON AND PENNE SALAD

Serves 8 as a first course

¾ pound salmon fillet
¾ pound penne
1 tablespoon coarse sea salt,
  for cooking pasta
1 tablespoon extra virgin olive oil
¼ medium onion, finely chopped
2 stalks celery, finely sliced crosswise
½ pound snow peas, sugar snap peas,
  or green beans, blanched 2 minutes
  and drained

2 bell peppers, roasted, peeled,
  seeded, and chopped
8 radishes, sliced
  fine sea salt and freshly ground
  pepper to taste
1 to 2 cups HomeChef's Light
  Yogurt "Mayonnaise" (p. 106)
4 tablespoons chopped fresh dill
  (or more or less, to taste)

1. Poach the salmon. Cool, remove and discard skin, crumble, and set aside.
2. Cook the penne in plenty of lightly salted boiling water until it is al dente, drain, and transfer to a large serving bowl. Toss with the olive oil and allow to cool.
3. Add the salmon, onion, celery, green vegetables, bell pepper, radishes, salt, and pepper to the cooled pasta and toss until well combined. Toss the salad with 1 cup of the mayonnaise, adding more if needed. Mix in the dill, adding more or less to taste. Chill until served.

Make It Ahead: You can make the salad up to 1 day in advance. The longer the salad is chilled, the more mayonnaise it will absorb, so you may wish to add more before serving.

SALAD DRESSINGS

The classic dressing for leafy green salads is a simple vinaigrette made with oil and vinegar, plus a little mustard for flavoring, and a pinch of salt and pepper. I always prefer a vinaigrette made with extra virgin olive oil and a wine vinegar, but you can substitute your own favorite oils and vinegars — just don't compromise on the quality. Always use cold-pressed, unprocessed oils, pure, undiluted vinegars, and full-flavored mustards.

Vinaigrettes are so easy to prepare, there's really no reason to buy ready-made dressings. The basic method is to whisk the oil and vinegar together, then stir in the flavorings (mustard, herbs, garlic).

All the following vinaigrettes will keep 2 weeks in the refrigerator. Let stand at room temperature 1 hour before serving, and always stir or shake before using.

HOMECHEF'S BASIC VINAIGRETTE

Makes about 1½ cups

1 cup extra virgin olive oil
¼ cup wine vinegar
1 tablespoon prepared mustard

1 teaspoon each fine sea salt,
freshly ground pepper, and sugar,
or to taste

Whisk the oil, vinegar, and mustard together in a small bowl until completely emulsified. Stir in the seasonings and optional herbs. (An alternative method is to put all the ingredients in a glass cruet with a rubber gasket or in a leakproof jar and shake well.) If you are not using the dressing immediately, refrigerate, then bring to room temperature, and stir (or shake) just before serving.

Variations:

(Note: all the following variations are to be prepared following the directions above for the Basic Vinaigrette. All will yield about 1 to 1½ cups.)

Herbs and Garlic: Add 2 teaspoons chopped fresh garlic and 2 teaspoons chopped fresh herbs to the Basic Vinaigrette (flat-leaf parsley, thyme, rosemary, tarragon, basil, and so on, or any combination that suits you).

Balsamic Garlic: Substitute ¼ cup balsamic vinegar for the wine vinegar and add 3 cloves finely chopped garlic

Hazelnut Balsamic: Substitute ¾ cup hazelnut oil, ¼ cup balsamic vinegar, and add 1 tablespoon hot and sweet prepared mustard.

Sherry Walnut: Substitute ¾ cup walnut oil, 2 to 3 tablespoons each sherry vinegar and sherry, and add 1 tablespoon hot and sweet prepared mustard.

Raspberry Walnut: Substitute ¾ cup walnut oil, ¼ cup raspberry vinegar, and add 1 tablespoon hot and sweet prepared mustard.

SUN-DRIED TOMATO DRESSING

Makes about 1½ cups

½ cup extra virgin olive oil
¼ cup each white table wine and
white wine vinegar
3 shallots, peeled and chopped finely
8 sun-dried tomatoes in oil,
drained and julienned

4 tablespoons chopped fresh
flat-leaf parsley
1 teaspoon each fine sea salt, freshly
ground white pepper, and sugar,
or to taste

Whisk together the wine, vinegar, and olive oil until completely emulsified. Stir in the remaining ingredients. (Or put all the ingredients in a glass cruet with a rubber gasket or a leakproof jar and shake well.)

Jalapeño chiles that have been smoked and dried are called chipotle chiles. You can purchase them in Mexican markets and gourmet food stores. Grind or chop them very fine in your spice grinder, mortar, or blender for this recipe.

CHIPOTLE DRESSING

Makes about 1 cup

3 tablespoons white wine vinegar
2 tablespoons fresh lime juice
1 teaspoon prepared mustard
1 teaspoon ground, finely chopped,
or puréed chipotle chiles

1 clove garlic, finely chopped
½ teaspoon each fine sea salt,
and sugar, or to taste
¾ cup extra virgin olive oil

Combine the vinegar and lime juice in a small bowl. Whisk in the mustard, chipotle chiles, garlic, salt, and sugar. Slowly whisk in the oil to emulsify.

HOMECHEF'S LIGHT SALAD DRESSING

Makes about 1½ cups

1 cup water
1 tablespoon arrowroot
dissolved in 1 tablespoon water
¼ cup extra virgin olive oil
1½ tablespoons each fresh lime juice
and red wine vinegar
⅛ teaspoon Tabasco sauce
1 teaspoon each fine sea salt and sugar

2 cloves garlic, squeezed through
a press
2 tablespoons each chopped fresh
basil, chopped fresh flat-leaf
parsley, and chopped chives
1 tablespoon hot and sweet
prepared mustard

In a small saucepan, bring the water to a boil, and whisk in the arrowroot. Remove from the heat, pour into a small bowl, and cool. Stir in the remaining ingredients and combine well.

I believe there is a huge difference in taste between store-bought and your own homemade mayonnaise. If you try it, I am certain you will agree, and, when you realize how simple the process is, you may never buy mayonnaise again. As with the vinaigrette, mayonnaise will taste different depending on what kinds of oils you use to make it, and, of course, you can add all kinds of herbs and seasonings to the basic recipe to create entirely different dressings, as we did with our Jalapeño-Lime Mayonnaise, below. Following are several mayonnaise recipes, including a completely fat-free version.

HOMECHEF'S BASIC MAYONNAISE

Makes about 2 cups

2 egg yolks
2 teaspoons prepared mustard
1 tablespoon lemon juice
  or wine vinegar
½ teaspoon each fine sea salt,
  freshly ground pepper, and sugar

1½ cups oil (olive, hazelnut, walnut,
  rice bran, or avocado oil,
  or any combination of these oils)

1. Have all ingredients at room temperature. Combine the egg yolks, mustard, lemon juice, salt, pepper, and sugar in a small deep mixing bowl.
2. Using a small sauce whisk, and whisking slowly, add the oil, drop by drop at first. When about ½ cup of the oil has been added, add the remaining oil in a steady stream, whisking continuously until thickened. Mayonnaise can be stored in the refrigerator up to 1 week.

JALAPEÑO-LIME MAYONNAISE

Makes about 1½ cups

1 cup HomeChef's Basic Mayonnaise
  (see preceding recipe)
½ teaspoon fine sea salt
1 teaspoon sugar
3 tablespoons freshly squeezed
  lime juice

zest of 1 lime, chopped
1 jalapeño chile, roasted, peeled,
  seeded, and finely chopped
2 tablespoons extra virgin olive oil
2 cloves garlic, squeezed through
  a press

Whisk all ingredients together until smooth.

This is a kind of "halfway step" to our totally fat-free yogurt "mayonnaise" which follows. You need to try them both, then make your own judgment as to which one to use, and what you will use them with.

MEDIUM-LIGHT MAYONNAISE

Makes about 2½ cups

1 egg
1 tablespoon hot and sweet
  prepared mustard
2 teaspoons raspberry vinegar
1 teaspoon each fine sea salt
  and sugar
½ teaspoon pepper

1 cup oil (olive, hazelnut, walnut,
  rice bran, or avocado oil, or
  any combination of these oils)
4 tablespoons each chopped fresh basil
  and chopped fresh flat-leaf parsley
3 shallots, finely chopped
1 cup low-fat Yogurt Cheese (p. 14)

1. Have all ingredients at room temperature. Combine the egg, mustard, vinegar, salt, sugar, and pepper in a small deep mixing bowl.
2. Whisking slowly with a small sauce whisk, add the oil, drop by drop at first. When about ½ cup of the oil has been incorporated, add the remaining oil in a slow steady stream, whisking continuously until thickened. Fold in the herbs, shallots, and Yogurt Cheese. Can be stored in the refrigerator up to 1 week.

As you can see, this next "mayonnaise" has no fat in it at all. You can change the way it tastes by using different prepared mustards, vinegars, and herbs. Refrigerated, this will keep up to 1 week.

HOMECHEF'S LIGHT YOGURT "MAYONNAISE"

Makes about 2 cups

1½ cups nonfat Yogurt Cheese (p. 14)
5 tablespoons balsamic vinegar
5 tablespoons concentrated
  Beef Stock (p. 12)
2 tablespoons prepared mustard
¼ teaspoon cayenne pepper

½ teaspoon each fine sea salt and
  sugar, or to taste
4 tablespoons chopped fresh flat-leaf
  parsley (or basil, tarragon, or thyme),
  or to taste

Combine all ingredients in a small deep bowl. Cover, and store in the refrigerator.

LIGHT ROQUEFORT DRESSING

1 cup nonfat Yogurt Cheese (p. 14)
2 ounces Roquefort cheese
   (about 4 tablespoons)
4 tablespoons concentrated
   Beef Stock (p. 12)

2 tablespoons red wine vinegar
1 tablespoon prepared mustard
1 teaspoon each fine sea salt,
   freshly ground pepper, and sugar

Whisk all ingredients together. Refrigerated, this will keep up to 1 week.

CHAPTER FOUR

BEANS, RICE, GRAINS, AND PASTA

Dried beans and rice have traditionally been regarded as peasant fare. This image undoubtedly reflects the fact that these foods play a central role in the diet of poor folk all over the world. Because of this, sophisticated diners have generally ignored these foods — until recently, that is. There is now a tremendous interest in all kinds of grains and beans, driven in part by an increased awareness of their nutritional value and their role in keeping a diet relatively low-fat. People have also discovered how delicious these humble foods can be. Our students certainly can't seem to get enough of them!

Most of the dishes in this category are appropriate as first courses or as side dishes to be served with a fish, chicken, or meat main course. However, many of them are substantial enough to serve as main courses, and are particularly good at times when you would like to serve a meatless meal. I have indicated this wherever it seemed apt.

Every time we make this chile in class, we get rave reviews. It seems to be a recipe with endless possibilities. For instance, you can add cooked meats or vegetables, or try substituting other varieties of beans, such as pintos or small white beans, or experimenting with the seasonings (a couple of suggestions are given below). This dish makes a superb main course: serve it with a salad and some French bread.

HOMECHEF'S BLACK BEAN AND SWEET CORN CHILE
Serves 8 to 10

1 **pound dried black beans, soaked overnight**
¼ **cup extra virgin olive oil**
2 **large yellow onions, finely chopped**
2 **medium carrots, finely chopped**
2 **stalks celery, finely chopped**
1 **bell pepper, seeded and chopped**
4 **cloves garlic, finely chopped**
2 **pounds tomatoes, chopped**
1 **cup each red table wine and Vegetable Stock (p. 13)**
1 **tablespoon coarse sea salt**
1 **teaspoon each freshly ground cumin seeds, coriander seeds, and black peppercorns**

½ **teaspoon each Hungarian paprika, dried oregano, and ground chile flakes**
4 **tablespoons each chopped fresh flat-leaf parsley and chopped fresh cilantro**
2 **tablespoons sugar**
2 **tablespoons tomato paste**
3 **ears fresh corn**
1 **medium red onion, finely chopped**
8 **ounces extra sharp Cheddar cheese, grated (about 2 cups)**
1 **cup sour cream**

1. Drain the beans, and put them in a pot with fresh water to cover. Bring to a boil, reduce to a simmer, cover partially, and cook until the beans are done, about 1½ to 2 hours. They should be tender but not mushy.

2. Heat the olive oil in an 8-quart soup pot, and sauté the onions, carrots, celery, bell pepper, and garlic for 5 minutes over medium heat. Add the tomatoes, wine, stock, salt, spices, herbs, sugar, tomato paste, and black beans. Stir well, and simmer covered, over very low heat for 1 hour. Cut the kernels off the ears of corn, stir them into the chile, and cook 15 minutes more. Taste for seasoning, and adjust according to taste.

3. Put the red onion, Cheddar cheese, and sour cream in separate bowls to pass around at the table. Serve the chile hot, in deep soup bowls.

Make It Light: Those who want to cut down on calories can forego the cheese and sour cream garnishes.

Make It Ahead: Chile may be finished up to 1 day in advance and refrigerated. When you are ready, reheat slowly over moderate heat. Chile freezes well for up to a month.

Variations: Add 4 ounces ground beef or sausage, cooked and crumbled, to the finished chile. Another possibility is to stir in about 2 cups of Roasted Vegetables (p. 218) to the finished chile (roasted zucchini and bell peppers are especially good).

Rebecca Ets-Hokin, the director of our cooking school, has developed a class that is devoted entirely to mushrooms. Her mushroom ragoût is a personal favorite of mine, perfectly suited to stand alone as a main dish. During asparagus season, I start with steamed asparagus dipped in Garlic Mayonnaise (p. 208), serve the ragoût with some crusty bread, and complete this special meal with one of our sorbets (p. 230).

WHITE BEAN AND WILD MUSHROOM RAGOÛT

Serves 4 to 6 as a main dish

½ pound dried small white beans
   (about 1¼ cups), soaked overnight
3 cups Vegetable Stock (p. 13)
   a bouquet garni
1 small onion
1 small carrot and 1 small stalk celery,
   each cut in half
2 ounces dried porcini mushrooms,
   soaked in warm water for 1 hour

3 tablespoons extra virgin olive oil
8 ounces yellow onions, chopped
¼ pound fresh mushrooms, sliced
½ cup white table wine
1 teaspoon each coarse sea salt, sugar,
   soy sauce, dried oregano, dried
   thyme, and chopped fresh rosemary
1 bay leaf

1. Drain and rinse the beans, and put them in a 6-quart pot together with the stock, bouquet garni, onion, carrot, and celery. Bring to a boil, cover the pot, leaving the cover slightly askew, lower the heat, and simmer until the beans are tender, about 1½ hours. Drain, discarding the vegetables and bouquet garni, and transfer the beans to a stoneware or clay casserole. Soak the mushrooms while the beans are cooking.
2. Drain the porcini, reserving the liquid. Rinse the porcini well and cut into a fine julienne. Strain the liquid and reserve. Heat the olive oil in a medium-sized skillet, and sauté the onions 2 or 3 minutes over medium heat. Add the fresh and dried mushrooms, and the reserved soaking water, and continue to cook until the liquid is reduced to ½ cup. Add remaining ingredients, and cook 1 minute.
3. Stir the sautéed mushroom mixture into the beans, cover, and bake in a preheated 350° oven 45 minutes, adding more wine or stock if necessary. Discard the bay leaf, and allow casserole to stand 15 minutes before serving.

Make It Ahead: You can finish this ragoût up to 1 day in advance and refrigerate. Reheat to serve.

I got this recipe from the gentleman from whom we purchase our Greek oils and seasonings. He is a wonderful cook and always brings us samplings of his marvelous dishes. He says it helps sell his products, and he is right!

BAKED BEANS À LA GRECQUE

Serves 8

1 pound dried white beans (medium or large), soaked overnight
3 tablespoons extra virgin olive oil
1 large onion, finely chopped
2 cloves garlic, finely chopped
2 pounds tomatoes, peeled and chopped
2 bay leaves

2 tablespoons sugar
2 teaspoons each dried oregano and coarse sea salt
1 teaspoon freshly ground pepper
juice of 1 lemon
3 tablespoons each chopped fresh mint leaves and chopped flat-leaf parsley

1. Drain the beans, and put them in a pot with fresh water to cover. Bring to a boil, reduce to a simmer, cover partially, and cook until the beans are done, about 1½ to 2 hours. They should be tender but not mushy.
2. Heat the oil in a skillet, and sauté the onion and garlic 2 minutes over medium heat, until softened. Transfer to a stoneware or clay casserole, and mix in the beans, bay leaves, tomatoes, oregano, sugar, salt, pepper, and lemon juice. Cover and bake in a preheated 350° oven for 1 hour.
3. Taste, adjust seasonings, and discard bay leaves. Stir in the mint and parsley. Serve warm or at room temperature.

Make It Light: Already light.

Make It Ahead: You can finish this dish up to 1 day in advance and refrigerate. Allow to stand 1 hour at room temperature before serving.

As you can probably guess from the title, this dish is meant to be cooked the day before you plan to serve it. Actually, it's cooked *overnight!* The long slow cooking seems to develop a flavor in this dish that is not there when it is cooked quickly. For best results, bake the beans in a stoneware or clay casserole.

SATURDAY NIGHT BAKED BEANS
FOR SUNDAY DINNER

Serves 8 to 10

1 pound small dried white beans, soaked overnight

8 ounces slab bacon, blanched 1 minute, drained, and coarsely chopped

3 onions, coarsely chopped

2 cloves garlic, finely chopped

5 cups hot water

½ cup dark molasses

½ cup tomato paste

2 tablespoons Worcestershire sauce

1 tablespoon each fine sea salt and dry mustard

¼ teaspoon cayenne pepper

Place beans in a stoneware or clay casserole in alternating layers with the bacon, onion, and garlic. Combine the water, molasses, tomato paste, Worcestershire sauce, salt, mustard, and cayenne, and pour over beans, adding more water if necessary to completely cover the beans. Cover the casserole and place in a 270° oven. Bake overnight or about 8 hours, replacing liquid if necessary. Serve from the casserole at the table.

Make It Light: Omit bacon.

Make It Ahead: You can finish this dish up to 1 day in advance, and refrigerate. When you are ready, reheat in a 350° oven for 45 minutes or until hot. If beans appear dry, add more liquid.

There are several types of lentils, and after trying them all, I've decided that the green lentils, or French lentils, as they are sometimes called, are the best tasting of all. Lentils can be cooked without soaking, although soaking speeds the cooking time a little. They are commonly used in Mediterranean and Middle Eastern countries to make soups, stews, and salads. I don't think you will miss the meat in this ragoût. Serve it as a main dish, accompanied with a green salad of your choice.

MEDITERRANEAN LENTIL-EGGPLANT RAGOÛT

Serves 6

1 large eggplant, cut into 1-inch cubes
coarse sea salt
4 cups water
7 ounces green lentils (about 1 cup),
soaked 30 minutes
3 tablespoons extra virgin olive oil
1 large onion, coarsely chopped
3 cloves garlic, coarsely chopped
6 tablespoons tomato paste
1 tablespoon each ground cumin and
Worcestershire sauce

½ cup dry red wine
2 cups Vegetable Stock (p. 13)
fine sea salt and cayenne pepper
to taste
2 tablespoons chopped fresh
flat-leaf parsley
4 ounces Monterey Jack cheese, grated
(about 1 cup)

1. Sprinkle the eggplant with salt and let stand for 1 hour. Meanwhile, bring 4 cups of water to a boil; add the lentils and 1 tablespoon olive oil. Lower the heat and simmer until the lentils are tender (but not mushy), about 35 minutes.
2. Rinse off the eggplant and pat dry. Heat the remaining 2 tablespoons oil in a skillet, add the eggplant, onion, and garlic, and sauté over medium heat for 10 minutes, stirring frequently. Stir in the tomato paste, cumin, Worcestershire sauce, wine, stock, salt, and cayenne pepper. Cover and cook about 15 minutes more, adding more liquid if necessary.
3. To serve, arrange the lentils on a warmed serving platter, spoon the eggplant on top, and garnish with chopped parsley and grated cheese.

Make It Light: Do not add any oil to the lentils, and use only 1 tablespoon olive oil to sauté the eggplant. Omit the Jack cheese.

Make It Ahead: You can make this dish up to 2 hours in advance through step 2. When you are ready, reheat the lentils and eggplant separately, and proceed with step 3.

All my children loved rice, so I figured out innumerable ways to include it in our meals. This one was so good I introduced it to the cooking school, and now it is a class favorite, too.

BASMATI RICE WITH VEGETABLES
Serves 6

2 tablespoons extra virgin olive oil	1 teaspoon each coarse sea salt
½ small onion, finely chopped	and sugar
1 clove garlic, finely chopped	½ teaspoon freshly ground pepper
1 tablespoon chopped fresh basil	2 carrots, peeled, coarsely chopped,
12 ounces basmati rice (about 1½ cups)	and blanched 1 minute
2 medium tomatoes, coarsely chopped	1 pound fresh green peas, shelled
3½ cups Vegetable Stock (p. 13)	(or a 10-ounce box frozen tiny peas)

Heat the oil in a saucepan, and sauté the onion, garlic, and basil 2 minutes over low heat. Stir in the rice, tomatoes, 2 cups of stock, salt, sugar, and pepper. Cover and cook over low heat 10 minutes. Add remaining stock, and sprinkle the carrots and peas over the rice. Cover, reduce heat to low, and cook about 10 minutes more. (If using frozen peas, do not add them at this time. Defrost and stir them in just before serving.)

Make It Light: Reduce oil to 1 tablespoon.

Make It Ahead: You can make this dish up to 1 hour in advance, and allow it to stand in the saucepan. Before serving, reheat over low heat for 1 minute.

An Indian *biriyani* is the equivalent of a Spanish paella or a Louisiana jambalaya. In other words, a *biriyani* is a dish that combines rice with other ingredients. The recipe for this delicious vegetarian dish comes from our Indian teacher, Suki Singh. *Garam masala*, which you can find in East Indian or Middle Eastern food markets, is an essential seasoning in this dish. Literally translated, *garam masala* means "hot mixture of spices" and typically it would contain ground cardamom, cloves, black peppercorns, cinnamon, and cumin. A *raita* is a refreshing Indian side dish made with yogurt and fruit or vegetables, commonly served with very spicy foods.

VEGETABLE *BIRIYANI*

Serves 6 to 8

14 ounces long-grain white rice
   (about 2 cups)
2 cups water
½ gram saffron threads
¼ cup milk
1 medium onion, chopped
4 cloves garlic
1 tablespoon grated fresh ginger
2 jalapeño chiles, stemmed and seeded
4 tablespoons unsalted butter (2 ounces)
2 teaspoons *garam masala* (available
   in Middle Eastern food stores)

2 ounces almonds
   (about ½ cup), ground
1 cup plain yogurt
½ cup heavy cream
1 red and 1 green bell pepper,
   seeded and chopped
2 carrots, chopped
2 zucchini, chopped
½ cup water
   fine sea salt to taste
   Cucumber *Raita* (recipe follows)

1. Soak the rice in the water for 1 hour. Soak the saffron threads in the milk for 1 hour. Meanwhile, go on to steps 2 and 3.
2. In a food processor or blender, process the onion, garlic, ginger, and chiles into a coarse paste. Heat the butter in a skillet, and sauté the onion mixture over medium heat until it turns a light brown. Stir in the *garam masala* and ground almonds, and sauté another 5 minutes.
3. Combine the yogurt and cream, and add this to the onions, little by little, stirring constantly. Add the bell peppers, carrots, zucchini, ½ cup water, and salt to taste. Bring to a boil, then reduce heat, cover, and cook for about 20 minutes. Turn off the heat and set aside.
4. Drain the rice and put it in a saucepan with 2 cups of water. Bring to a boil, lower the heat, and simmer uncovered for 10 minutes; remove from the heat, and drain. Transfer the rice to a stoneware or clay casserole, add the cooked vegetables, and gently combine. Pour the saffron-milk over all.
5. Cover and bake in a 350° oven for 30 minutes. Allow to rest 10 minutes, and serve from the casserole, with Cucumber *Raita* on the side.

Make It Light: Substitute 1½ cups nonfat yogurt for the plain yogurt and heavy cream called for in the recipe.

Make It Ahead: You can make this dish up to 4 hours in advance through step 4 and refrigerate. Put it in the oven about 45 minutes before serving (step 5).

CUCUMBER *RAITA*

3 large cucumbers, peeled
  about 1 teaspoon coarse sea salt
1 cup plain yogurt
1 tablespoon extra virgin olive oil

1 tablespoon white wine vinegar
  fine sea salt and freshly ground
  black pepper, to taste
2 tablespoons chopped fresh mint leaves

1. Cut the cucumbers in half lengthwise, and remove the seeds. Slice the halves into thin half moons. Place on paper towels, sprinkle with coarse salt, and allow to drain for 1 hour. Pat dry, brushing off any salt remaining.
2. In a small bowl, combine the yogurt, oil, vinegar, salt, pepper, and mint. Toss with the cucumbers.

Make It Light: Use nonfat yogurt.

Make It Ahead: Best made and served within an hour.

The next two recipes came from a Greek friend of mine. They both make superb side dishes for grilled meats, chicken, or fish. The Greek Lemon Rice is a particularly good accompaniment for Grilled Fish Teriyaki (p. 187).

GREEK LEMON RICE

Serves 8

¼ cup extra virgin olive oil
1 medium yellow onion,
  finely chopped
14 ounces long-grain white rice
  (about 2 cups)
2 cups Chicken Stock (p. 12)
2 cups water

  juice of 3 lemons
4 lemon slices
2 teaspoons coarse sea salt
  freshly ground black pepper to taste
2 bay leaves
4 cloves

1. In a 3-quart saucepan, heat the oil, and sauté the onion over medium heat for 3 minutes. Stir in the rice, and sauté, stirring, for 5 minutes more.
2. In a small pot, combine the stock, water, lemon juice, lemon slices, salt, pepper, bay leaves, and cloves and bring to a boil. Stir into the rice, cover, and cook over low heat for 20 to 25 minutes, or until the liquid is absorbed. Remove from the heat and let stand covered until ready to serve.

Make It Light: Reduce olive oil to 2 tablespoons.

Make It Ahead: You can make this dish up to 2 hours in advance. Before serving, return to a low heat for 1 minute.

GREEK PILAF

Serves 8

3 tablespoons extra virgin olive oil
2 ounces toasted pine nuts
(about ½ cup)
1 small onion, finely chopped
2 cloves garlic, finely chopped
2 carrots, finely chopped
10 ounces long-grain white rice
(about 1⅓ cups)
3 cups Chicken Stock (p. 12)

2 ounces dried currants (about ½ cup)
1 teaspoon each dried oregano and
chopped fresh rosemary
2 teaspoons fine sea salt
½ teaspoon freshly ground
black pepper
1 tablespoon chopped fresh
mint leaves

Heat the oil in a large sauté pan, add the pine nuts, onion, garlic, and carrots, and sauté 3 minutes over medium heat. Add the rice, and cook, stirring, 2 minutes. Stir in the stock, currants, oregano, rosemary, salt, and pepper. Bring to a boil, then cover and reduce the heat. Simmer over low heat until all the liquid is absorbed, about 25 minutes. Sprinkle with chopped mint and serve.

Make It Light: Reduce oil to 1 tablespoon

Make It Ahead: You can make this dish up to 2 hours in advance. Before serving, return to a low heat for 1 minute.

Variation:
Wild Rice Pilaf: substitute wild rice for the long-grain rice, and increase the Chicken Stock to 6 cups. Simmer 45 to 55 minutes, or until all the stock is absorbed.

This is my version of a dish I learned at the Beijing Culinary School, the year I led a cooking tour to China. You can make it with Chinese sausage, or any of the newer chicken sausages, like chicken-and-apple, or chicken-and-ginger. (Chinese sausage, which you can find in Asian markets, is a dried sausage made with pork.) Try serving this dish with a couple of vegetable dishes like Sautéed Artichokes with Pancetta and Thyme (p. 198) or Carrots and Wild Mushrooms Madeira (p. 202) for an interesting combination of Eastern and Western cuisines.

RICE WITH SAUSAGE AND BABY BOK CHOY, SHANGHAI STYLE

Serves 3 to 4

4 ounces sausage
4 tablespoons rice bran oil
¾ pound baby bok choy, trimmed and cut into ½-inch strips
3 scallions, chopped

7 ounces long-grain white rice (about 1 cup)
2 teaspoons coarse sea salt
2 tablespoons sherry
1¾ cups Chicken Stock (p. 12)

1. Steam the sausage and cut into 1-inch-thick diagonal slices. Set aside.

2. Heat the oil in a wok or large sauté pan. Over high heat, add the bok choy and scallions and toss until coated with oil and starting to wilt, about 30 seconds. Stir in the sausage, rice, salt, and wine. Add the stock, bring to a boil, and boil 30 seconds. Cover the pot, reduce the heat to low, and simmer 20 minutes. Remove from the heat and test for doneness. Correct seasonings if necessary, cover, and let stand at least 15 minutes before serving.

Make It Light: Reduce oil to 2 tablespoons.

Make It Ahead: You can make this dish up to 2 hours in advance. Before serving, return to a low heat for 1 minute.

I like this dish because it allows so much freedom for improvisation. You can use leftovers to create a new dish that is really delicious.

"TODAY'S" FRIED RICE
Serves 4 to 6

4 tablespoons rice bran oil
2 eggs, lightly beaten
½ cup cooked green vegetables, chopped (asparagus, broccoli, green beans, peas, etc.)
¼ cup cooked meat, chopped (shrimp, pork, ham, etc.)

3 cups cooked rice
2 scallions, finely chopped
   soy sauce and chile oil to taste
2 tablespoons each chopped fresh flat-leaf parsley and chopped cilantro

1. Heat 2 tablespoons of the oil in a wok or skillet over medium heat. Add the eggs, tossing lightly until set and fluffy. Transfer the eggs to a cutting board and when cool, cut into thin ribbons.
2. Wipe the wok or skillet clean, and heat the remaining 2 tablespoons of oil over high heat; add the vegetables and meat, tossing them quickly, just long enough to coat them with oil, about 30 seconds. Add the rice and scallions and toss to combine with other ingredients. Taste for seasoning and add soy sauce and chile oil to taste.
3. Add the eggs, parsley, and cilantro, and toss everything over high heat just long enough to heat through. Transfer to a warmed serving platter.

Make It Light: Omit the eggs and reduce the oil to 1 tablespoon.

Make It Ahead: You can make this recipe through step 2 up to 2 hours in advance. When you are ready, proceed with step 3.

The popularity of risotto dishes has increased about 500% in the past ten years at our school. For the uninitiated, risotto is a special rice cooked in a particular way. The rice is a short grain variety called Arborio rice, and it is only grown in northern Italy. It has a pearly white spot on it that remains firm even after the rice is cooked. This is the only rice suitable for risotto and it may be purchased in Italian markets or specialty food shops. Always use Arborio rice, a good home-made stock, and real Parmigiano-Reggiano cheese, and even if you add nothing else, the result will be absolutely delicious. The next two dishes will give you some idea of how the basic dish can be embellished. In Italy, risotto is served as a first course.

RISOTTO WITH BABY ARTICHOKES

Serves 8 to 10

6 tablespoons unsalted butter
   (3 ounces)
3 tablespoons extra virgin olive oil
2 cloves garlic, chopped
½ small onion, chopped
15 baby artichokes, trimmed and
    quartered (p. 219)
6 tablespoons chopped fresh
   flat-leaf parsley

   fine sea salt and freshly ground
   black pepper to taste
½ cup white table wine
14 ounces Arborio rice (about 2 cups)
6 to 8 cups Beef Stock (p. 12), heated
4 ounces Parmigiano-Reggiano,
   grated (about 1 cup)

1. In a large heavy sauté pan or skillet, heat half the butter with the olive oil, and add garlic, onion, artichokes, half the parsley, and salt and pepper to taste. Sauté gently over low heat about 5 minutes, until artichokes are tender. Add the wine, and continue cooking until the wine has all disappeared. Add the rice and stir to combine all ingredients.
2. Add 1 cup of hot stock, or enough to just barely cover the rice. Cook over low heat, stirring often, until the rice has absorbed almost all the stock. Add another cup of stock, and cook and stir again. Continue in this manner until the rice is al dente and creamy, about 15 to 20 minutes. You may not need all the stock or you may need more.
3. Remove from the heat and stir in the remaining butter and parsley, and half the Parmigiano-Reggiano. Serve the risotto in shallow soup bowls with the remaining cheese on the side.

Make It Light: Reduce butter and olive oil to 2 tablespoons each, reduce cheese to 1 ounce (about ¼ cup)

Make It Ahead: You can make the risotto up to 2 hours in advance through step 2. When you are ready, heat the risotto, stir in ¾ to 1 cup additional stock, and proceed with step 3.

This risotto is another of Rebecca's creations.

RISOTTO WITH SUN-DRIED TOMATOES, PISTACHIOS, AND BASIL

Serves 8

6 tablespoons extra virgin olive oil
1 small onion, coarsely chopped
14 ounces Arborio rice (about 2 cups)
¾ cup dry white wine
6 to 8 cups Chicken Stock
    (p. 12), heated
15 sun-dried tomatoes packed in oil,
    drained and coarsely chopped

1 teaspoon fine sea salt
½ teaspoon freshly ground pepper
2 ounces pistachios (about ¼ cup),
    toasted and coarsely chopped
15 fresh basil leaves, cut in thin strips
2 ounces freshly grated
    Parmigiano-Reggiano (about ½ cup)
2 tablespoons unsalted butter

1. In a large sauté pan or skillet, heat the olive oil, and sauté the onion over medium heat about 1 minute, until it begins to soften. Add the rice and cook, stirring, for 1 minute. Add the wine, and stir until it is absorbed by the rice.

2. Ladle 1 cup of stock into the pan, and cook over low heat, stirring so it is slowly absorbed. Add the tomatoes, salt, and pepper, stirring gently. Add another cup of stock, and cook and stir again until it has been absorbed. Continue in this manner until the rice is al dente and creamy, about 15 to 20 minutes You may not need all the stock or you may need more.

3. Remove the pan from the heat, and stir in the pistachios, basil, Parmigiano, and butter. Serve the risotto in shallow soup bowls.

Make It Light: Reduce olive oil to 3 tablespoons, Parmigiano to 1 ounce, and omit butter.

Make It Ahead: You can make the risotto up to 2 hours in advance through step 2. When you are ready, heat the risotto, stir in ¾ to 1 cup additional stock, and proceed with step 3.

When I was growing up, we had "mush" for breakfast everyday. Some days it was Cream of Wheat, other days it was oatmeal, and sometimes we'd have cornmeal mush. Little did I know that this same cornmeal mush would later become a staple dish in the trendiest restaurants in town! It may be called *polenta* on the menu, and the dish may be dressed up with additional ingredients, and served for lunch or dinner, but it's basically the same thing I ate for breakfast as a child. There is both yellow and white cornmeal, and they can be found finely ground or coarsely ground. I think coarse-grained yellow cornmeal from Italy (also called *polenta*) has the most flavor, but you can use any cornmeal you wish. Cooked polenta can be used in many ways, in a first or second course, as a side dish, or as an appetizer. Sometimes seafood or roasted meats are served on a bed of polenta, and then it becomes part of a sturdy main course, as in the following dish.

POLENTA AND SAUSAGE

Serves 8

2 tablespoons extra virgin olive oil
1 small onion, chopped
1 stalk celery, chopped
2 small carrots, chopped
4 ounces pancetta, cut into
  ½-inch strips
1½ pounds sweet Italian sausage,
  cut into 3-inch pieces
1½ pounds Roma tomatoes,
  coarsely chopped with their juice

1 teaspoon each sugar, fine sea salt,
  and freshly ground pepper
7 cups water
1 tablespoon coarse sea salt
14 ounces cornmeal (about 2 cups)
6 tablespoons unsalted butter
  (3 ounces)
2 ounces Parmigiano-Reggiano,
  grated (about ½ cup)

1. Heat the oil in a skillet or sauté pan, add the onion, carrot, celery, and pancetta. Cover the pan and sauté over low heat for 3 minutes. Add the sausage and sauté 5 minutes more. Stir in the tomatoes and their juices, and cook uncovered over low heat about 15 minutes more. Stir in the sugar, fine sea salt, and pepper. Set aside until ready to reheat and serve.

2. Bring the water to a boil in a 6-quart saucepan, add the coarse salt, and turn the heat down to a simmer; add the cornmeal in a very thin stream, stirring with a wooden spoon. Cook over low heat, stirring often, for about 25 to 30 minutes. Polenta is done when it comes away from the sides of the pot. Stir in the butter and grated Parmigiano, and turn the polenta out onto a warmed serving platter. Make a well in the center and spoon in the warm sausage in tomato sauce.

Make It Light: Substitute one of the low-fat sausages such as chicken or turkey. Reduce the butter to 2 tablespoons and the cheese to 1 ounce (¼ cup).

Make It Ahead: You can make this dish through step 1 up to 2 hours in advance. Start cooking the polenta (step 2) about 30 minutes before you plan to serve. When the polenta is almost done, reheat the sausage.

This recipe comes from my Moroccan friends, the Himys. We are forever on the lookout for good vegetarian recipes, and when I tasted their couscous, I knew it would be well received at our school. Couscous, which is actually a cereal, is very easy to prepare because you simply add boiling water to it, let it stand briefly, and it's ready. Because couscous has little flavor of its own, it is usually served with highly seasoned vegetables and/or meat. To add flavor to the couscous itself, put the soaked couscous into a steamer insert on top of the saucepan in which the vegetables are cooking so it can absorb the flavors of the vegetables. (There is a special pot for this called a *couscousier,* but the steamer insert works well enough. Just be sure it fits the pot.) This dish goes very well served with Sliced Tomato and Roasted Bell Pepper Salad (p. 87).

MOROCCAN COUSCOUS
WITH SAFFRON-FLAVORED VEGETABLES

Serves 6 to 8

2 cups boiling water
2 tablespoons unsalted butter
¾ pound couscous (about 2 cups)
3 tablespoons extra virgin olive oil
1 medium onion, coarsely chopped
3 cloves garlic, coarsely chopped
1 jalapeño chile, seeded and
   coarsely chopped
2 teaspoons grated fresh ginger
4 small carrots, quartered lengthwise
4 baby artichokes, quartered
4 small turnips peeled and quartered
4 small zucchini, quartered lengthwise

1 red and 1 green bell pepper,
   seeded and cut into ½-inch strips
2 large tomatoes, coarsely chopped
½ teaspoon each freshly grated
   nutmeg and freshly ground cumin
2 teaspoons each Hungarian paprika,
   sugar, and fine sea salt, or to taste
1 teaspoon freshly ground pepper
2 cups cooked garbanzo beans
   (canned and drained are okay)
¼ gram saffron threads,
   soaked 10 minutes in
   1 cup Chicken Stock (p. 12)

1. In a large ovenproof bowl, combine the boiling water and butter; add the couscous, stir, cover, and let stand for 5 minutes.
2. Heat the oil in a large soup pot over medium heat, and add the onion, garlic, jalapeño, ginger, carrots, artichokes, turnips, zucchini, bell peppers, tomatoes, nutmeg, cumin, paprika, sugar, salt, and pepper. Sauté vegetables for 5 minutes, and mix in the garbanzos, saffron, and stock. Place the couscous in a steamer insert above the vegetables, cover, reduce heat, and cook for 15 minutes, stirring the vegetables occasionally.
3. To serve, spoon the couscous onto a warmed deep platter and spoon the vegetables over it.

Make It Light: Reduce the butter and oil to 1 tablespoon each.

Make It Ahead: You can complete the couscous through step 2 up to 2 hours in advance. When you are ready, reheat the couscous and vegetables briefly and serve as described in step 3.

The interest in pasta dishes has risen to an extraordinary level in the United States. Even the smallest markets sell both fresh and dried pasta in dozens of shapes and colors, and most restaurants, Italian or not, will have at least one pasta dish on the menu. At HomeChef, we have a workshop called "Pasta: How to Make it, Cook it, and Sauce it." Not everyone has time to make their own pasta, of course, so we also have classes where we present three or four pasta dishes using store-bought pasta. You can do very well with the fresh and dried pastas from your local grocery store, but you should try some of the pastas imported from Italy. I think they are superior. I also like the Italian custom of eating pasta as a first course, so the servings in the recipes that follow are based on first course portions.

If you want to make your own pasta, consult *The HomeChef* cookbook for directions. Remember, whether it's homemade or store-bought, pasta should be cooked in plenty of boiling water (6 to 8 quarts per pound of pasta). Add a little salt to the water, and cook the pasta until it is al dente — firm, not soft and mushy, and not hard.

Agnolotti is a small half-moon-shaped filled pasta with a ruffled edge. It comes frozen or vacuum-packed (look for it in the dairy section of your supermarket or in an Italian market). For variety, try substituting other small filled pastas, like ravioli, or tortellini. This makes a lovely first course or side dish served with grilled meats, fish, or poultry. It is very quick and easy to make, and can be served warm or cold. It is our single most popular pasta dish ever!

AGNOLOTTI IN AN HERBED YOGURT SAUCE

Serves 8

3 tablespoons extra virgin olive oil
3 tablespoons each chopped
  fresh flat-leaf parsley and
  chopped fresh basil
1 clove garlic, squeezed through
  a press
¾ cup plain yogurt
½ cup HomeChef's Basic
  Mayonnaise (p. 105)

1 tablespoon fresh lemon juice
1 teaspoon freshly ground
  white pepper
1 teaspoon plus 1 tablespoon
  fine sea salt
1 pound agnolotti

1. In a serving bowl, combine everything except 1 tablespoon of salt and the agnolotti.
2. Put 8 quarts water in a large pot with the tablespoon of salt; bring to a boil. Drop in the agnolotti and boil until tender, about 3 to 5 minutes. Drain and toss with the sauce. Serve warm or cold.

Make It Light: Substitute nonfat yogurt for all or some portion of the yogurt and mayonnaise.

Make It Ahead: If you wish to serve this cold, you can make it up to 4 hours in advance and refrigerate. To serve warm you can complete step 1 up to 2 hours in advance. When you are ready, proceed with step 2.

Tortelloni is a large filled pasta, sometimes as big as 3 inches square or round. You can substitute smaller filled pastas for the tortelloni, if you wish, such as ravioli, tortellini, or agnolotti. Follow this dish with a simple grilled, poached, or roasted meat.

TORTELLONI WITH PANCETTA AND ROSEMARY

Serves 8

4 tablespoons unsalted butter (2 ounces)
4 tablespoons extra virgin olive oil
4 cloves garlic, finely chopped
1 tablespoon finely chopped fresh rosemary
½ pound pancetta, cut into ¼-inch strips
freshly ground pepper to taste
¼ pound freshly grated Parmigiano-Reggiano (about 1 cup)
1 pound tortelloni, frozen or fresh, with vegetable or cheese filling
1 tablespoon coarse sea salt, for the pasta

1. Heat the butter and oil in a large skillet or sauté pan, and sauté the garlic and rosemary over low heat for 1 minute. Set aside.

2. In a separate skillet, sauté the pancetta until lightly colored, but not crisp. Drain off the fat, or leave it as part of this dish, as you like. Add the garlic mixture to the pan; stir, and season with pepper to taste. Transfer to a large deep bowl.

3. Put about 6 quarts water in a large pot with the tablespoon of salt; bring to a boil, and drop in the tortelloni. Cook until barely tender, but still firm, about 3 to 5 minutes. Drain, transfer to the large bowl, and toss with the rosemary and pancetta sauce and half the cheese. Serve in large shallow soup bowls. Pass the remaining cheese at the table.

Make It Light: Reduce the butter and olive oil to 2 tablespoons each.

Make It Ahead: You can make this dish through step 2 up to 2 hours in advance. Shortly before serving, cook the tortelloni and finish the dish (step 3).

As you can tell by the title, this dish is best made in the summer when tomatoes and basil are at their peak.

ANGEL HAIR PASTA
WITH SUMMER TOMATOES AND BASIL
Serves 8

½ cup plus 2 tablespoons extra virgin olive oil

4 tablespoons each chopped fresh flat-leaf parsley and chopped fresh basil

juice of 2 lemons

2 cloves garlic, finely chopped

5 large ripe tomatoes, peeled, cored, and each cut into 4 thick slices

1 teaspoon sugar

fine sea salt and freshly ground pepper to taste

1 pound angel-hair pasta

1 tablespoon coarse sea salt, for cooking the pasta

4 tablespoons unsalted butter (2 ounces)

2 tablespoons extra virgin olive oil

2 ounces Parmigiano-Reggiano, grated (about ½ cup)

1. Heat ½ cup oil in a large skillet or sauté pan. Warm the parsley, basil, lemon juice, and chopped garlic in the oil over low heat 1 minute. Add the tomato slices and heat 1 minute more, turning once. Season with sugar, salt, and pepper, and remove from heat.

2. Cook the pasta in a large pot of lightly salted boiling water until just al dente. Drain and transfer to a warm pasta bowl and toss with butter and remaining 2 tablespoons of olive oil. Spoon the pasta into warm, shallow soup bowls and garnish each serving with tomato slices. Spoon the sauce over the tomatoes. Pass the grated Parmigiano-Reggiano at the table.

Make It Light: Reduce olive oil to 5 tablespoons (4 for the sauce, and 1 for the pasta) and reduce the butter to 2 tablespoons.

Make It Ahead: You can complete this recipe through step 1 up to 2 hours in advance. When you are ready, reheat the tomatoes and proceed with step 2.

Sometimes I think there is no combination that could taste better than prosciutto and morels. Morels are wild mushrooms that have a meaty texture and an earthy, nut-like taste; prosciutto is so sweet and tender that it leaves a veil of flavor on the tongue. Add some cream and you have a dish that is both creamy rich; and rich in flavor. Serve this in small portions as a first course, followed by a lean grilled fish or meat.

FETTUCCINE WITH PROSCIUTTO AND MORELS

Serves 8

2 ounces dried morels,
    soaked in warm water for 1 hour
3 tablespoons unsalted butter
3 shallots, finely chopped
4 ounces thinly sliced prosciutto,
    cut into fine strips
½ cup crème fraîche (p. 14)
1 cup heavy cream

½ bunch chives, chopped
½ teaspoon each fine sea salt and
    freshly ground pepper
1 pound fettuccine
1 tablespoon coarse sea salt,
    for cooking the pasta
2 ounces Parmigiano-Reggiano,
    grated (about ½ cup)

1. Drain the mushrooms (you may wish to reserve the liquid for another use) and rinse well; slice into strips.

2. Melt the butter in a skillet and sauté the shallots 1 minute over medium heat. Add the mushrooms and prosciutto, and sauté 1 more minute. Stir in the crème fraîche, cream, chives, salt, and pepper, and remove from heat .

3. Cook the pasta in plenty of lightly salted boiling water until just al dente. Reheat the sauce, if necessary. Drain the pasta and toss it with the sauce in a warm serving bowl. Sprinkle with half the cheese and serve, passing the remainder of the cheese at the table.

Make It Light: Substitute half-and-half for both the crème fraîche and heavy cream.

Make It Ahead: You can make this recipe through step 2 up to 2 hours in advance. When you are ready, proceed with step 3.

PENNE WITH ROASTED SWEET PEPPERS

Serves 8

4 tablespoons extra virgin olive oil
6 cloves garlic, coarsely chopped
5 red bell peppers, roasted, peeled, seeded, and cut into ½-inch strips
½ teaspoon each fine sea salt and freshly ground pepper
1 pound penne, or other short tubular pasta

1 tablespoon coarse sea salt, for cooking the pasta
6 tablespoons unsalted butter (3 ounces), melted
20 fresh basil leaves, cut into strips
4 ounces Parmigiano-Reggiano, grated (about 1 cup)

1. Heat the olive oil in a large skillet; and sauté the garlic and bell peppers over low heat 2 minutes. Season with salt and pepper, and set aside.

2. Cook the pasta in plenty of lightly salted boiling water until it is cooked al dente. Drain and place in a warm serving bowl. Add the peppers and all the oil from the pan, the melted butter, basil, and half the grated cheese, and toss thoroughly. Serve in warmed shallow soup bowls, and pass the rest of the cheese at the table.

Make It Light: Reduce olive oil to 2 tablespoons, butter to 2 tablespoons, and cheese to 2 ounces (about ½ cup).

Make It Ahead: You can finish step 1 up to 3 hours in advance. Finish the dish when you are ready to serve (step 2). The peppers will be warmed by the hot pasta, so it's not necessary to reheat them separately.

As a young bride, I had the good fortune to live in the same building as a very kind 85-year-old woman from Genoa, Italy. She used to invite my husband and me down for supper now and then, and this was my favorite dish, especially when she served it with her very special fried chicken (p. 172).

POTATOES AND FETTUCCINE WITH PESTO
Serves 8

2 pounds tiny new red potatoes,
   scrubbed and quartered
1 tablespoon extra virgin olive oil
3 bunches basil, stems removed
3 cloves garlic
½ teaspoon coarse sea salt plus
   1 tablespoon for cooking the pasta

1 tablespoon toasted pine nuts
1 ounce Pecorino Romano,
   freshly grated (¼ cup)
3 ounces Parmigiano-Reggiano,
   freshly grated (¾ cup)
1 cup extra virgin olive
1 pound fettuccine

1. Arrange the potatoes in an open roasting dish, sprinkle with the olive oil, and roast in a 400° degree oven until tender, about 25 to 30 minutes. Set aside.
2. To make the pesto sauce, put the basil, garlic, ½ teaspoon salt, pine nuts, Pecorino Romano, and ½ cup of the Parmigiano in a blender or food processor, and finely purée. When the purée is smooth, slowly add the olive oil in a steady stream with the blender or processor still running, until the oil is incorporated into the sauce.
3. Cook the fettuccine in plenty of lightly salted boiling water until it is cooked al dente, and drain. Combine the fettuccine and potatoes, and toss the two together with the pesto (the hot pasta will warm everything to just the right temperature). Serve in shallow warm soup bowls; pass the remaining Parmigiano at the table.

Make It Light: Substitute HomeChef's Light Pesto (p. 217) for the pesto sauce specified in the recipe.

Make It Ahead: You can make this dish through step 2 up to 2 hours in advance, leaving potatoes and pesto at room temperature. When you are ready, proceed with step 3.

CHAPTER FIVE

MEATS

My parents believed that at least one substantial portion of meat per day was not only American, but necessary for your health, so I grew up on a diet that featured steaks, chops, and roasts. In the last two decades, though, my eating habits have changed considerably, and I have seen a similar shift in the diets of Americans in general. Years ago, it was not uncommon for people to put away fourteen- or sixteen-ounce steaks, or two-inch-thick cuts of prime rib in a single sitting, but now we have become a little bit more like the rest of the world. While we have not given up meat, we have cut down on the amount we consume, and five- or six-ounce portions of meat are now considered more than adequate. Judging from the students at HomeChef, I'd say that, like me, most people still love and crave meat — there is really nothing to take its place — but are quite happy with scaled-down portions.

BEEF

A longtime friend of mine from Mexico taught me to prepare steaks this way. It's so simple, but so good!

GRILLED STEAKS À LA RAMÓN

Serves 6

4 pieces skirt steak, about
6 ounces each
juice of 1 lemon
12 fresh corn tortillas
½ teaspoon each fine sea salt and

freshly ground pepper, or to taste
6 sprigs cilantro
6 tiny dry red chile peppers
Guacamole (p. 46)
Salsa (p. 46)

1. Place the steak in a nonreactive dish, sprinkle with lemon juice, and marinate for 10 minutes. Preheat grill or broiler. Wrap the tortillas in foil, and place in a 250° oven for 15 minutes.

2. Remove steak from marinade, pat dry, and season with salt and pepper. Broil or grill under a preheated broiler or on a preheated grill for 2 to 3 minutes each side for rare, slightly longer for medium-rare. Let stand 10 minutes before slicing across the grain and at an angle, into thin strips. Garnish each serving with cilantro and dry chile peppers. Pass the Guacamole, Salsa, and warmed tortillas.

Make It Light: Skip the Guacamole.

Make It Ahead: Both the Guacamole and Salsa can be made up to a day in advance and refrigerated. If you wish, the steak can be grilled up to 2 hours in advance and served at room temperature. Warm the tortillas 15 minutes before serving. Do not slice the meat until ready to serve.

This is as light as the previous recipe, Grilled Steaks à la Ramón, but the marinade is somewhat more robust.

MARINATED GRILLED FLANK STEAK

Serves 6

1 flank steak (about 1 pound)
   freshly ground pepper
2 tablespoons extra virgin olive oil
3 tablespoons cabernet vinegar
½ cup red table wine
3 cloves garlic, crushed
4 tablespoons chopped fresh
   flat-leaf parsley

1 tablespoon each chopped fresh basil
   and chopped fresh oregano
1 bay leaf, broken in half
   fine sea salt and freshly ground
   black pepper to taste

1. With a sharp knife, make shallow crisscross cuts on one side of the steak, and place in a nonreactive dish, cut side up. Combine the pepper, olive oil, vinegar, wine, garlic, parsley, basil, oregano, and bay leaf. Pour marinade over steak, cover, and refrigerate for 6 hours, turning occasionally.
2. Preheat the grill or broiler. Remove steak from marinade, pat dry, and season with salt and pepper. Grill (or broil) about 4 minutes each side for rare, slightly longer for medium-rare. Let stand 10 minutes, then slice on the diagonal.

Make It Ahead: Allow 6 hours for the steak to marinate. It can then be grilled up to 2 hours in advance and served at room temperature. Do not slice the meat until ready to serve.

This is HomeChef's version of a classic Chinese stir-fried dish. The plum sauce, which is available in Asian food markets — or in the ethnic sections of well-stocked supermarkets — is a sweet and spicy condiment that will give the dish an interesting flavor. Because this dish is cooked very quickly, you should have all the ingredients ready and at hand before you start, and then cook it just before you're ready to serve it.

SESAME BEEF
Serves 4 to 6

4 ounces flank steak,
 thinly sliced across the grain
1 tablespoon plus 2 teaspoons
 soy sauce
3 tablespoons sesame oil

1 clove garlic, thinly sliced
1 teaspoon plum sauce
1 tablespoon each sherry and sugar
2 teaspoons sesame seeds,
 toasted 5 minutes in a 300° oven

1. Marinate the beef in 1 tablespoon soy sauce for 1 hour. Heat the sesame oil in a wok or skillet until smoking, and sauté the beef over high heat for 30 seconds, tossing constantly. Transfer meat to a dish.
2. Lower the heat, and sauté the garlic with the remaining soy sauce, plum sauce, sherry, and sugar for 30 seconds, stirring all the while. Return the beef to the sauce, and toss 10 seconds more. Serve garnished with sesame seeds.

Make It Ahead: Marinate the beef an hour ahead (step 1), and assemble all the ingredients. Then it will take you less than 1 minute to finish the dish and serve it.

David Crosby, one of our students, assured us that this favorite recipe of his would fit into our book. We tried it and agreed. An integral part of his recipe is a pasta accompaniment that's prepared with a sauce of sun-dried tomatoes and olives, giving the whole dish a Mediterranean identity. Oh, and it *is* definitely worth the time it takes to toast and grind the coriander seeds.

DAVID'S MEDITERRANEAN ROASTED TENDERLOIN OF BEEF

Serves 6

2 teaspoons coriander seeds, toasted and coarsely ground
½ teaspoon black peppercorns, coarsely ground
1 tablespoon fine sea salt
½ cup plus 2 tablespoons extra virgin olive oil
a 2-pound beef tenderloin, trimmed of excess fat
2 large shallots, thinly sliced

1 large clove garlic, thinly sliced
½ cup thinly sliced oil-packed sun-dried tomatoes
⅓ cup black olives, preferably Kalamata
⅓ cup chopped fresh flat-leaf parsley
1 tablespoon coarse sea salt, for cooking the pasta
12 ounces tubular pasta, such as penne
¼ teaspoon additional freshly ground pepper

1. Combine the ground coriander, peppercorns, and salt; and stir in 2 tablespoons olive oil to make a paste. Place the beef in a small roasting pan; rub the spice paste over the meat and let stand 1 hour.
2. In a medium-sized saucepan, heat 1 tablespoon of olive oil over low heat. Add the shallots and garlic and sauté slowly until they are softened but not browned, about 5 minutes. Stir in the sun-dried tomatoes, olives, parsley, and remaining olive oil. Set aside.
3. Roast the meat in a preheated 450° oven to the desired degree of doneness, approximately 25 to 30 minutes for medium-rare. Remove the meat to a carving board, cover loosely with foil, and let rest for 10 minutes. Strain any pan juices into the sun-dried tomato sauce.
4. Meanwhile, cook the pasta in a large pot of boiling salted water, until just al dente, about 12 minutes. Drain, return the pasta to the pot, and stir in the sun-dried tomato sauce. Season with pepper and cover to keep warm.
5. To serve, carve the meat across the grain into ¼-inch-thick slices and arrange on a serving platter. Transfer the pasta to a serving bowl and serve the two together. Pour any meat juices from the carving board over the tenderloin.

Make It Light: Reduce the olive oil by half.

Make It Ahead: Boil the pasta up to an hour ahead, toss lightly in a little olive oil, and keep warm in a covered casserole. Prepare the sauce up to an hour ahead, reheating just before pouring over pasta.

For many years, now, I have been serving this as a special "company" dish. It tastes and looks elegant, yet, as you can see, it is actually quite quick and easy to prepare. Even people who are unaccustomed to eating calves liver love it.

SAUTÉED CALVES LIVER WITH PORT WINE SAUCE
Serves 8

1 cup ruby port	8 slices calves liver
juice of 1 orange	4 or 5 tablespoons flour
1½ cups Beef Stock (p. 12)	4 tablespoons rice bran oil,
½ cup crème fraîche	or other light oil
salt and freshly ground white	
pepper to taste	

1. In a heavy saucepan, over medium heat, reduce the port and orange juice to 2 tablespoons. Add the stock, and reduce sauce by half. Add the crème fraîche and reduce to about ½ cup. Season to taste with salt and pepper, and set aside.

2. Trim the liver of any surrounding tissue and slash the edges of each piece in 4 or 5 places to keep it from curling up when you sauté it; season with salt and pepper, and dredge lightly in flour. Heat the oil in a skillet, and sauté the liver quickly over very high heat, about 1 minute each side for rare. Serve on warm plates, with a little sauce spooned over each serving.

Make It Light: Eliminate the crème fraîche.

Make It Ahead: Prepare the sauce up to an hour in advance, and reheat over low heat before serving.

VEAL

Veal used to be a rarity in the average American home — we ate it seldom, if at all, and when we did, it was usually in a French or Italian restaurant. Today, with America's interest in lowering its dietary fat, milk-fed veal has become more popular, and is currently being marketed nationwide. Veal is lean and delicate and is generally cooked more like chicken than beef. I have selected outstanding examples of veal dishes we have done in our classes, including a stew, scallops (or scaloppine, as they are usually called), chops (my personal favorite), and an outstanding roasted veal.

This traditional Italian stew has become one of HomeChef's contemporary classics. It is wonderful served with wide buttered egg noodles ·

VEAL RAGOÛT

Serves 8 to 10

2 ounces dried porcini mushrooms, soaked in 2 cups water for 1 hour	fine sea salt and freshly ground pepper to taste
3 pounds boneless veal shoulder, cut into 2-inch cubes	¾ cup port
3 tablespoons unsalted butter	½ teaspoon dried thyme
3 tablespoons extra virgin olive oil	2 tablespoons tomato paste
5 tablespoons flour	1½ pounds peas, shelled
1 medium onion, finely chopped	½ cup crème fraîche

1. Drain the porcini, reserving the liquid. Rinse the porcini well and strain the reserved liquid. Set both aside.
2. Dust the veal with flour. Heat the butter and oil in a large skillet, and brown the onion and veal together over medium-high heat. Season with salt and pepper, and transfer to an ovenproof casserole.
3. Pour off any oil remaining in the skillet, and add the port, thyme, tomato paste, strained mushroom-soaking liquid, and mushrooms. Bring to a boil, and pour over the veal, mixing well. Cover and braise in a preheated 375° oven about 1 hour, or until veal is tender.
4. Blanch the peas in boiling water for 2 minutes; drain and set aside. When the veal is done, stir in the peas and crème fraîche. Taste for seasoning and correct.

Make It Light: Reduce butter and oil to 2 tablespoons each and omit the crème fraîche.

Make It Ahead: You can make the veal through step 3 up to a day in advance, and refrigerate. Before reheating, allow the casserole to stand at room temperature for 1 hour. Reheat in a 350° oven for 30 minutes, and proceed with step 4.

Marsala is the sweet amber dessert or aperitif wine from Sicily that this classic dish is named after. It is a blended wine that must be aged in casks for at least two years: the longer it is aged, the more mellow it becomes. Using a well-aged Marsala will make this classic dish a memorable one. I love this served with Carrot-Potato Purée (p. 203).

VEAL SCALOPPINE MARSALA

Serves 6

6 boneless veal cutlets
4 to 5 tablespoons flour
3 tablespoons extra virgin olive oil
   fine sea salt and freshly ground
   pepper to taste

¾ cup Marsala
2 tablespoons unsalted butter
2 tablespoons chopped fresh
   flat-leaf parsley

1. Lay the veal between two pieces of waxed paper, and flatten each cutlet with the flat end of a meat pounder until about ¼ inch thick. Dredge lightly with the flour. Heat the oil in a heavy skillet, and sauté the scaloppine over high heat for less than 1 minute each side (they cook very quickly). Transfer to a warm platter and season with salt and pepper.
2. Pour off any oil left in pan, and still over high heat, add the Marsala and simmer until it has reduced slightly, about 2 minutes. Off the heat, swirl in the butter and any juices from the scaloppine platter. Return the scaloppine to the skillet, and baste them with sauce. Serve warm, garnishing each plate with parsley.

Make It Light: Reduce both the butter and the olive oil by half.

Make It Ahead: You can make this dish through step 1 up to an hour in advance, and finish the sauce just before serving.

The great appeal of this dish lies in the combined flavors of the rosemary, sage, and garlic. Leftovers of this roasted veal make superb sandwiches.

ROASTED LEG OF VEAL
WITH ROSEMARY, SAGE, AND GARLIC

Serves 8 to 10

1 leg of veal (about 4 to 5 pounds),
  boned
2 tablespoons each chopped fresh
  rosemary, chopped fresh sage,
  and chopped garlic

fine sea salt, freshly ground pepper,
  and Hungarian paprika to taste
1 cup dry white wine

1. Lay the veal out flat and sprinkle with rosemary, sage, garlic, salt, pepper, and paprika. Roll the meat up and tie securely. Sprinkle the outside of the roast with additional salt, pepper, and paprika, and place on a rack in a shallow roasting pan.
2. Pour the wine over the meat and roast uncovered in a preheated 375° oven 1½ to 2 hours, or until tender, basting occasionally with the pan juices, adding more wine if necessary.
3. Allow roast to stand, loosely covered with foil, for 20 minutes before carving into thin slices. If serving warm, serve with a little of the pan juices over each serving.

Make It Ahead: If you intend to serve this cold, the meat can be roasted up to a day in advance and refrigerated until you are ready to slice and serve it.

Absolutely simple and absolutely delicious. Serve these chops with grilled eggplant, zucchini, and tiny new potatoes (see p. 222).

GRILLED VEAL CHOPS ROSEMARY

Serves 8

8 veal loin chops (about 5 to 6 ounces each)
¼ cup extra virgin olive oil
1 tablespoon finely chopped fresh
  rosemary leaves

juice of 2 lemons
fine sea salt and freshly ground
  pepper to taste

1. Brush the veal chops with oil. Press the rosemary onto both sides of the chops, sprinkle with the lemon juice, and refrigerate 1 hour.
2. Preheat the grill, and grill the chops for 4 minutes each side (they can also be broiled). Season with salt and pepper and serve.

Make It Ahead: You can season the chops (step 1) up to 2 hours in advance.

LAMB

This lamb stew is best made a day in advance, then served the next day. It'll have a richer and more flavorful taste.

BRAISED LAMB WITH BABY ARTICHOKES

Serves 6 to 8

2½ pounds boneless lamb shoulder, cut into 2-inch cubes
 3 or 4 tablespoons flour
 ¼ cup extra virgin olive oil
 coarse sea salt and freshly ground pepper to taste
 1 onion, chopped

 1 tablespoon each finely chopped garlic and fresh rosemary
 ¾ cup red table wine
 4 tablespoons tomato paste
 ¾ cup Chicken Stock (p. 12)
32 baby artichokes, trimmed and quartered (p. 219)

1. Dust the lamb lightly with flour. Heat the oil in a skillet; and brown the lamb over high heat on all sides. Season with salt and pepper and transfer to an ovenproof casserole. In the same skillet, over medium heat, sauté the onion, garlic, and rosemary for 2 minutes. Stir in the wine, tomato paste, and stock, simmer 1 minute, and pour over the lamb.
2. Cover the casserole and braise the lamb in a 375° oven about 1 hour or until the lamb is tender. Stir in the artichokes, and continue cooking until all is tender, about 20 to 30 minutes more.

Make It Light: Reduce olive oil to 2 tablespoons.

Make It Ahead: You can make this dish up to a day in advance, and refrigerate. Let stand at room temperature 1 hour before reheating. Reheat in a preheated 350° oven 30 minutes before serving.

Juniper berries are probably best known for their use in the production of gin, but they also have their place in the kitchen, as a traditional seasoning for game. I tried these fragrant blue-green berries with lamb, and I loved the result. Like all braised dishes this will taste better the day after it's made.

BRAISED LAMB WITH JUNIPER BERRIES

Serves 6

2½ pounds leg of lamb,
    cut into 2-inch cubes
 3 to 4 tablespoons flour
 ¼ cup extra virgin olive oil
    fine sea salt and freshly ground
    pepper to taste
 1 carrot, finely chopped
 1 stalk celery, finely chopped
 ½ medium onion, finely chopped

 1 cup red table wine
 ¼ cup balsamic vinegar
 3 cloves garlic, finely chopped
 1 teaspoon fresh rosemary leaves,
    finely chopped
 2 teaspoons juniper berries, crushed
 4 tablespoons finely chopped fresh
    flat-leaf parsley

1. Lightly dust the meat with flour. Heat the oil in a skillet and brown the meat over high heat on all sides. Season with salt and pepper and transfer to an ovenproof casserole. In the same skillet, sauté the carrot, celery, and onion over medium heat for 2 minutes. Add the remaining ingredients, stir, bring to a boil, and pour over the lamb in the casserole.
2. Cover the casserole, and braise in a preheated 375° oven approximately 1½ hours, or until meat is tender. If the casserole appears dry, add more wine or some water.

Make It Ahead: You can make this dish up to a day in advance, and refrigerate. Let stand at room temperature 1 hour before reheating. Reheat in a preheated 350° oven 30 minutes before serving.

The combined flavors of the peppercorns, rosemary, sage, and mint permeate the lamb with a wonderful fresh flavor. Typically, a leg of lamb is boned, then rolled, and tied, but for this dish, I prefer to leave the meat flat because it is much easier to carve. It also reduces the cooking time.

ROASTED BUTTERFLIED LEG OF LAMB AU POIVRE
Serves 8 to 10

1 small leg of lamb, boned and left untied
3 tablespoons each white, green, and black peppercorns, coarsely ground
1 tablespoon each chopped fresh rosemary, sage, and mint
5 cloves garlic, crushed

½ cup raspberry vinegar
¼ cup soy sauce
¾ cup dry white wine
4 tablespoons Dijon mustard sprigs of fresh rosemary and mint for garnish

1. In a nonreactive dish large enough to hold the lamb, combine half the ground peppercorns, and all the rosemary, sage, mint, garlic, vinegar, soy sauce, and wine. Place the lamb in the dish, and marinate overnight in the refrigerator, turning once.
2. When ready to roast, remove the lamb from the marinade and pat dry; place the meat on a rack in a shallow roasting pan, skin side up. Reserve the marinade. Combine the remaining peppercorns and mustard to make a paste; spread the paste over the top of the meat, and spoon the reserved marinade all around the lamb.
3. Roast in a preheated 450° degree oven 10 minutes per pound for rare, 12 minutes for medium. Baste 2 or 3 times during the roasting. Transfer the roast to a carving board, preferably one with a well. Cover lightly with foil and let stand at least 20 minutes before carving. To serve, arrange overlapping slices of lamb on warmed plates, spoon pan juices over all, and garnish with sprigs of rosemary and mint.

Make It Ahead: Marinate the lamb and prepare it for roasting up to 2 hours in advance (steps 1 and 2). Put the lamb in the oven about an hour before serving (step 3).

As the lamb roasts, its juices fall onto the potatoes and onions. All the flavors blend harmoniously to create a unique dining experience.

ROASTED LEG OF LAMB
WITH POTATOES AND ONIONS ·
Serves 8

2 medium onions, coarsely chopped
4 pounds new potatoes, peeled
   and cut into ¼-inch slices
   fine sea salt, freshly ground pepper,
   and Hungarian paprika to taste

2 cups Beef Stock (p. 12)
6 cloves garlic, slivered
6 sprigs fresh sage
1 small leg of lamb, boned
   and left untied

1. Spread the potatoes and onions in a large roasting pan, and season with salt, pepper, and paprika. Bring the stock to a boil, and pour it over the potatoes and onions. Bake in a preheated 425° oven for 30 minutes.

2. Cut tiny slits into the skin side of the lamb and insert the slivers of garlic and sprigs of sage. Place a rack in the pan over the potatoes and onions, and put the lamb skin side up on the rack. Season generously with additional salt, pepper, and paprika.

3. Roast the lamb 10 minutes a pound for rare, and about 12 minutes a pound for medium. Transfer the lamb to a carving board, cover lightly with foil, and let stand at least 20 minutes before slicing. Put 2 or 3 slices of lamb on each plate, surrounded by roasted potatoes and onions.

Make It Ahead: You can have the potatoes and onions in the roasting pan and the lamb all seasoned about 2 hours before serving time. An hour before serving, heat the stock and proceed as described above.

I used to prepare these ribs all the time for my young children. They seemed to love picking up the small ribs and chewing on them. By the way, adults love them, too! The marinade contains Chinese five-spice powder, which is a combination of aromatic spices, and brown bean paste, a sweet and salty condiment. Both are available in Asian food markets.

SAVORY LAMB RIBLETS

Serves 4 to 6

1 teaspoon each ground peppercorns, sugar, and Chinese five-spice powder

2 tablespoons each soy sauce, sherry, sesame oil, and water

1 tablespoon each finely chopped fresh ginger and finely chopped garlic

1 tablespoon brown bean paste (available in Asian food markets)

2 racks of lamb ribs, trimmed of extra fat and halved crosswise

1. Put all the ingredients except the lamb ribs in a small bowl, and combine well. Place the ribs in a shallow container, and spread the sauce over the ribs, rubbing it into the meat on all sides. Cover and refrigerate overnight.

2. Preheat the broiler and broiler pan. Place the ribs meat side down on the broiler pan, and broil for 3 minutes. Turn and broil another 3 minutes. Let the ribs stand covered lightly with foil for 5 minutes. Cut the ribs apart before serving.

Make It Ahead: You can make the ribs up to 1 hour in advance. Place them on a warm platter, and cover loosely with foil; put them in a warm, turned-off oven with the door left ajar.

Eggplant and lamb make ideal partners, especially when seasoned with the herbs that typify Greek cooking — basil, mint, rosemary, and oregano.

GREEK LAMB RAGOÛT

Serves 8

2 large eggplants, peeled and
  cut into 2-inch cubes
½ cup extra virgin olive oil
3 pounds boneless lamb shoulder,
  cut into 2-inch cubes
4 to 5 tablespoons flour
2 pounds tomatoes, chopped with juice
½ cup white table wine
2 large onions, finely chopped

2 cloves garlic, finely chopped
3 tablespoons tomato paste
1 teaspoon each ground cumin,
  turmeric, and pepper
1 teaspoon each finely chopped fresh
  basil, mint, rosemary, and oregano
½ cup coarse fresh bread crumbs
3 tablespoons finely chopped fresh
  flat-leaf parsley

1. Sprinkle the eggplant with coarse sea salt and drain for 1 hour. Pat dry with paper towels, toss with 4 tablespoons of the olive oil, and place on an oiled baking sheet. Bake in a preheated 375° oven until softened, about 20 minutes.
2. Dust the lamb with flour; heat the remaining 4 tablespoons oil in a large skillet, and brown the lamb on all sides over high heat. Transfer the lamb to an ovenproof casserole. Discard any oil remaining in the skillet, and add the tomatoes, wine, onions, garlic, tomato paste, cumin, turmeric, pepper, and chopped herbs. Simmer and stir for 2 minutes, then pour over the lamb. Add the eggplant, mix well, cover, and braise in a preheated 375° oven for approximately 1½ hours, or until the lamb is tender.
3. Combine the bread crumbs and parsley, and sprinkle the mixture over the lamb. Lower the heat to 350° and return the casserole to the oven uncovered. Continue to braise for 30 minutes, or until crumbs are lightly browned.

Make It Light: Reduce the olive oil by half.

Make It Ahead: You can make the lamb up to a day in advance through step 2, and refrigerate it in the casserole. Let stand at room temperature for 1 hour then proceed with step 3.

PORK

The interesting news about pork is that the animals are being bred to produce very lean meat. In fact, a well-trimmed pork chop now is actually leaner than chicken. The pork tenderloin, which corresponds to the filet mignon cut of beef, is particularly lean. It is excellent for roasting, sautéing, or grilling. In the dish following, the tenderloin is quickly roasted, cut into small round slices, and served with a wild mushroom sauce. This is an extremely elegant dish, and is suitable for very special occasions. People will tell you that you really ought to open a restaurant!

ROASTED PORK TENDERLOIN
WITH WILD MUSHROOM PAN GRAVY

Serves 8

3 pork tenderloins, about ¾ pound each
1 cup bourbon
2 ounces dried morels, rinsed well
1 cup Beef Stock (p. 12)
1 tablespoon soy sauce

1 tablespoon unsalted butter
6 shallots, finely chopped
1 cup crème fraîche
fine sea salt, freshly ground pepper, and Hungarian paprika to taste

1. Put the meat in a nonreactive dish, pour the bourbon over the meat, and marinate 2 hours at room temperature. Combine the stock and soy sauce in a small saucepan and bring to a boil. Pour over the morels and marinate for 2 hours.
2. Remove the mushrooms from the stock, rinse again to eliminate all the sand, and chop finely. Strain the stock through a fine strainer and reserve. Remove the meat from the bourbon, reserving the bourbon.
3. In a skillet, heat the butter and sauté the shallots 1 minute over low heat. Add the bourbon, remove from the heat and ignite, shaking the pan until the flames die. Add the reserved stock and chopped mushrooms, return to the heat, and cook over low heat until reduced to approximately ½ cup. Stir in the crème fraîche and reduce until slightly thickened. Season with salt and pepper, and set aside.
4. Season the meat with salt, pepper, and paprika, and roast on a rack in a preheated 450° oven approximately 35 minutes for rare, 45 minutes for medium. Transfer the meat to a cutting board (preferably one with a well to catch the juices), and cover lightly with foil. Let stand 20 minutes, then slice. Stir any juices from the meat into the sauce and reheat the sauce. Arrange overlapping slices of meat on each warmed plate, with sauce spooned down the middle of the slices.

Make It Light: Omit the crème fraîche.

Make It Ahead: Be sure to allow 2 hours for the meat and morels to marinate. The mushroom sauce can be made while the meat is roasting.

Try this one for your next picnic or outdoor potluck. After the meat is roasted, allow it to cool, wrap in foil, and chill. Before packing it for your picnic, slice it, and wrap it back up in foil. Bring along some crusty bread or rolls, and I think you will agree, you will not find a better sandwich at any picnic.

BOURBON AND HONEY MARINATED PORK TENDERLOIN

Serves 8–10

1 cup extra virgin olive oil
½ cup each bourbon and
   red wine vinegar
3 tablespoons honey
2 tablespoons each, finely chopped
   garlic, finely chopped fresh ginger,
   and finely chopped fresh sage

¼ cup soy sauce
½ small onion, thinly sliced
3 pork tenderloins, about ¾ pound each
   fine sea salt, freshly ground pepper,
   and Hungarian Paprika

1. Combine the oil, bourbon, vinegar, honey, garlic, ginger, sage, soy sauce, and onion, and mix well. Put the tenderloins in a nonreactive dish and pour the marinade over them. Cover and marinate in the refrigerator overnight, turning the meat several times.
2. Remove meat from the refrigerator and let stand at room temperature for 1 hour. Remove from marinade, pat dry, and season with salt, pepper, and paprika. Reserve the marinade.
3. Roast in a preheated 450° degree oven about 15 minutes per pound for medium, basting 2 or 3 times during the roasting with the reserved marinade. Let the roast stand on a carving board lightly covered with foil for 20 minutes before slicing. Serve warm, at room temperature, or cold.

Make It Ahead: To serve cold, roast the meat a day ahead. Wrap and refrigerate it unsliced. Slice before serving.

Follow some common sense kitchen safety rules when flaming food. First of all, clear the area of pot holders and towels or any other objects that might catch fire. Always turn off the stove and remove the pan from the heat source; ignite with long matches, and stand back after igniting. As soon as the alcohol has burned off, the flames will die out on their own, usually in less than 30 seconds. What's left is the savory taste of the gin, without the alcohol. With all that as an introduction, you're probably wondering if it's worth the effort. One taste, and I'm sure you'll agree with me that it is.

GIN-FLAMED PORK SPARERIBS

Serves 6 to 8

5 **pounds baby back pork ribs**	1 **tablespoon sugar**
4 **cloves garlic, cut in half**	½ **cup gin, warmed**
fine sea salt and freshly ground pepper	

1. Rub garlic over both sides of the ribs. Season one side of the ribs with salt and pepper, and place in a shallow baking pan. Roast in a preheated 375° oven 35 minutes. Drain off fat in pan; turn and season the other side of the ribs with salt and pepper, and roast 30 to 35 minutes more, until nicely browned.

2. Remove the pan from the oven and drain off any fat. Sprinkle the ribs with sugar, pour the gin over, and ignite. When the flames die out, transfer ribs to a board, cut the ribs apart, and serve.

Make It Ahead: You can roast the ribs (step 1) up to 2 hours in advance. When you are ready, reheat ribs in a 350° oven for 15 minutes, then proceed with step 2.

I picked up this recipe on a winter's trip to Normandy, on the northern coast of France. The weather was cold and gray, there were virtually no other tourists in sight, and we were the only guests in a small family-run hotel. The proprietors were very attentive, and served us many wonderful meals. This was one of them.

PORK CHOPS STUFFED WITH
SMOKED HAM, GRUYÈRE, AND SAGE

Serves 8

8 center-cut pork chops,
  cut 1¼ inch thick
  fine sea salt and freshly ground
  pepper to taste
2 tablespoons coarsely chopped fresh
  sage leaves
8 thin slices smoked ham,
  trimmed to fit the chops

8 thin slices Swiss Gruyère,
  trimmed to fit the chops
3 tablespoons unsalted butter
½ cup white table wine
½ cup Chicken Stock (p. 12)

1. Cut a small pocket in each chop. Sprinkle the chop inside with salt, pepper, and chopped sage. Place a slice of ham and a slice of cheese in the opening and close the chop. Season the outside lightly with salt and pepper.
2. Heat the butter in a large skillet and sauté the chops, covered, over low heat, 5 minutes each side. Remove to a warm serving dish and cover lightly with foil.
3. Pour out any fat remaining in the pan and add the wine and stock. Reduce rapidly over high heat to about ½ cup. Taste for seasoning and correct if necessary. To serve, spoon a little sauce over each chop.

Make It Light: Omit the cheese.

Make It Ahead: You can have the chops stuffed, ready to sauté up to 2 hours in advance. About 20 minutes before serving, sauté the chops and make the sauce (steps 2 and 3).

Serve this one-dish meal in deep bowls, accompanied by warm tortillas. If you can't find fresh tomatillos, you can substitute a 14-ounce can of tomatillos, in which case it is not necessary to roast them.

GREEN CHILE PORK RAGOÛT

Serves 6

10 tomatillos, husked and rinsed
1 serrano chile, roasted, peeled, and seeded
1 clove garlic, chopped
¼ onion, chopped
½ cup Chicken Stock (p. 12)
1 teaspoon sugar
¼ teaspoon salt, or to taste
1 tablespoon finely chopped fresh cilantro

½ teaspoon each ground cumin and ground peppercorns
2 teaspoons water
2 tablespoons extra virgin olive oil fine sea salt and freshly ground pepper to taste
2½ to 3 pounds boneless pork shoulder, cut into 2-inch cubes

1. Place the tomatillos in a roasting dish and roast in a 350° oven until softened, about 10 minutes. Put them in a blender or food processor, together with the serrano chile, garlic, onion, stock, sugar, and about ¼ teaspoon salt, and process until smooth. Stir in the cilantro and set aside.
2. Combine the cumin, peppercorns, and water, and mix to a paste. Season the pork with salt and pepper. Heat the olive oil in a sauté pan, and brown the meat over high heat on all sides. Remove any excess fat from the pan and stir in the spice paste and the tomatillo sauce. Reduce heat to medium-low, cover, and simmer until meat is tender, approximately 40 minutes more, stirring occasionally.

Make It Ahead: You can make this dish up to 1 day in advance and refrigerate. Reheat before serving.

RABBIT

Rabbit is so popular today, that most markets carry it year round. Our students like rabbit as a great alternative to chicken. It is just as tender and lean, but is more flavorful, and is delicious braised or roasted. Serve this dish with wide buttered noodles, if you like.

BRAISED RABBIT IN A TARRAGON MUSTARD SAUCE
Serves 8

2 young rabbits, about 2 pounds each
4 or 5 tablespoons flour
3 tablespoons extra virgin olive oil
   fine sea salt and freshly ground
   pepper to taste
1 onion, finely chopped
2 cloves garlic, finely chopped
3 shallots, finely chopped

⅓ cup Cognac
1 cup each white table wine and
   Chicken Stock (p. 12)
1 tablespoon chopped fresh tarragon
2 tablespoons Dijon mustard
1 cup crème fraîche
4 tablespoons chopped fresh
   flat-leaf parsley

1. Cut each rabbit into 8 pieces and dust with flour. In a large skillet, heat the olive oil, and brown the rabbit lightly over high heat, about 2 or 3 minutes each side. Season with salt and pepper, and transfer to an ovenproof casserole. Pour off any oil remaining in the skillet, and add the onion, garlic, and shallots. Reduce the heat to medium and stir and sauté 1 minute. Remove the skillet from the heat, add the Cognac, and ignite. When the flame dies, add the wine, stock, and 2 teaspoons of the tarragon. Pour over the rabbit in the casserole, cover, and braise in a preheated 425° oven for 30 to 40 minutes, until tender.

2. Remove the rabbit to a warmed serving platter. Pour the braising liquid into a saucepan and reduce over high heat to about ½ cup. Whisk in the mustard. Stir in the crème fraîche and remaining tarragon, and simmer the sauce until it thickens slightly. Stir in the parsley, pour the sauce over the rabbit, and serve.

Make It Light: Omit the crème fraîche.

Make It Ahead: You can make this dish up to 1 hour in advance through step 1. Let the casserole stand in a warm, turned-off oven with the door left ajar. When you are ready, proceed with step 2.

Most of the garlic in this recipe gets roasted with the skin on. When you serve the dish, each person can squish the garlic out of its skin by pressing it with the tines of their fork, then mix it with the potatoes and rabbit meat. I love this in the summertime, served with Caesar Salad (p. 80).

ROSEMARY ROASTED RABBIT
WITH GARLIC AND POTATOES
Serves 8

2 young rabbits, 2 pounds each	16 small new potatoes, scrubbed
24 cloves garlic	and quartered
2 cups red table wine	coarse sea salt, finely ground pepper,
¼ cup extra virgin olive oil	and Hungarian paprika, to taste
2 tablespoons chopped	sprigs of rosemary for garnish
fresh rosemary	

1. Cut each rabbit into 8 pieces, and place in a nonreactive dish. Peel and crush 8 cloves of garlic, and combine with the wine, olive oil, and rosemary to make a marinade. Pour the marinade over the rabbit, and marinate overnight in the refrigerator.

2. Place the potatoes and unpeeled cloves of garlic in a large roasting pan, season with salt, pepper, and paprika, and spoon in 4 tablespoons of the marinade. Bake in a preheated 350° oven 30 minutes.

3. Remove the rabbit from the marinade, pat dry, and season with salt, pepper, and paprika. Raise the oven heat to 375°, arrange the rabbit over potatoes, and spoon 3 or 4 more tablespoons of the marinade over all. Roast 45 to 50 minutes, until tender, basting once or twice with the juices in the pan, adding more marinade if necessary. To serve, arrange the rabbit on a warm platter; surround with roasted potatoes and roasted garlic, and garnish with sprigs of rosemary.

Make It Ahead: You can make this up to 1 hour in advance, and arrange on a platter. Cover loosely with foil and place in a warm oven with the heat turned off and the door left ajar until serving.

GROUND MEATS

When I was growing up, meat loaf was a standard once-a-week dinner at our house (and a standard once-a-week sandwich in my school lunch box). Meat loaf is such a comforting food, I'm happy that it has become very chic to serve it these days. This is good with Garlic Mashed Potatoes (p. 210).

MEAT LOAF WITH TOMATO SAUCE

Serves 8

1 thick slice of French or Italian bread
¼ cup milk
1 onion, chopped
1 clove garlic, chopped
2 teaspoons tomato paste
¼ cup HomeChef's Basic
   Mayonnaise (p. 105)
2 teaspoons fine sea salt

1 teaspoon freshly ground pepper
3 tablespoons chopped fresh
   flat-leaf parsley
1 pound ground beef
4 ounces each ground veal and
   ground pork
   Tomato Sauce, warmed (p. 14)

1. Soak the bread in the milk to soften it. In a blender or food processor, combine the onion, garlic, tomato paste, mayonnaise, salt, pepper, parsley, and soaked bread; process until thick and creamy.
2. Combine the meats in a large mixing bowl. Add the onion mixture to the meats, and mix thoroughly with your hands.
3. Pack into a greased loaf pan, and bake in a preheated 375° oven for 1 hour and 10 minutes. Allow to stand 20 minutes before turning it out onto a cutting board. Cut into ½-inch slices, arrange on a warm serving platter, and surround with warm Tomato Sauce.

Make It Light: For a light meat loaf, see the following recipe.

Make It Ahead: You can bake the meat loaf up to 1 hour ahead. Leave it in the pan, cover lightly with foil, and place in a warm oven with the heat turned off and the door left ajar until serving. Remove from the pan, cut, and serve as described above.

This light alternative is so good, our students were adamant that we include it here. I think it is great to have an option like this.

"LIGHT" MEAT LOAF
Serves 8

1 ounce old-fashioned oats, uncooked (about ½ cup)
½ cup nonfat milk
¾ pound each ground turkey and ground beef chuck
1 carrot, finely shredded
½ small onion, finely chopped

1 clove garlic, finely chopped
4 tablespoons chopped fresh flat-leaf parsley
2 teaspoons fine sea salt
1 teaspoon freshly ground pepper
½ cup canned strained tomatoes or tomato purée

1. In a large bowl, combine the oats and milk. Add the remaining ingredients except the tomatoes and combine well.
2. Pack into a lightly greased loaf pan and cover with strained tomatoes or tomato purée. Bake at 350° for 1 hour and 20 minutes. Let stand 10 minutes before unmolding, slicing, and serving.

Make It Ahead: You can bake the meat loaf up to 1 hour ahead. Leave it in the pan, cover lightly with foil, and place in a warm oven with the heat turned off and the door left ajar until serving. When you are ready, unmold, slice, and serve.

Homemade sausage is easy to make (especially this kind, which does not involve casings), and really is superior to any you can buy. I always make this sausage in large batches. It freezes very well, and makes an excellent spur-of-the-moment weekend brunch that everyone loves.

SPICY SAUSAGE PATTIES
WITH BRANDIED APPLESAUCE

Serves 10

1 pound each ground pork,
   ground beef, and ground veal
4 cloves garlic, finely chopped
6 scallions, finely chopped
1 bell pepper, roasted, peeled, seeded,
   and chopped
1 teaspoon each ground cumin,
   ground fennel seeds, dried thyme,
   and chopped fresh sage

¼ teaspoon freshly ground nutmeg
¼ teaspoon hot sauce
1 tablespoon fine sea salt
3 tablespoons clarified butter
   Brandied Applesauce
   (see recipe below)

1. In a large bowl, combine all ingredients except the clarified butter and applesauce. Mix well with your hands. Divide the mixture in half and roll each half into a log about 2 inches in diameter. Wrap well, and refrigerate overnight.
2. Slice the sausage into patties. Heat the butter in a large skillet and fry the patties until well browned on both sides. Arrange the patties on a warmed serving platter; pass the Brandied Applesauce.

Make It Ahead: You can make the sausage up to a day ahead (step 1) and store in the refrigerator. The patties can be sautéed up to 30 minutes in advance and arranged on a warm serving platter: Cover lightly with foil, then place in a warm oven with the heat turned off and the door left ajar until serving. (The uncooked sausage logs can also be wrapped airtight in foil or freezer wrap, and stored in the freezer, where they will keep for up to a month.)

BRANDIED APPLESAUCE

8 large tart apples, peeled, cored,
   and quartered
2 oranges, peeled and sectioned

3½ ounces sugar (about ½ cup)
¼ cup brandy, rum, or Cognac

Combine the apples, oranges, and sugar in a saucepan; cover and simmer until soft, about 25 to 30 minutes. Cool slightly and pass through a food mill or coarse strainer. Stir in the brandy, rum, or Cognac, and allow to stand 2 hours before serving. Serve at room temperature.

Make It Ahead: Applesauce can be prepared up to 2 days in advance, and refrigerated. Bring to room temperature before serving.

CHAPTER SIX

POULTRY

When it comes to "great cooking in minutes," chicken fits in perfectly, because with chicken, you don't have to resort to elaborate, time-consuming preparations to create wonderfully delectable dishes. Besides that, it can be cooked in so many ways, and is compatible with so many different kinds of seasonings, that you could easily prepare a different chicken dish every day for years and never repeat yourself. There is more good news — chicken is low in fat, can be purchased everywhere, and is relatively inexpensive.

A favorite technique at HomeChef is to use fillets of chicken breast meat, sauté them quickly, and add a light sauce. Most dishes made with chicken breast fillets can be prepared in less than fifteen minutes, and your family and friends are guaranteed to fall in love with them. Many times, innocent guests have said to me, after sampling one of these dishes, "This is the *best* veal I have *ever* had! *Where* do you buy your *veal*?" The first five recipes in this chapter are made with these fillets of chicken breast. They cook very quickly, so be sure to follow the cooking times exactly.

CHICKEN

CHICKEN BREAST FILLETS
WITH SHERRY CHIVE SAUCE

Serves 8

6 tablespoons clarified butter
8 half chicken breasts, boned,
   skinned, and filleted
   fine sea salt and freshly ground
   white pepper to taste
¾ cup concentrated Chicken Stock (p. 12)
¾ cup sherry

1 cup white table wine
4 shallots, finely chopped
1 cup crème fraîche
1 tablespoon tomato paste
2 tablespoons fresh chives,
   finely chopped

1. Heat the butter in a large skillet and sauté the chicken fillets over medium-high heat, no more than 1 minute each side. Season with salt and pepper, and transfer to a warm serving platter.
2. Pour off any fat remaining in the pan. Stir in the Chicken Stock, sherry, white wine, and shallots, and reduce the sauce by half. Stir in the crème fraîche and tomato paste, and reduce to about ¾ cup, or until slightly thickened. Season to taste with salt and pepper, and add the chives. Return the fillets to the pan and warm for 1 minute.

Make It Light: Omit the creme fraîche.

Make It Ahead: You can make the chicken and sauce up to 1 hour in advance, but do not combine them. (Both sauce and chicken can stand at room temperature for 1 hour.) When ready to serve, reheat the sauce, and warm the chicken in the sauce for 1 minute.

HOW TO PREPARE
CHICKEN BREAST FILLETS

Start with chicken breast halves; remove the skin, then gently separate the meat from the bone with a sharp knife and the help of your fingers. The breast will naturally separate into two pieces. The smaller piece, which lies on the underside of the breast and can easily be pulled away, makes one fillet. Holding the larger piece flat on the cutting board with one hand, cut it into two thinner pieces, slicing it horizontally with the knife. Now you have three fillets from one half breast of chicken.

CHICKEN BREAST FILLETS
WITH ROASTED GARLIC ROSEMARY SAUCE

Serves 8

2 whole heads roasted garlic (p. 220)
¼ cup extra virgin olive oil
2 tablespoons butter
8 half chicken breasts, boned,
   skinned, and filleted
   fine sea salt and freshly ground
   pepper to taste

1 tablespoon each chopped fresh
   rosemary and flat-leaf parsley
½ cup white table wine
¼ cup fresh lemon juice
6 tablespoons unsalted butter
   (3 ounces), at room temperature
   zest of 2 lemons for garnish

1. Squeeze the pulp out of the cloves of garlic and mash; set aside. Heat the oil and butter in a large skillet and sauté the chicken fillets over medium-high heat, no more than 1 minute each side. Season with salt and pepper, and transfer to a warm serving platter.

2. Pour off any fat remaining in the skillet, and add the roasted garlic, rosemary, parsley, wine, and lemon juice. Stir with a whisk over moderate heat until well combined, then reduce until thickened to about ⅓ cup. Off the heat, or over very low heat, whisk in the butter. Arrange the chicken on warm plates, spoon the sauce over the chicken, and garnish with lemon zest.

Make It Light: Eliminate the butter from the sauce.

Make It Ahead: You can make the chicken and sauce up to 1 hour in advance, but do not combine them. (Both sauce and chicken can stand at room temperature for 1 hour.) When ready to serve, reheat the sauce, and warm the chicken in the sauce for 1 minute. Serve garnished with lemon zest.

I first sampled this dish years ago while traveling in Italy, and it has become one of my favorites. It's best made with fresh young artichokes that are no bigger than 2 inches in diameter (the whole thing is edible then, because the choke has not yet developed). If you can't get baby artichokes, substitute fresh artichoke bottoms or frozen baby artichokes.

CHICKEN BREAST FILLETS WITH BABY ARTICHOKES

Serves 6

30 baby artichokes, trimmed and halved or quartered (p. 219)
5 or 6 tablespoons flour
¼ cup extra virgin olive oil
fine sea salt and freshly ground pepper to taste

6 half chicken breasts, boned, skinned, and filleted
1 cup white table wine
6 lemon wedges for garnish

1. Dust the artichokes lightly with flour. Heat the olive oil in a skillet and sauté the artichokes over medium heat for about 10 minutes, or until tender. Season with salt and pepper, and transfer to a warm serving platter, leaving the oil in the skillet.
2. Lightly flour the chicken fillets, and sauté over medium-high heat in the remaining oil, no more than 1 minute each side. Season with salt and pepper, and transfer to the artichoke platter.
3. Pour off any fat remaining in the skillet, add the wine, and reduce by half, scraping up the juices stuck on the bottom of the skillet. Arrange the artichokes around the chicken, and pour wine sauce over all. Garnish with lemon wedges.

Make It Ahead: Prepare the artichokes, chicken, and sauce up to 1 hour in advance, but keep the sauce separate. (Everything can stand at room temperature for 1 hour.) Shortly before serving, reheat artichokes and chicken in a 350° oven for 5 minutes; reheat sauce, and proceed as described above to serve.

This dish was adapted from a recipe that is Mexican in origin. It is a little spicy and very low calorie; it would go really well with Old-Fashioned Mashed Potatoes (p. 210).

CHICKEN BREAST FILLETS PICANTÉ

Serves 8

2 serrano chiles, roasted, peeled, seeded, and chopped
2 cloves garlic, peeled
2 teaspoons cumin seed
1 teaspoon each chile powder, Hungarian paprika, and coriander seed
2 cardamom seeds

juice of 1 lime
1 teaspoon hot sauce
8 half chicken breasts, boned, skinned, and filleted
6 tablespoons clarified butter
fine sea salt to taste
1 cup concentrated Chicken Stock (p. 12)

1. Place chiles, garlic, and all the spices in a spice grinder or mortar and pestle, and grind to a fine paste. Stir in the lime juice and hot sauce and rub this paste all over the chicken fillets. Cover and marinate 2 hours in the refrigerator.
2. Heat the butter in a large skillet and sauté the chicken fillets over medium-high heat, no more than 1 minute each side. Season with salt, and transfer to a warm serving platter.
3. Pour off any fat remaining in the pan, stir in the Chicken Stock, and reduce to ½ cup. Spoon the sauce over the chicken to serve.

Make It Ahead: The fillets can be sautéed, and the sauce prepared up to 1 hour in advance, but do not combine them. (Both sauce and chicken can stand at room temperature for 1 hour.) When you are ready to serve, reheat the sauce, and warm the chicken breasts in the sauce for about 1 minute, until heated through.

This marvelous dish also borrows from Mexican cuisine. For the sauce, use raw hulled pumpkin seeds (available in Latin markets or at health food stores). Tomatillos, which look like small green tomatoes, are also sold in Latin markets, or you may even find them at your local supermarket.

CHICKEN BREAST FILLETS
WITH PUMPKIN SEED SAUCE

Serves 6

½ cup extra virgin olive oil
½ medium onion, coarsely chopped
2 cloves garlic, coarsely chopped
1 jalapeño chile, seeded and coarsely chopped
4 tomatillos, coarsely chopped (canned are okay if you can't find fresh)
2½ ounces raw hulled pumpkin seeds (about ½ cup), toasted

8 shelled almonds, toasted
2 tablespoons sesame seeds, toasted
10 sprigs cilantro
½ teaspoon each ground cumin, fine sea salt, and pepper
1 to 2 cups Chicken Stock (p. 12)
6 half chicken breasts, boned, skinned, and filleted
3 jalapeño chiles, seeded and halved lengthwise, for garnish

1. Heat half the oil in a skillet over medium heat and sauté the onion, garlic, jalapeño, and tomatillos for 2 minutes. Transfer all to a blender or food processor. Set aside 2 tablespoons of the pumpkin seeds for garnish, and put the rest in the blender or food processor, along with the almonds, sesame seeds, 4 sprigs of cilantro, cumin, salt, and pepper. Process, adding enough Chicken Stock to create a thick, smooth paste.
2. Heat the remaining oil in the skillet and sauté the chicken fillets over medium-high heat, no more than 1 minute each side. Transfer to a warm serving platter.
3. Pour off any fat remaining in the skillet, and add the blended ingredients. Cook over low heat for 2 minutes, stirring and scraping up any juices stuck on the bottom of the skillet. If the sauce seems too thick, add a little more Chicken Stock.
4. Arrange the chicken on warm plates, spoon the sauce over the chicken, and garnish each serving with a sprig of cilantro, pumpkin seeds, and jalapeños.

Make It Ahead: You can make this up to 1 hour in advance, but keep the chicken and sauce separate. (Both sauce and chicken can stand at room temperature for 1 hour.) When ready to serve, heat the sauce, then warm the chicken in the sauce for 1 minute. Garnish as described above.

When I broil or grill chicken breasts, I remove the bone, but leave the skin on because this keeps the chicken from drying out as it cooks. Guests who wish can always remove the skin later. This dish is exceptionally good served at room temperature, so it's ideal for buffets. Serve it with some grilled vegetables (p. 218) and a hot side dish, like Roquefort-Potato Gratin (p. 213).

GRILLED CHICKEN BREASTS ROSEMARY

Serves 8

⅓ cup extra virgin olive oil
¼ cup sherry vinegar
3 cloves garlic, chopped
1 tablespoon chopped fresh rosemary
2 tablespoons chopped fresh
  flat-leaf parsley

8 half chicken breasts, boned,
  skin left on
  fine sea salt, freshly ground pepper,
  and Hungarian paprika to taste

1. In a nonreactive bowl, combine the olive oil, sherry vinegar, garlic, and herbs. Marinate the chicken breasts in this overnight in the refrigerator.
2. When ready to serve, remove the chicken from the marinade, and season with salt, pepper, and paprika. Grill on a preheated grill 4 minutes each side (or broil the chicken, if you prefer). Do not overcook. Serve warm or at room temperature.

Make It Ahead: Don't hesitate to make this up to 1 to 2 hours in advance and serve at room temperature. In fact, I think it tastes better this way.

In Spanish this could be called *pollo borracho* (drunken chicken)!

GRILLED CHICKEN BREASTS TEQUILA
Serves 6

2 tablespoons extra virgin olive oil
8 jalapeño chiles, roasted, peeled,
   and seeded
¾ cup fresh orange juice
¼ cup each fresh lemon juice
   and tequila
¼ teaspoon hot sauce

1 medium onion, chopped
2 cloves garlic, finely chopped
6 half chicken breasts, boned,
   skin left on
   fine sea salt, freshly ground black
   pepper, and Hungarian paprika to taste

1. Heat the oil in a skillet, and over low heat, gently sauté the jalapeños for 10 minutes. Place in a blender or food processor with the orange juice and purée until smooth. Transfer to a nonreactive container, and combine with the lemon juice, tequila, hot sauce, onion, and garlic, and mix well. Marinate the chicken in the sauce overnight in the refrigerator.
2. One hour before grilling, remove the chicken from the marinade and season with salt, pepper, and paprika. Grill on a preheated grill 4 minutes each side (or broil the chicken, if you prefer), basting with the marinade. Do not overcook. Serve warm or at room temperature.

Make It Ahead: Don't hesitate to make this up to 1 to 2 hours in advance and serve at room temperature. In fact, I think it tastes better this way.

Poussin is the French term for what we call a spring chicken or young broiler. They weigh about 2 pounds each, and you can substitute squabs or Cornish hens if you wish. Since both are smaller than *poussins,* you may wish to serve 1 per person.

GRILLED *POUSSINS* WITH FRESH HERBS AND MUSTARD

Serves 8

4 *poussins* (or 8 squab or Cornish hens), split in half, rinsed, and patted dry
6 tablespoons prepared mustard
1½ tablespoons each finely chopped fresh tarragon, fresh basil, and fresh thyme

2 teaspoons Hungarian paprika, or to taste
1 teaspoon each fine sea salt and freshly ground pepper, or to taste
1¼ cups dry table wine, red or white

1. Place the *poussins* in an open dish, and brush half the mustard over them. Combine the tarragon, basil, thyme, paprika, salt, and pepper, and sprinkle half this mixture over the chicken. Turn the pieces over and repeat the process.
2. Preheat the grill to highest temperature possible, and place the rack so that the *poussins* are 4 inches from the heat. Grill the *poussins* skin side down for about 10 minutes, or until nicely browned, basting them with wine, two or three times. Turn them over and repeat. (The *poussins* can also be broiled, if you prefer.) Serve warm or at room temperature.

Make It Ahead: You can finish the *poussins* up to an hour in advance. Serve at room temperature or reheat in a preheated 350° oven 5 minutes.

A few years ago, I led a tour to Beijing, where we attended the prestigious Beijing Culinary School. This is one of the recipes we learned there, and that I have adapted somewhat to our Western style of cooking. It involves the technique of "velveting" the chicken (coating it with egg white and cornstarch and blanching it), which affects the texture of the chicken, making it very smooth yet firm. Serve this accompanied by "Today's" Fried Rice (p. 120).

HOISIN STIR-FRIED CHICKEN

Serves 4 to 8

1 egg white, very lightly beaten
1 tablespoon plus 2 teaspoons sherry
1 tablespoon cornstarch
1 teaspoon coarse sea salt
1 whole breast of chicken, skinned, boned, and cut into 1-inch cubes
4 cups water
2 teaspoons plus 3 tablespoons rice bran oil
1 medium red and 1 medium yellow bell pepper, seeds removed, cut into 1-inch squares

2 cloves garlic, finely chopped
1 tablespoon finely chopped fresh ginger
2 scallions, finely chopped
6 drops chile oil, or to taste
3 tablespoons hoisin sauce (available in Asian markets)
2 teaspoons soy sauce
3 ounces cashews (about ½ cup), toasted

1. Combine the egg white, 1 tablespoon of the sherry, cornstarch, and salt, mixing until smooth and thick. Stir in the chicken and marinate overnight in the refrigerator.
2. Bring the water and 2 teaspoons rice bran oil to a boil in a saucepan. Drop in the chicken, blanch for 15 seconds, and drain.
3. Heat 2 tablespoons of rice bran oil in a wok or skillet, and stir-fry the bell peppers briskly over high heat for 2 minutes. Remove and set aside. Heat the remaining table-spoon of rice bran oil, and stir-fry the garlic, ginger, scallions, and chile oil 15 seconds. Stir in the hoisin sauce, remaining 2 teaspoons sherry, and soy sauce, raise the heat, and add the chicken and bell peppers. Toss 20 to 30 seconds; taste and adjust seasonings. Add the cashews, toss, then turn onto a warmed platter.

Make It Ahead: You can make this dish up to 2 hours in advance through step 2. Have everything prepared, and proceed with step 3 just before serving. It should take you just a few minutes to finish the dish.

This is a dish I learned when I studied cooking in Florence, Italy, a few years ago. I have made it often since then, and am not a bit tired of it! For a menu that will bring you rave reviews, start with the Romaine Salad with Feta Cheese, Fresh Figs, and Pine Nuts (p. 84), serve Potatoes and Fettuccine with Pesto (p. 130) next, and finish on a high note with this dish.

BRAISED CHICKEN FLORENTINE

Serves 6 to 8

1 ounce dried porcini mushrooms, soaked in warm water to cover for 1 hour
½ cup extra virgin olive oil
  a 3- or 4-pound chicken, cut into 8 pieces
1 clove garlic, crushed
2 slices salt pork, finely chopped

1 onion, finely chopped
½ cup Marsala
4 large tomatoes, peeled, seeded, and chopped
½ teaspoon each sugar, fine sea salt, and freshly ground pepper, or to taste
2 tablespoons chopped fresh flat-leaf parsley

1. Drain the mushrooms, reserving the liquid. Strain the mushroom liquid through a fine strainer, and set aside. Rinse the mushrooms well, making sure all the sand is gone, and cut into a fine julienne.
2. Heat the oil in a skillet and brown the chicken with the crushed garlic, salt pork, and onion over medium-high heat. Transfer to an ovenproof casserole, and pour off any fat remaining in the skillet. Turn up the heat to high, stir in the Marsala, tomatoes, mushrooms, and mushroom liquid, scraping up the juices stuck to the bottom of the pan, and cook 1 minute. Season with sugar, salt, and pepper, and pour over the chicken.
3. Cover the casserole and braise in a 375° oven, for 30 to 35 minutes, until chicken is tender. Allow casserole to stand 15 minutes before serving. Garnish with chopped parsley.

Make It Light: Omit salt pork.

Make It Ahead: You can make this dish up to a day in advance, and refrigerate. When you are ready, remove from the refrigerator, allow to stand 1 hour at room temperature, then reheat in a 375° oven for 15 minutes, or until hot.

Calvados, a special apple brandy that comes from the Normandy region of France, gives this dish its distinctive taste. Use a little caution when cooking with it, and make certain you have no flammable items nearby. It has a high alcohol content and may ignite spontaneously when you add it to a hot pan. Don't panic, though, the flames will die in a matter of seconds, as soon as the alcohol burns off.

CHICKEN NORMANDY
Serves 8

6 tablespoons unsalted butter (3 ounces)
2 small chickens, cut into 6 pieces each
1 pound fresh mushrooms, cleaned and thinly sliced
3 shallots, finely chopped
¾ cup Calvados
1 bay leaf

1 tablespoon chopped fresh thyme
3 tablespoons chopped fresh flat-leaf parsley
½ cup crème fraîche
fine sea salt and freshly ground pepper to taste

1. Heat the butter in a skillet, and brown the chicken lightly over medium-high heat, 5 minutes each side. Season with salt and pepper and transfer to an ovenproof casserole. Pour off any fat remaining in the skillet, and add the mushrooms, shallots, and Calvados. Cook 1 minute, tossing frequently. Pour this mushroom mixture over the chicken and add the bay leaf, thyme, and 1 tablespoon chopped parsley (reserve the rest for garnish). Cover and braise in a 375° oven 35 minutes, or until chicken is tender.
2. Combine the crème fraîche with the juices in the casserole, and return to the oven for another 10 minutes. Remove and allow to stand 15 minutes before serving. Garnish each serving with a little parsley.

Make It Light: Omit the crème fraîche.

Make It Ahead: You can make this chicken up to 1 hour in advance through step 1. When you are ready, proceed with step 2.

This exotic dish comes from Sicily.

ROASTED CHICKEN WITH ORANGE SAUCE

Serves 6 or 8

a 4- or 5-pound chicken,
cut into 8 pieces
1½ cups white table wine
Hungarian paprika, fine sea salt,
and freshly ground pepper to taste
2 tablespoons white raisins

2 slices dry white bread,
crusts removed
zest and juice of 4 oranges
½ teaspoon grated fresh ginger
⅛ teaspoon each ground cinnamon,
ground cloves, and ground saffron

1. Place the chicken pieces on a rack in a roasting pan, skin side up; pour 1 cup of the wine over the chicken, season with paprika, salt and pepper, and roast uncovered in a 375° oven for approximately 1 to 1¼ hours, basting occasionally with the wine and juices from the pan.

2. Soak the raisins in the remaining ½ cup wine and set aside. Process the bread, orange zest, juice, ginger, cinnamon, cloves, and saffron in a food processor or blender until smooth. Transfer to a saucepan.

3. When the chicken is tender, remove from the oven and add all the pan juices to the saucepan, along with the wine-soaked raisins. Bring to a boil, stirring until the sauce is smooth. Remove from the heat, and adjust seasonings.

4. When ready to serve, arrange the chicken on a warmed serving platter, pour the sauce over the chicken, and heat in a 350° oven 10 minutes.

Make It Ahead: You can make this up to 1 hour in advance through step 3. When you are ready, proceed with step 4.

When I was a young bride, one of our neighbors was a charming 85-year-old Italian woman who was a wonderful cook. After tasting her fried chicken, I told her I had never tasted better. She was very pleased, and consequently invited us over and served it to us often. She frequently served it with Potatoes and Fettuccine with Pesto (p. 130), which was an unbeatable combination. When we moved away, she gave me her recipes. I still feel as I did then: this is the best fried chicken there is.

Note: The key to making fried chicken is to have the oil at the right temperature — between 365° and 375° on a deep-fry thermometer. Hook the thermometer onto the side of your deep-fryer or deep sauté pan, so that you can keep track of the temperature.

MARIA'S FRIED CHICKEN

Serves 8

2 chickens, about 2 to 2½ pounds each
10 ounces flour (about 2 cups)
4 eggs, lightly beaten
2 tablespoons extra virgin olive oil
4 tablespoons chopped fresh flat-leaf parsley

2 teaspoons each Hungarian paprika, fine sea salt, and freshly ground pepper
½ cup water
   vegetable oil, enough to fill your pan to a depth of 3 inches
3 lemons cut into wedges

1. Cut each chicken into 8 pieces, rinse, and pat dry. Mix together the flour, eggs, olive oil, parsley, paprika, salt, and pepper in a bowl. Gradually add the water, and whisk for only as long as it takes to produce a smooth batter. Do not overbeat. Allow the batter to stand for 1 hour at room temperature, so it will cling to the chicken evenly.
2. Heat the oil in a deep-fryer or sauté pan to 365°. Dip the chicken pieces into the batter, and fry the chicken in the oil in small batches until golden and crisp all over, 10 to 15 minutes. Place the chicken on paper towels to drain. Serve hot or at room temperature, garnished with lemon wedges.

Make It Ahead: You can make this up to 2 hours in advance and serve it at room temperature.

TURKEY

I love turkey and think it should be enjoyed all year long. Recently, the availability of turkey parts has made that possible. I like to use the turkey breast, which is available whole, or half, with the bone or boneless. This recipe was contributed by my step-daughter Emily, who is a wife and the mother of two small girls, and holds down a full-time job, too. She does not have a lot of time to cook, but is a wonderful cook nevertheless, and loves good food. She created this wonderful grilled turkey breast dish to fit her busy life. She likes to serve it hot with Old-Fashioned Mashed Potatoes (p. 210) or Roquefort-Potato Gratin (p. 213). It also makes fabulous sandwiches — serve it cold or at room temperature on crusty French bread with a little Garlic Mayonnaise (p. 208). Purchase your turkey breast fresh, and follow the cooking times carefully.

EMILY'S GRILLED TURKEY BREAST

Serves 6

2 cups orange juice
½ cup extra virgin olive oil
2 tablespoons chopped fresh sage
6 cloves garlic, crushed

1 half turkey breast, with the bone
  (about 3 pounds)
  fine sea salt, freshly ground pepper,
  and Hungarian paprika to taste

1. In a nonreactive container, combine the orange juice, olive oil, sage, and garlic. Marinate the turkey breast 1 day in the refrigerator, turning 2 or 3 times.
2. Remove breast from marinade, season with salt, pepper, and paprika, and place on a rack in an open roasting pan. Roast 1 hour in a preheated 400° oven, basting 2 or 3 times with the marinade. Remove from the oven, and place on a preheated grill for 5 to 7 minutes each side, basting frequently with the marinade. Let stand 20 minutes before carving.

Make It Ahead: You can make this turkey 2 or 3 hours in advance and serve it at room temperature.

This is a perfect dish to make after Thanksgiving, to use up the leftover turkey. However, I think you will probably find that it is so tasty, you will not want to wait a year in between each time you make it. With turkey parts so easily available, you can start buying and roasting turkey just so you can make these tacos.

ROASTED TURKEY AND FRESH CORN TACOS

Serves 8

16 corn tortillas
2 ears fresh corn
3 tablespoons vegetable oil
2 medium onions, finely chopped
2 cloves garlic, finely chopped
2 to 3 cups diced roasted turkey meat
2 cups Fresh Tomato Salsa (p. 46)

½ cup white table wine
½ teaspoon salt
4 tomatoes, coarsely chopped
½ head lettuce, shredded
8 ounces Monterey Jack cheese, grated (about 2 cups)
1 cup sour cream

1. Wrap the tortillas in foil, and place in a 250° oven for about 15 minutes to warm. Cut the corn kernels off the cobs and set aside. Heat the oil in a large frying pan, and sauté the onions, garlic, and turkey over medium-high heat for 1 minute. Add the corn, 4 tablespoons of tomato salsa, wine, and salt, and cook until the liquid disappears, about 5 minutes.
2. Spread some filling in the middle of each tortilla. Top with some of the remaining salsa, chopped tomatoes, shredded lettuce, cheese, and sour cream. Fold and serve.

Make It Light: If you eliminate the cheese and sour cream, this dish will be very light.

Make It Ahead: You can make the filling (step 2) up to 1 hour in advance. Have all the remaining ingredients prepared; warm the tortillas shortly before serving, reheat the filling, and assemble the tacos.

CHAPTER SEVEN

FISH AND SHELLFISH

Like poultry, seafood fits in perfectly with everything we currently want to incorporate into our diets. It has a naturally delicious and fresh flavor, cooks quickly, is relatively low in fat, and is readily available in our local markets, even if we don't live near water. The most important rule to remember when it comes to cooking fish is *don't overcook it*. Overcooking fish (or cooking it until it is "opaque and flaking," as some cookbooks may put it) will make it dry or give it a strong "fishy" taste. Shellfish that is cooked too long will be tough and dry. In order to avoid this, follow the cooking times exactly as they are specified in the recipes that follow.

Our local supermarket once asked if I would donate a recipe to be printed on their shopping bags, and this is the one I gave them. It circulated throughout the neighborhood, via the bags, and we got lots of calls thanking us for such a "great recipe in minutes."

GRILLED HERBED SALMON

Serves 4

1 tablespoon each chopped fresh basil, fresh thyme, and fresh rosemary
5 cloves garlic, crushed
1 teaspoon coarsely ground peppercorns
6 tablespoons extra virgin olive oil

4 salmon fillets, about 6 or 7 ounces each coarse salt and freshly ground pepper to taste
4 sprigs rosemary
2 lemons, cut in half

1. Combine the herbs, garlic, peppercorns, and olive oil. Add the salmon fillets and marinate them in the refrigerator overnight.
2. Remove the salmon from the marinade and season with salt and pepper. Cook on a preheated grill, 4 minutes each side (or broil it if you prefer). Garnish each serving with a sprig of rosemary and half a lemon.

Make It Ahead: You can grill the fish up to 1 hour in advance, and serve it at room temperature.

Here is another of my friend Ramón's super recipes. Garlic, tomatoes, and olives give this dish a Mediterranean feeling, but it is actually from Mexico.

BAKED SNAPPER VERACRUZ
Serves 8

8 red snapper fillets, about 6 ounces each
½ teaspoon freshly ground pepper
3 tablespoons fresh lime juice
¼ cup extra virgin olive oil
1 medium onion, coarsely chopped
4 cloves garlic, sliced
2 pounds ripe tomatoes, peeled and coarsely chopped

10 large pitted green olives, cut in half
1 tablespoon each capers and chopped jalapeño chiles
½ teaspoon chopped fresh oregano
½ teaspoon each fine sea salt and sugar
1 large bay leaf

1. Place the snapper fillets in a 12-inch stoneware or glass baking dish, sprinkle both sides with pepper and lime juice, and marinate 30 minutes to 1 hour at room temperature.
2. Heat the oil in a large skillet or sauté pan, and sauté the onion and garlic over medium-low heat for 5 minutes. Add the tomatoes, olives, capers, jalapeños, oregano, salt, sugar, and bay leaf; stir and cook another 5 minutes over medium heat.
3. Pour the sauce over the fish and bake uncovered in a preheated 375° oven for 10 minutes. Remove the bay leaf before serving.

Make It Light: Reduce the oil to 2 tablespoons

Make It Ahead: You can make this recipe up to 1 hour in advance through step 2. When you are ready, proceed with step 3.

I love this exciting combination of tastes and textures, which includes aromatic fennel, the perfect accompaniment for fish. Fennel is frequently used in Italian kitchens, so you can probably guess that this recipe is Italian in origin.

RED SNAPPER BAKED OVER FENNEL

Serves 6

1 head fennel
1 medium zucchini, cored to remove seeds, and coarsely chopped
1 red bell pepper, coarsely chopped
1 small turnip, coarsely chopped
1 small dry hot red chile, stemmed
1 clove garlic, lightly crushed
¼ cup extra virgin olive oil

3 tablespoons vermouth
1 teaspoon finely chopped fresh oregano
juice of 1 lemon
8 fennel stalks, cut into 2-inch pieces
6 red snapper fillets, about 6 ounces each fine sea salt and freshly ground pepper to taste
8 sprigs of oregano

1. Cut the stalks off the fennel bulb; cut 8 of them into 2-inch pieces and set aside. Coarsely chop the fennel bulb. Blanch the zucchini, bell pepper, turnip, and chopped fennel for 30 seconds and drain.

2. Combine the blanched vegetables, hot chile, and garlic clove in a small bowl. Add the olive oil, vermouth, oregano, and lemon juice. Cover and marinate at room temperature for 1 hour to blend flavors.

3. Spread the fennel stalks on the bottom of a large baking dish. Season fish with salt and pepper, and place over fennel stalks in one layer. Sprinkle 4 tablespoons of marinade over the fish.

4. Bake uncovered in a preheated 475° oven, 10 minutes. Remove the chile and garlic from the vegetable mixture and discard. In a small saucepan, heat the mixture until lukewarm. Season with salt and pepper to taste.

5. Transfer fish fillets to warm plates, leaving fennel stalks behind. Drain the vegetables and sprinkle over fillets. Garnish with sprigs of oregano.

Make It Light: Reduce the olive oil to 3 tablespoons.

Make It Ahead: You can make this dish up to 1 hour in advance through step 3. When you are ready, proceed with steps 4 and 5.

This dish is a bit unconventional, not because the fish is poached, but because it's poached in red wine. Usually, the rule is white wine with fish. You can always substitute white wine if you wish, but try it this way first, and see what you think. This would be good with Oven-Baked "French Fries" (p. 210) and a green salad.

SOLE POACHED IN RED WINE

Serves 6

1 cup red wine
2 medium shallots, finely chopped
½ cup Beef Stock (p. 12)

6 sole fillets, about 6 ounces each
4 tablespoons unsalted butter
   (2 ounces)

1. In a nonreactive skillet or sauté pan, combine the wine, shallots, and stock. Bring to a boil, simmer 5 minutes, and carefully add the sole fillets. Remove from the heat after 1 minute, and let stand 1 minute. Carefully transfer sole to a warmed serving platter.
2. Turn up the heat under the pan, and reduce the liquid to ½ cup. Remove the pan from the heat and swirl in the butter. Pour the sauce over the fish and serve warm.

Make It Light: Delete the butter

Make It Ahead: This is such a quick recipe, it is better made just before serving. If you have everything ready, it should take you about 10 minutes from start to finish.

Be very careful to follow the marinating time and cooking time for the sole; it is a delicate fish and, if overcooked, will fall apart. Served together with Carrot-Potato Purée (p. 203), this will make a memorable meal.

FILLET OF SOLE WITH SHRIMP AND ARTICHOKES

Serves 6

6 sole fillets, about 6 ounces each
½ cup extra virgin olive oil
¼ cup fresh lemon juice
¼ teaspoon each fine sea salt and
  freshly ground white pepper
4 tablespoons unsalted butter
  (2 ounces)

24 baby artichokes, trimmed and
  quartered (p. 219)
½ cup dry vermouth
6 scallions, finely chopped
½ teaspoon black pepper
½ cup crème fraîche
8 ounces tiny cooked shrimp

1. Place the sole in a shallow glass or porcelain baking dish. Mix the olive oil, lemon juice, salt, and white pepper together, and pour over sole; marinate in the refrigerator for 1 hour.
2. Heat the butter in a skillet, and sauté the baby artichokes over medium-high heat until tender, about 5 to 10 minutes. Transfer the artichokes to a warm platter.
3. Drain the sole and discard the marinade; add the fillets to the skillet, pour the vermouth over the sole, and sprinkle on the scallions and black pepper. Bring to a boil, and immediately transfer sole to the artichoke platter. Reduce the juices in the skillet to ¼ cup, stir in the crème fraîche, and simmer 2 minutes. Remove from the heat and stir in the shrimp.
4. To serve, arrange the artichoke hearts and sole attractively on the platter and top with the shrimp sauce.

Make It Light: Omit crème fraîche.

Make It Ahead: The artichokes can be sautéed up to 1 hour in advance (do it during the time the fish is marinating). When you are ready, reheat the artichokes in a 300° oven for 5 minutes, and proceed with steps 3 and 4.

The lean, fine-textured flesh of the halibut blends beautifully with this elegant rich sauce. The halibut can be grilled or broiled, as you wish.

GRILLED HALIBUT WITH CILANTRO CREAM

Serves 6

¼ cup extra virgin olive oil
5 tablespoons chopped fresh cilantro
6 halibut fillets, about 6 ounces each
4 shallots, chopped
1 cup each white table wine, Fish Stock, and Vegetable Stock (p. 13)

1 cup crème fraîche
fine sea salt and freshly ground white pepper to taste
2 tablespoons chopped fresh flat-leaf parsley

1. Combine the oil and 3 tablespoons of chopped cilantro in a shallow glass or stoneware dish, and marinate the halibut 1 hour.

2. In a small saucepan, combine the wine, stocks, and shallots, and reduce over medium heat to approximately ½ cup. Stir in the crème fraîche and simmer over low heat until sauce is slightly thickened, about 5 minutes. Season with salt and pepper to taste, stir in the parsley and remaining cilantro, and set aside.

3. Preheat the grill. Grill the halibut about 2 minutes each side (the fish can also be broiled). Place the halibut on individual warmed plates, rewarm the sauce over low heat, and spoon a little over each serving of fish.

Make It Light: Omit crème fraîche.

Make It Ahead: You can make this recipe up to 1 hour in advance through step 2. When you are ready, proceed with step 3.

Saffron is the thread-like stigma of the crocus flower. If possible, buy dried whole saffron threads as they are better quality, then grind them yourself in a mortar. This is wonderful served with buttered wide egg noodles; you will have enough sauce so that you can spoon a little over the noodles as well. I think you will find this to be a very elegant dish, deserving of your best china.

POACHED HALIBUT FILLETS
IN TOMATO SAFFRON CREAM
Serves 8

1 cup Fish Stock (p. 13)	8 halibut fillets, about 6 ounces each
½ cup white table wine	1½ cups crème fraîche
3 bay leaves	¼ teaspoon ground saffron, or more
2 cups vacuum-packed strained or	to taste
puréed tomatoes	½ teaspoon fine sea salt
3 tablespoons unsalted butter	¼ teaspoon freshly ground white pepper

1. In a large sauté pan, combine the stock, wine, bay leaves, tomatoes, and butter. Bring to a boil, add the halibut, bring back to a boil, cover, remove from the heat, and let stand 5 minutes.
2. Remove the fish from the poaching liquid with a slotted spoon, and set aside. Add the crème fraîche and saffron to the liquid and over medium heat, reduce by half. Discard the bay leaves, and season with salt and pepper.
3. Return the fish to the sauce, reheat for 20 seconds. Place a portion of fish in the center of each warmed plate, and spoon sauce around the fish.

Make It Light: Omit crème fraîche and butter.

Make It Ahead: You can make this dish through step 2 up to 1 hour in advance. When you are ready, bring the sauce back to a boil, and reheat the fish briefly (step 3).

It takes a little extra time to thread everything onto skewers, but doing this allows you to offer each person an interesting variety of seafood with a minimum of fuss. The combination I've suggested below will give you an attractive array of textures and flavors.

MIXED GRILLED SEAFOOD ON SKEWERS
Serves 8

¼ cup lemon juice
½ cup walnut oil
2 cloves garlic, crushed
8 ounces each cod, sea bass,
  red snapper, and halibut fillets
8 ounces mushrooms, cleaned,
  each cut in half

8 large shrimp, peeled and deveined
8 ounces scallops
  fine sea salt and freshly ground
  pepper to taste
2 red onions, quartered and separated
8 lemon wedges

1. Cut fish into 8 pieces each. Blanch the mushrooms for 10 seconds, and drain. In a large shallow glass or stoneware baking dish, mix together the lemon juice, walnut oil, and garlic. Put the fish, mushrooms, scallops, shrimp, and onions in the marinade, keeping each group together in the dish, if possible. Marinate for 1 hour.
2. Thread the onions, seafood, and mushrooms onto 8- to 10-inch skewers, distributing them evenly. Use 2 pieces of onion together, and try to have at least one of everything on each skewer.
3. Preheat the grill. Brush each skewer with marinade, and season with salt and pepper. Grill for approximately 3 minutes each side (or you can broil this, if you prefer). Arrange the skewers on a warm platter, surrounded by lemon wedges.

Make It Ahead: Marinate everything and thread the skewers up to an hour in advance (step 2). Put them on the grill (or broil them) shortly before serving. When you are ready, proceed with step 3.

Cioppino is San Francisco's answer to the European bouillabaisse. The derivation of the name is said by some to come from the fisherman encouraging each other to "chip in, chip in" to the pot. Here is my rendition of that seafood stew. As with all fishermen's stews, it's open to interpretation, depending, for one thing, on what the catch of the day is. By the way, you can decide for yourself whether to peel the prawns or serve them in the shell.

CIOPPINO

Serves 8 to 10

¾ pound mushrooms, sliced
2 pounds snapper fillets, cut into 2-inch pieces
1 pound each large prawns and scallops
3 cloves garlic, finely chopped
2 cups each white table wine and Fish Stock (p. 13)
1 pound small clams, scrubbed
2 cups chopped tomatoes

8 ounces each cooked tiny shrimp and cooked crab meat
1 tablespoon chopped fresh oregano
6 tablespoons chopped fresh flat-leaf parsley
1 tablespoon sugar
fine sea salt and freshly ground pepper to taste

1. In a large soup pot, combine the mushrooms, fish, prawns, scallops, garlic, wine, Fish Stock, clams, and tomatoes. Cover, bring to a boil, reduce the heat, and simmer 5 minutes, or until the clams open.

2. Stir in the tiny shrimp, crab meat, oregano, parsley, sugar, salt, and pepper. Taste and adjust accordingly. Serve in large deep bowls accompanied by crusty French or Italian bread.

Make It Ahead: You can finish this up to 1 hour in advance. When you are ready to serve, reheat it over medium heat for 2 or 3 minutes, until it is heated through.

Teriyaki is the Japanese cooking method of marinating foods in a mixture of soy sauce, *mirin* (a sweet rice wine used in cooking), and *sake,* and then broiling or grilling them. I love to serve this fish warm, together with a chilled, crisp green salad; the contrasts in temperature, texture, color, and taste are wonderful. Chicken, steak, and fish are all delicious cooked this way.

GRILLED FISH TERIYAKI

Serves 6

6 halibut, swordfish, or cod fillets or steaks, about 2½ pounds in all
¾ cup each soy sauce, mirin, and sake

3 tablespoons superfine sugar
1 clove garlic, finely chopped

1. Combine the soy sauce, mirin, sake, and sugar in a small saucepan and bring to a boil. Add the garlic, and remove the pan from the heat. Allow to cool for 5 minutes, then pour the hot teriyaki sauce over the fish fillets, and marinate 10 minutes.
2. Cook the fish on a preheated grill 3 minutes each side, brushing with the marinade several times. (You can broil the fish, if you prefer.) Serve warm or at room temperature.

Make It Ahead: You can marinate the fish up to 1 hour in advance of grilling or broiling.

Don't let the notion of Brussels sprouts keep you from trying this dish. When they are bought fresh, and cooked with care, Brussels sprouts have a delicate, subtle, nutty taste; puréed with potatoes, as they are in this dish, they come close to perfection. Whenever I want to make a special impression on my guests, this is the dish I always make. It is luxurious, rich, delicious, and beautiful looking, but surprisingly easy to make, and best of all, can be made in advance.

SHELLFISH WITH PURÉED BRUSSELS SPROUTS AND POTATOES
Serves 4

1 pound Brussels sprouts, cooked until tender, about 15 minutes

8 ounces baking potatoes, peeled, cut into quarters, and cooked until soft fine sea salt and freshly ground pepper to taste

6 tablespoons unsalted butter (3 ounces)

8 ounces scallops, halved crosswise

8 ounces large shrimp, peeled, deveined, and halved lengthwise

½ cup each white wine, crème fraîche, and Fish Stock (p. 13) Hungarian paprika to taste

⅛ teaspoon cayenne pepper or to taste

2 tablespoons chopped fresh flat-leaf parsley

1. Purée the sprouts in a blender or food processor until thick and smooth. Purée the potatoes in a ricer or food mill. Combine the sprouts and potatoes in a saucepan, season to taste with salt and pepper, and over low heat, stir in 3 tablespoons butter, using a wooden spoon. Set aside.

2. Heat the remaining butter in a skillet and over medium heat, sauté the scallops about 30 seconds. Remove the scallops, leaving the butter in the skillet. Return the skillet to a medium heat, sauté the shrimp 30 seconds, and remove them from the skillet. Pour off any remaining butter, and stir in the wine, crème fraîche, and stock. Reduce by half, and season to taste with salt, pepper, paprika, and cayenne.

3. Arrange the purée on the bottom of 6 oval or round individual ovenproof serving dishes; add the scallops and shrimp and spoon on a little sauce. Place the individual dishes on a baking sheet, cover with foil, and bake in a preheated 350° oven for 10 minutes, until heated through. Garnish each serving with parsley.

Make It Light: Reduce the amount of butter by half, adding only 1 tablespoon to the purée, and using only 2 tablespoons to sauté the shellfish. Crème fraîche can be eliminated.

Make It Ahead: You can make this dish through step 2 up to 1 hour in advance. When you are ready, proceed with step 3.

This preparation may seem too simple and commonplace to you, but I have found that shrimp, plain or fancy, is a perennial favorite. I've served this dish many times to friends and family, and there has never been a single shrimp left on a plate.

GRILLED GIANT SHRIMP

Serves 6

4 tablespoons unsalted butter (2 ounces), melted
½ cup extra virgin olive oil
1 tablespoon fresh lemon juice
1 tablespoon each finely chopped garlic, shallots, and scallions
½ teaspoon each coarse sea salt, freshly ground pepper, and Hungarian paprika, or to taste

36 large shrimp (12 to 16 to the pound), peeled and deveined
6 lemon wedges
4 tablespoons finely chopped flat-leaf parsley

1. In a nonreactive bowl, combine melted butter, olive oil, lemon juice, garlic, shallots, scallions, salt, pepper, and paprika. Add the shrimp and marinate 1 hour at room temperature.
2. Preheat the grill. Grill the shrimp 2 minutes each side, brushing with marinade as they are cooking. Do not overcook. (The shrimp can also be broiled.) Serve garnished with lemon wedges and parsley.

Make It Light: Omit butter, and reduce olive oil to 4 tablespoons (¼ cup).

Make It Ahead: You can grill the shrimp up to 1 hour in advance. Transfer to a warmed platter, and cover lightly with foil. When ready to serve, place in a preheated 350° oven for 5 or 6 minutes, just until warm.

I call my longtime friend Lois, a wonder-cook. She spent a year in Leningrad for a year with her art collector husband, and this recipe was one of the "treasures" she brought back with her. It's named after the Neva River, which runs through Leningrad into the Gulf of Finland. The recipe is now a standard in our seafood classes.

SAUTÉED SHRIMP NEVA

Serves 6

2 tablespoons extra virgin olive oil
1½ pounds large shrimp (12 to the pound), peeled and deveined
2 tablespoons unsalted butter
1 clove garlic, crushed

fine sea salt, freshly ground pepper, and Hungarian paprika to taste
juice of 2 lemons
¼ cup vodka

1. Heat the olive oil in a skillet and sauté the shrimp over high heat for about 30 seconds, until they turn pink. Off the heat, add the butter, garlic, salt, pepper, and paprika. Toss well, and allow shrimp to stand covered off the heat for 1 hour.
2. Just before serving, return the skillet to a high heat, add the lemon juice and vodka, and toss 20 seconds. Remove from the heat, ignite, and when the flame dies, serve.

Make It Light: Omit butter.

Make It Ahead: You can make this up to 1 hour in advance through step 1. Finish the dish just before serving (step 2).

This dish is adapted from one I learned at the Beijing Culinary Academy, when I led a cooking tour to China. Our master teacher described it perfectly: "After the cooking of this dish is completed, the shrimp look beautiful and glossy, their meat [is] tender and uniquely tasty. The entire dish is a miraculous mixture of saltiness, sweetness, alluring smell, and delicious taste."

GINGER-SCALLION SHRIMP WITH TANGY NOODLES

Serves 4

½ cup Chicken Stock (p. 12)
2 tablespoons each dry sherry
  and soy sauce
4 scallions, cut into ¼-inch pieces
1 tablespoon (or more) chopped
  fresh ginger

1 teaspoon sugar
½ teaspoon (or more) coarse sea salt
1 pound shrimp (25 to a pound),
  peeled and deveined
  Tangy Noodles (see recipe below)

1. Combine the stock, sherry, soy sauce, scallions, ginger, sugar, and salt in a wok or skillet. Bring to a boil, lower the heat, and simmer 2 minutes.

2. Add the shrimp and toss lightly. Cover the wok and simmer 1 minute. Arrange the shrimp on a serving plate, and spoon the juices over the shrimp. Serve with Tangy Noodles.

Make It Ahead: If you plan to serve the shrimp and noodles at room temperature or chilled, you can cook both the shrimp and noodles up to 2 hours in advance, arrange on a platter, and set aside in a cool place or refrigerate. If you prefer to serve the dish warm, prepare it shortly before serving.

TANGY NOODLES

¾ pound thin egg noodles
2 tablespoons each soy sauce and
  balsamic vinegar
1 tablespoon each sesame oil and
  rice bran oil
1 tablespoon each sugar and
  coarse sea salt

½ teaspoon (or more) hot chile oil
3 scallions, cut into 2-inch long
  fine julienne
2 tablespoons each chopped fresh
  cilantro and flat-leaf parsley

Boil the noodles until just done and drain. Combine the soy sauce, vinegar, sesame oil, rice bran oil, sugar, salt, and chile oil in a large warm serving bowl. Add the noodles, and toss gently, separating the noodles and evenly distributing the sauce. Can be served immediately, or at room temperature, or chilled. To serve, garnish with the scallions, cilantro, and parsley.

A classic, very rich, very delicious, wonderful way to eat oysters. Just be careful not to boil or overcook this stew, or the oysters will get tough.

HOT OYSTER STEW

Serves 8

1 **quart shucked oysters, with their liquor**
6 **cups half-and-half**
fine sea salt, freshly ground white pepper, and Hungarian paprika to taste

4 **tablespoons chopped fresh flat-leaf parsley**
4 **tablespoons unsalted butter (2 ounces)**

1. Put the oysters and their liquor in a saucepan and simmer over medium heat for 2 minutes; remove from the heat.
2. Put the cream in another saucepan, and bring it just barely to a boil. Combine with the oysters and their liquor, and season to taste with salt, pepper, and paprika. Off the heat, swirl in the parsley and butter. Serve in shallow soup bowls as the butter is melting .

Make It Light: Omit the butter.

Make It Ahead: You can cook the oysters up to an hour in advance ((step 1). When you are ready, proceed with step 2.

Serve this as is or spoon it over spaghetti or linguini. It's nice to have a few clam shells for effect, but I suggest you discard half of them so that they don't get in the way.

CLAMS IN A WHITE SAUCE

Serves 4 to 6

48 small clams, scrubbed clean
2 cups white table wine
1 teaspoon each chopped fresh thyme and chopped fresh oregano

1 tablespoon unsalted butter
1 tablespoon flour
4 tablespoons chopped fresh flat-leaf parsley

1. Put the clams in a large saucepan along with the wine and herbs. Cover and simmer over high heat until clams open, about 5 to 10 minutes. Discard any clams that do not open. Remove the clams to a bowl, and discard half the shells.
2. Strain the stock through a fine strainer (to get rid of the sand) into a small saucepan. With your fingers, knead the butter and flour together into a ball. Over a medium heat, add the kneaded butter and flour in small pieces to the clam liquor, stirring constantly until thickened slightly. Stir in the parsley.
3. Return the clams to the sauce, and heat 1 minute. Serve clams and sauce in deep bowls.

Make It Light: Eliminate the butter and flour.

Make It Ahead: You can make this through step 2 up to 1 hour in advance. When you are ready, reheat and serve (step 3).

This wonderful dish is perfect in the summer when tomatoes and basil are at their peak. The tomatoes are seeded and barely cooked to retain their sweet fresh taste. Accompany this dish with buttered linguini.

STEAMED MUSSELS WITH FRESH TOMATOES AND BASIL
Serves 8

½ cup extra virgin olive oil
2 cloves garlic, finely chopped
8 large tomatoes (about 3 pounds), peeled, seeded, and chopped
1 tablespoon tomato paste
1 cup white table wine
1 cup water

6 dozen mussels, scrubbed well, and bearded just before steaming them
4 tablespoons unsalted butter (2 ounces)
1 teaspoon each fine sea salt, freshly ground pepper, and sugar
6 tablespoons coarsely chopped fresh basil leaves

1. Heat the oil in a skillet and sauté the garlic 30 seconds over medium heat. Add the tomatoes and tomato paste and sauté a minute longer. Stir in ½ cup wine and cook 3 more minutes; set aside.

2. Put the water and remaining wine in a large deep pot and bring to a boil. Add the mussels, bring back to the boil, cover, and simmer until mussels have opened, about 5 minutes. Transfer the mussels to a warmed serving platter, discarding any that have not opened, and cover lightly with foil. Strain the mussel-cooking liquid , and add about ½ cup of it to the tomato sauce.

3. Reheat the sauce over low heat for 2 minutes, remove from the heat, and swirl in the butter, salt, pepper, sugar, and basil. Pour the sauce over the mussels.

Make It Light: Reduce the oil to ¼ cup and the butter to 2 tablespoons.

Make It Ahead: You can complete the dish up to 1 hour in advance (pour the sauce over the mussels and cover again with foil). Just before serving, place the platter in a preheated 300° oven for 10 minutes.

Until recently if you wanted to cook squid at home, it meant going through a lengthy cleaning process. Now, in most fish markets, you can buy squid (also known as calamari) all cleaned and ready to cook. Here is one of our favorite recipes for squid: if you like spicy food, add a little more cayenne.

SQUID IN A SPICY TOMATO SAUCE

Serves 4 to 6

1½ pounds small squid, cleaned, bodies cut into rings
½ cup extra virgin olive oil
1 clove garlic, crushed
1 cup Tomato Sauce (p. 14)

½ cup white table wine
⅛ teaspoon (or more) cayenne pepper
1 teaspoon fine sea salt
2 tablespoons chopped fresh flat-leaf parsley

Heat the oil in a large skillet or sauté pan; brown the garlic over medium-high heat and discard. Add the squid; cover and cook over low heat 10 minutes. Add the Tomato Sauce, wine, cayenne, and salt, and stir. Cover and cook over low heat 5 minutes more. Serve in shallow soup bowls, garnished with parsley

Make It Light: Reduce the oil to 2 tablespoons.

Make It Ahead: You can make this recipe up to 1 hour in advance. Just before serving, reheat over low heat for 2 minutes.

CHAPTER EIGHT

VEGETABLES

In Asia and the Middle East, vegetables have always been prized as highly as meats, and treated accordingly — prepared with care, and served with pride. In America however, they have in years past been handled unimaginatively, often appearing as tasteless, canned products, overcooked greens or plain boiled potatoes. No wonder, as a child, I would sneak them off my plate, hide them in my napkin, then dump them into the garbage. When I was caught, my punishment was to have a double portion! How things have changed! We've learned just how delicious properly cooked vegetables can be, and are gradually becoming more adventurous in our outlook. In addition, we've become highly aware of the importance of eating lighter and consuming less meat. For instance, many of our students are choosing to make vegetables the focus of their meals, and are pushing the meat aside, rather than the vegetables! And our Vegetarian Basics class is one of the best attended of all the classes we offer! Grocery stores have responded to this new demand by offering an incredible array of beautiful fresh produce, and I, in turn, am offering here an incredible array of marvelous vegetable dishes.

Note: For general information on preparing vegetables before they are cooked, see pages 219–222.

Baby artichokes have become more common in the markets now, especially in the springtime. When you see them, buy them, the smallest you can find, preferably around 1½-inches in diameter. The following dish is a great accompaniment to poultry and fish and is also wonderful, cooled and combined with a green salad. Substitute artichoke bottoms if you are unable to find baby artichokes (p. 219).

SAUTÉED ARTICHOKES WITH PANCETTA AND THYME
Serves 8

2 pounds baby artichokes, trimmed and halved (p. 219)
6 tablespoons extra virgin olive oil
  fine sea salt and freshly ground pepper to taste

5 ounces pancetta, sliced and cut into ¼-inch julienne
1 teaspoon chopped fresh thyme
2 tablespoons chopped fresh flat-leaf parsley

1. Marinate the artichokes in 4 tablespoons of olive oil for 1 hour.
2. Heat 2 tablespoons of the oil in a skillet, and sauté artichokes over medium heat until tender, about 8 to 12 minutes. Season to taste with salt and pepper, and transfer to a cutting board to cool. Meanwhile, in the same skillet, sauté the pancetta until lightly browned. Drain off and discard the fat.
3. Quarter the artichokes lengthwise, and return them to the skillet with the pancetta; add the thyme and parsley. Sauté over medium heat 1 minute, or until heated through; taste and adjust seasonings, if necessary. Serve warm or at room temperature.

Make It Light: Use only 2 tablespoons olive oil to marinate the artichokes, 1 tablespoon to saute them.

Make It Ahead: You can make this dish up to 2 hours in advance through step 2. When you are ready, proceed with step 3.

This is a great side dish to serve with simple grilled meats, fish, or poultry. It can also be a light main course, wonderful served with sliced tomatoes and crusty bread, and one of my favorite ways to prepare asparagus. Be generous with the pepper, and, if you like, you can increase the Parmigiano.

ASPARAGUS AND CHARD GRATIN

Serves 8

1½ pounds asparagus, peeled
 1 tablespoon extra virgin olive oil
 3 pounds Swiss chard, stalks only, leaves reserved for another use
 4 tablespoons unsalted butter (2 ounces)

fine sea salt and freshly ground pepper to taste
 4 ounces freshly grated Parmigiano-Reggiano (1 cup)

1. Blanch the asparagus 30 seconds, drain, and set aside. Heat the olive oil in a skillet and sauté the chard stalks over medium heat until tender, about 5 minutes.

2. Spread a little butter over the bottom and sides of a baking dish and line the bottom with a layer of chard stalks. Season with salt and pepper, then top with a layer of asparagus. Repeat until you have used up both vegetables. Sprinkle the grated cheese on top, and dot with remaining butter.

3. Bake in a preheated 375° oven until a light brown crust forms on the top, about 20 minutes. Let rest 5 minutes before serving.

Make It Light: Reduce butter to 2 tablespoons.

Make It Ahead: You can make this recipe up to 2 hours in advance through step 2. When you are ready, proceed with step 3.

I am so happy that bok choy (Chinese Cabbage) is now available in most produce markets. It is a truly delicious, flavorsome vegetable, that is always wonderful with chicken or seafood, or just about anything else you could have. Buy "baby" bok choy, if you can find it, as it is even better than its more mature relative. You could use this recipe as a model to sautéing other vegetables. Try substituting asparagus, green beans, snow peas, or broccoli, for instance. (Blanch them briefly, first. Leafy greens do not need to be blanched.)

SAUTÉED BOK CHOY

Serves 6

¼ cup extra virgin olive oil
1 clove garlic, finely chopped
1 teaspoon grated fresh ginger
1 large head bok choy or 6 heads
   baby bok choy, rinsed and
   cut crosswise into ½-inch slices

fine sea salt and freshly ground
pepper to taste

Heat the oil in a large skillet or wok over high heat. Add the garlic and ginger and stir and sauté 1 minute over high heat. Add the bok choy and toss until wilted and dark green, about 2 minutes. Season to taste with salt and pepper.

Make It Light: Reduce the oil to 2 tablespoons.

Make It Ahead: Have all your ingredients prepared; it will only take you a few minutes to cook this.

Broccoli has become quite popular these days, and for very good reasons: high-quality broccoli is available year round, is always a good buy, and there are dozens of ways to prepare it. But the best news is that broccoli, along with other cruciferous vegetables such as cabbage, cauliflower, and Brussels sprouts, is associated with lower cancer rates in those who eat it regularly. We have it at least twice a week in my household, and our students love it too.

RAMÓN'S BROCCOLI

Serves 6

2 pounds broccoli, cut into florets
2 large tomatoes, coarsely chopped
2 cloves garlic, peeled
¼ medium onion
2 tablespoons extra virgin olive oil

¼ to ½ cup Chicken Stock (p. 12)
1 bay leaf
½ teaspoon each cumin, sugar, fine
   sea salt, and freshly ground pepper
⅛ teaspoon ground cinnamon

1. Blanch the broccoli for 2 minutes, drain, and set aside.
2. In a blender or food processor, process the tomatoes, garlic, and onion until smooth. In a skillet, heat the olive oil over medium heat, add the purée, and cook 1 minute. Add ¼ cup of stock, the bay leaf, cumin, sugar, salt, pepper, and cinnamon, and cook 2 minutes, stirring from time to time. Sauce should lightly coat a wooden spoon. If too thick, add more stock.
3. Add the broccoli, cover, and cook over medium-low heat 3 minutes more. Discard the bay leaf before serving.

Make It Light: Reduce oil to 1 tablespoon.

Make It Ahead: You can make this recipe up to 2 hours in advance through step 2. When you are ready, proceed with step 3.

I usually serve this dish with roast lamb, but it's substantial enough to be a light main course, if served with roasted potatoes or rice.

CARROTS AND WILD MUSHROOMS MADEIRA

Serves 8 to 10

2 ounces dried morel or porcini mushrooms
1 cup Madeira
3 tablespoons extra virgin olive oil
1½ pounds slender carrots, peeled and cut diagonally into ½-inch pieces
fine sea salt to taste

2 cloves garlic, chopped
4 thin slices prosciutto, finely julienned
freshly ground pepper to taste
2 tablespoons chopped fresh flat-leaf parsley

1. Soak the mushrooms in the Madeira for 2 hours. Drain the mushrooms, reserving the liquid. Strain the Madeira through a fine strainer, and set aside. Rinse the mushrooms well, making sure all the sand is gone; then cut them into a fine julienne.
2. Heat the oil in a skillet or sauté pan and sauté the carrots over medium heat for 5 minutes. Season lightly with salt. Add the Madeira, mushrooms, and garlic, and simmer mixture until liquid has evaporated and carrots begin to brown, about 5 minutes. Add prosciutto and ground pepper, and stir. Taste and correct seasonings, if necessary. Serve garnished with parsley.

Make It Light: Reduce the olive oil to 1 tablespoon.

Make It Ahead: You can make this dish up to 2 hours in advance. Just before serving, reheat until warmed through, and add the parsley garnish.

I got the recipe for this dish many years ago from an accomplished Swiss cook. It is really wonderful with Sautéed Calves Liver with Port Wine Sauce (p. 138), however, I think you will find that anything you serve it with will be enhanced.

CARROT-POTATO PURÉE
Serves 8

8 medium-sized carrots, peeled and cut into chunks
6 baking potatoes, peeled and cut into chunks
1 cup crème fraîche
4 tablespoons unsalted butter (2 ounces)

1 tablespoon hot and sweet prepared mustard
fine sea salt and freshly ground white pepper to taste

Boil the carrots and potatoes until very soft (it's okay to cook them together). Put them through a ricer, or pass them through the medium blade of a food mill and transfer them to a pot. Over a low heat, stir in the crème fraîche and butter, a little at a time, stirring until all is absorbed. Stir in the mustard, salt, and pepper.

Make It Light: Substitute nonfat milk for the crème fraîche, and reduce the butter to 1 tablespoon.

Make It Ahead: You can make the purée up to 2 hours in advance. Warm over low heat before serving.

"Comfort foods" are usually very simple dishes, the kind of thing your mother made for you when you were feeling under the weather. Since we all have different childhood experiences, they tend to be a very personal thing. Creamed corn is one of my comfort foods, which is why I just could not leave it out of this collection. I love it with grilled steak, fish, or chicken.

CREAMED CORN

Serves 4 to 6

6 ears fresh sweet corn	1½ cups milk
4 tablespoons unsalted butter (2 ounces)	1 teaspoon sugar
½ small onion, finely chopped	Hungarian paprika, fine sea salt,
2 tablespoons unbleached white flour	and freshly ground pepper to taste

Cut the kernels off the ears of corn and set aside. Melt the butter in a saucepan and sauté the onion over low heat for 2 minutes. Add the flour and cook, stirring, for an additional 2 minutes. Raise the heat, stir in the milk, and continue cooking and stirring until sauce thickens, about 5 minutes more. Stir in the corn kernels, sugar, paprika, salt, and pepper, then continue to cook 1 minute more. Let stand covered, off the heat for 5 minutes, before serving.

Make It Light: Reduce the butter to 2 tablespoons, and substitute nonfat milk for whole milk.

Make It Ahead: You can make this dish up to 2 hours in advance. When you are ready, return saucepan to a low heat until corn is heated through.

For a change of pace, try this rich, sweet vegetable custard. Serve it with barbecued or grilled meats.

CORN, LEEK, AND BELL PEPPER PUDDING
Serves 8

6 ears fresh sweet corn
2 tablespoons unsalted butter
3 large leeks, whites only, cleaned
  and chopped
1 large red bell pepper, seeded
  and chopped
2 cups each crème fraîche and
  whipping cream

6 egg yolks
1 tablespoon hot and sweet
  prepared mustard
½ teaspoon each fine sea salt, freshly
  ground pepper, and sugar, or to taste
3 tablespoons chopped fresh
  flat-leaf parsley

1. Cut the kernels off the ears of corn. Melt the butter in a large skillet, and sauté the corn, leeks, and bell pepper over medium heat for 5 minutes. Sprinkle the mixture over the bottom of a 12- or 14-inch baking dish.
2. Whisk together the crème fraîche, whipping cream, egg yolks, mustard, salt, pepper, sugar, and parsley. Pour this into the baking dish and bake in a preheated 350° oven for 45 minutes, until just set. Let stand 10 minutes before serving.

Make It Light: Substitute low-fat milk for both the crème fraîche and cream, and 3 whole eggs for the yolks.

Make It Ahead: You can complete step 1 up to 2 hours in advance. About an hour before serving, whisk the custard together and bake (step 2).

The more eggplant I eat, the more I love it! And there seems to be no end to the number of ways it can be prepared. This rendition is especially good with lamb. It also can be served as an appetizer

GRILLED EGGPLANT
WITH GARLIC, BASIL, AND PARSLEY
Serves 8

2 medium eggplants, about 1 pound each
   coarse sea salt
½ cup extra virgin olive oil
1 tablespoon chopped garlic

3 tablespoons each chopped fresh
   basil and fresh flat-leaf parsley
   freshly ground pepper to taste

1. Cut each eggplant lengthwise into ¼-inch-thick slices (about 16 slices in all). Place on paper towels and sprinkle with coarse sea salt. Let stand 1 hour; brush or rinse off any remaining salt and pat dry with paper towels.
2. Brush the bottom of a large baking dish with olive oil. Place the eggplant in the dish, brushing the tops with olive oil, and bake in a preheated 450° oven 15 minutes. Remove the eggplant from the oven, and using a pair of tongs, hold each piece over the burner flame 10 seconds or so, just until it begins to char. Be sure not to exceed 10 seconds. (If you don't have a gas range, you can also do this on an indoor grill, or under an electric broiler). This step gives the eggplant a grilled taste.
3. Return the eggplant to the baking dish, lower the heat to 375°, and sprinkle the garlic, basil, parsley, and pepper over all. Brush on the remainder of the olive oil, and bake 10 minutes more, or until the eggplant feels soft and creamy when touched. Can be served warm, but is even better at room temperature.

Make It Light: Reduce the olive oil to 5 tablespoons.

Make It Ahead: You can make this up to 3 hours in advance and serve at room temperature.

Dried wild mushrooms have such concentrated flavor, that just 2 ounces of them combined with 1½ pounds of fresh mushrooms, creates the illusion that the entire dish is made with wild mushrooms, which would be a very extravagant undertaking, indeed.

SAUTÉED MUSHROOMS WITH GARLIC
Serves 8

2 ounces dry porcini or morels, soaked in warm water to cover for 1 hour
4 tablespoons extra virgin olive oil
5 cloves garlic, crushed
1½ pounds fresh mushrooms, cleaned and quartered

fine sea salt and freshly ground pepper to taste
3 tablespoons chopped fresh flat-leaf parsley

Drain and rinse the soaked mushrooms well, and cut into matchstick julienne. In a large skillet, heat the olive oil, and sauté the garlic over low heat until it begins to brown. Discard the garlic, turn heat to high, and add all the mushrooms. Season with salt and pepper, and toss over high heat 2 minutes. (Do not overcook). Sprinkle with parsley and serve.

Make It Light: Reduce the oil to 3 tablespoons.

Make It Ahead: Allow 1 hour to soak the dried mushrooms. Then, if you have the garlic and fresh mushrooms ready, it will only take you a few minutes to cook this.

If you've never had any experience with portobello mushrooms, you're in for a surprise. For one thing, they're big — about the size of a saucer. For another, their texture is like meat (actually I think they taste better than meat). Dan Phipps, an assistant in one of our basic series, grills them, and serves them just as you would a hamburger. (They also make good hors d'oeuvres.)

DAN'S GRILLED PORTOBELLO MUSHROOM BURGERS

Serves 8

8 portobello mushrooms, cleaned, stems removed
3 red onions, sliced ¼ inch thick
½ cup extra virgin olive oil, more or less fine sea salt and freshly ground pepper to taste
8 large crusty rolls, cut in half

1 cup Garlic Mayonnaise (see recipe below)
2 red bell peppers, roasted, peeled, seeded, and cut into 4 pieces each
8 inner leaves of romaine, trimmed to fit burgers

1. Brush the mushrooms and onion slices with olive oil and season with salt and pepper. Cook on a preheated grill or under the broiler until the mushrooms are soft, about 5 minutes each side, and the onions are done as you like. Remove to a platter. Brush the insides of the rolls with olive oil, and toast until lightly browned.
2. To build the burgers, spread the rolls with plenty of Garlic Mayonnaise, place a mushroom on the bottom half of each roll, followed by a piece of bell pepper, a slice of onion, a lettuce leaf, and the top half of the roll. Cut each burger into quarters and hold each quarter together with an hors d'oeuvre toothpick.

Make It Light: Use little or no Garlic Mayonnaise on the burgers.

Make It Ahead: The burgers can be completely assembled up to 1 hour in advance and served at room temperature

GARLIC MAYONNAISE

1 egg yolk
2 teaspoons fresh lemon juice
1 teaspoon sugar
2 teaspoons hot and sweet prepared mustard
2 cloves garlic, squeezed through a press

1 cup extra virgin olive oil
1 tablespoon chopped fresh flat-leaf parsley
fine sea salt and freshly ground pepper to taste

In a small deep bowl, whisk together the egg yolk, lemon juice, sugar, mustard, and garlic. Slowly drizzle in the olive oil, whisking slowly and gently all the while. Continue whisking until thickened. Stir in the parsley, and season with salt and pepper.

Make It Ahead: You can make the Garlic Mayonnaise up to a day in advance and refrigerate.

This combination is a happy marriage between East and West. Try it with Grilled Steaks à la Ramón (p. 134).

SHIITAKE MUSHROOMS AND CORN
Serves 4 to 6

4 tablespoons sesame oil
1 clove garlic, chopped
2 tablespoons grated fresh ginger
8 ounces fresh shiitake mushrooms, rinsed, stems removed, and sliced
1½ cups fresh corn kernels, cut from the cob (about 3 ears)

½ teaspoon each fine sea salt, freshly ground black pepper, and sugar
1 tablespoon soy sauce
¼ cup dry vermouth
1 teaspoon finely chopped orange zest

1. Heat the sesame oil over high heat in a large skillet or sauté pan; add the garlic and ginger, and sauté for 1 minute, stirring frequently. Add the mushrooms and the corn, season with salt and pepper, and continue tossing over medium heat for 2 minutes. Add the soy sauce, vermouth, and orange zest, cover, and cook 2 minutes. Remove from the heat and allow to stand covered 5 minutes.
2. Remove the cover, toss over high heat 2 minutes to reduce liquid, and serve.

Make It Light: Reduce the sesame oil to 2 tablespoons.

Make It Ahead: You can make this dish through step 1 up to 1 hour in advance. Just before serving, proceed with step 2.

These onions are sweet, yet slightly piquant — wonderful as a condiment on hamburgers, or as an accompaniment to grilled steak. They're also good as a pizza topping or tossed with noodles.

CARAMELIZED RED ONIONS
Serves 8

¼ cup extra virgin olive oil
1½ pounds red onions, halved and sliced ¼ inch thick
2 teaspoons sugar

1 teaspoon coarse sea salt
½ teaspoon freshly ground pepper
3 tablespoons sherry wine vinegar, or more to taste

1. Heat olive oil in a large saucepan or sauté pan, add the onions, sugar, salt, and pepper. Cook over a low heat, covered, for 35 minutes, letting the onions turn a pale brown.
2. Stir in the vinegar, cover, and cook over a low heat another 30 minutes. The onions should be very soft. Taste and adjust seasoning, adding more vinegar if you wish.

Make It Light: Reduce the oil to 1 tablespoon.

Make It Ahead: The cooked onions can be refrigerated for up to 2 days. They also freeze well. Reheat over a medium heat for 2 minutes, if desired.

There are definitely two groups of mashed potato lovers, those who like lumps and those who like perfect smoothness. Both sides are "correct" — it's just a matter of personal preference. This recipe should satisfy either camp:

OLD-FASHIONED MASHED POTATOES
8 servings

2 pounds baking potatoes, peeled (or scrubbed well)
½ cup milk
1 cup crème fraîche
3 tablespoons butter

1 teaspoon each fine sea salt and Hungarian paprika, or to taste
½ teaspoon freshly ground white pepper, or to taste

Cut potatoes into chunks and boil about 30 minutes, or until tender. Drain, and pass them through a food mill or ricer, or mash them leaving lumps. Transfer to a large saucepan. Add the remaining ingredients and beat with an electric mixer or mash until well mixed. Taste and correct seasoning.

Make It Light: Reduce the butter to 1 tablespoon and substitute nonfat milk and Yogurt Cheese (p. 14) for the milk and crème fraîche.

Make It Ahead: You can make this dish up to 2 hours in advance. Reheat, stirring over low heat when you are ready to serve.

Variation:
Garlic Mashed Potatoes: Beat in the pulp from a whole head of roasted garlic (p. 220).

A lighter version of everyone's favorite. When you make these, allow 1 potato per person.

OVEN-BAKED "FRENCH FRIES"
Serves 4 to 6

2 pounds unpeeled baking potatoes, scrubbed and cut into ¼-inch lengthwise strips
5 tablespoons extra virgin olive oil

1 tablespoon unsalted butter
1 teaspoon each Hungarian paprika and coarse sea salt, or to taste
½ teaspoon freshly ground pepper

1. In a large bowl, combine all ingredients and toss thoroughly.
2. Arrange potatoes in a single layer on a parchment-lined baking sheet, and bake in a preheated 425° oven for about 20 minutes, until the potatoes are soft and lightly browned. Serve hot.

Make It Light: Reduce the oil to 2 tablespoons.

Make It Ahead: You can season the potatoes (step 1) up to 2 hours in advance. Put them in the oven about 25 minutes before serving (step 2).

Twice-baked potatoes are one of those dishes that allows enormous room for creativity. You can have a wonderful time experimenting with the stuffing, using all kinds of different cheeses and vegetables. Depending on what you add to the stuffing, these potatoes can serve as anything from a snack to a light meal.

TWICE-BAKED POTATOES
WITH SPINACH AND CHEESE

Serves 6

6 large baking potatoes (about 8 ounces each), scrubbed	1 cup each milk and crème fraîche
1 pound spinach, cleaned, stems removed	1 teaspoon each fine sea salt and Hungarian paprika
1 clove roasted garlic	freshly ground white pepper to taste
2 tablespoons unsalted butter	2 ounces Parmigiano-Reggiano, freshly grated (about ½ cup)

1. Prick the skin of each potato in several places, and place directly on the rack of a preheated 400° oven for approximately 1 hour, or until they test done. Allow to cool, then cut the top off the potato lengthwise, and carefully remove the insides, leaving a ¼-inch shell. Transfer the potato pulp to a large mixing bowl; set the skins aside.
2. Rinse the spinach and drain but don't dry it. Put it in a heavy pan, cover, and cook over medium heat for 2 or 3 minutes, shaking the pan once or twice. (There will be enough water left on the spinach to cook it.) Drain off the excess water and season with salt and pepper. Chop coarsely and add to the potatoes.
3. Mash the potatoes and spinach together with the garlic, butter, milk, crème fraîche, salt, paprika, pepper, and grated cheese until well combined. Stuff the potato mixture into the reserved potato skins.
4. Place the potatoes in a baking dish, and bake in a preheated 350° oven until heated through, about 20 minutes.

Make It Light: Substitute nonfat milk and Yogurt Cheese (p. 14) for the milk and crème fraîche called for in the recipe. Reduce the butter to 1 tablespoon and the Parmigiano to 1 ounce (about ¼ cup).

Make It Ahead: You can prepare the potatoes through step 3 up to 2 hours in advance. Put them in the oven about 20 minutes before serving (step 4).

Variations:

Twice-Baked Potatoes with Ancho Chiles and Brie: Substitute 2 dried ancho chiles and 8 ounces of Brie for the spinach and Parmigiano-Reggiano. Remove the skin from the Brie, dice, and chill 1 hour. To prepare the chiles, roast them at 375° until puffed and fragrant, about 5 minutes. Remove the stems, seeds, and veins, cover with hot water and let stand for 1 hour. Purée in a blender or food processor, using just enough of the soaking water to make a smooth purée.

Twice-Baked Potatoes with Corn: Substitute corn for the spinach: Drop 3 ears of corn into boiling water for 3 minutes. Drain and cool. When cool enough to handle, cut the kernels off the cob.

Whenever I'm a guest on the local radio shows, someone invariably calls in to ask how to make oven-roasted potatoes. They taste so good, I guess people think there's some complicated technique involved. But there's really nothing to it.

OVEN-ROASTED POTATOES

Serves 8

3 **pounds tiny boiling potatoes, scrubbed**
4 **tablespoons unsalted butter (2 ounces)**
4 **tablespoons extra virgin olive oil**

coarse sea salt, Hungarian paprika, and freshly ground pepper to taste

Cut the potatoes into serving pieces, halves or quarters, depending on their size (very small ones can be left whole). Toss with the remaining ingredients in a 12-inch roasting dish and bake in a preheated 400° oven until nicely browned and tender, approximately 1¼ hours. Allow to stand 15 minutes before serving.

Make It Light: Reduce butter and olive oil to 2 tablespoons each.

Make It Ahead: You can assemble this dish up to 2 hours in advance of baking. Put it in the oven about 1½ hours before serving (see above).

Variations:

Oven-Roasted Potatoes with Red Onions: Peel 2 large red onions, cut them in half, and thinly slice. Toss well with the potatoes and other ingredients, and roast.

Rosemary Garlic Oven-Roasted Potatoes: Combine 1 tablespoon each chopped fresh rosemary and chopped fresh garlic and ½ cup Chicken Stock (p. 12) or Vegetable Stock (p. 13). Pour this over the potatoes after the potatoes have roasted for 45 minutes, continue to roast until the liquid has disappeared and the potatoes are nicely browned, about 30 minutes more.

I especially like serving this gratin as the only hot dish on an otherwise room-temperature buffet. Another suggestion is to serve it with Grilled Chicken Breasts Rosemary (p. 165) and Roasted Red, Golden, and Purple Bell Pepper Salad (p. 89).

ROQUEFORT-POTATO GRATIN

Serves 8

3 ounces Roquefort cheese (about ⅓ cup)
½ cup crème fraîche
4 tablespoons unsalted butter (2 ounces)
3 pounds baking potatoes, peeled
  and thinly sliced

freshly grated nutmeg to taste
coarse sea salt and freshly ground
  black pepper to taste
4 cups milk

1. Combine the Roquefort and crème fraîche in a small bowl. Use 1 tablespoon of butter to grease the sides and bottom of a 12- or 14-inch baking dish.
2. Evenly arrange half the potatoes in the dish. Sprinkle with half the Roquefort cream, and a little nutmeg, salt, and pepper. Repeat the process with the remainder of the potatoes, Roquefort, butter, and seasonings. Pour the milk over all.
3. Bake in a preheated 375° oven until the gratin is crisp and golden on top, and the potatoes are soft, about 1½ hours. Let the gratin rest 20 minutes before serving.

Make It Light: Reduce the Roquefort to 2 ounces (¼ cup), substitute Yogurt Cheese (p. 14) for the crème fraîche, and nonfat milk for all or part of the milk called for in recipe.

Make It Ahead: You can do steps 1 and 2 up to 4 hours in advance. About 2 hours before serving, put the dish in the oven (step 3).

Here are a couple of uncomplicated recipes that came up time and again in our menus for entertaining. If you bake tomatoes for a short time, they hold their shape and stay intact. If you bake them for a longer time, they will soften and become almost saucelike, and the flavors will become very intense. They are excellent either way — following are directions for both versions:

BAKED HERBED TOMATOES I

Serves 8

8 tomatoes
2 cups fresh bread crumbs
2 tablespoons each chopped fresh
   flat-leaf parsley, chopped fresh basil,
   and chopped fresh garlic

1 teaspoon each sugar, coarse sea salt,
   and freshly ground pepper
3 tablespoons extra virgin olive oil

1. Cut the tops off the tomatoes and scoop out the seeds and juice. Mix the bread crumbs, parsley, basil, garlic, sugar, salt, and pepper together. Stuff the tomatoes loosely with this mixture, and place them in a shallow baking dish.
2. Sprinkle with olive oil, and bake in a preheated 350° oven 20 to 30 minutes, until the tomatoes are soft and the tops are golden brown. Serve warm or at room temperature. Delicious either way.

Make It Light: Reduce the oil to 1 tablespoon.

Make It Ahead: You can complete step 1 up to 2 hours in advance. Put the tomatoes in the oven about 45 minutes before serving (step 2).

BAKED HERBED TOMATOES II
Serves 8

8 small tomatoes
1 tablespoon each chopped fresh
  flat-leaf parsley, fresh basil,
  fresh sage, and fresh oregano
2 tablespoons chopped fresh garlic

1 teaspoon each coarse sea salt, sugar,
  and freshly ground pepper
½ cup each balsamic vinegar and
  extra virgin olive oil

1. Stem the tomatoes, then beginning at the top, carefully cut each tomato into fourths without cutting all the way through so that the quarters remain joined at the bottom. Place the tomatoes in a single layer in a shallow baking dish; sprinkle with the herbs and garlic, season with salt, sugar, and pepper, and drizzle with the vinegar and olive oil.
2. Bake in a preheated 350° for 50 or 60 minutes. Remove from the oven and cool in the dish. Serve at room temperature.

Make It Light: Reduce the oil to ¼ cup.

Make It Ahead: You can complete step 1 up to 3 hours in advance. Start baking the tomatoes about 1½ hours before serving (step 2).

Frittatas are Italy's answer to the omelet, the difference being that with frittatas, the fillings are mixed into the eggs, and they are usually baked in the oven. Frittatas can be served hot right out of the dish they are baked in. They are also good served at room temperature, which makes them the perfect brunch food, especially when you have a lot of people to serve. Tom Vitanza, the assistant director at our San Francisco school, contributed this recipe. I added our "light" pesto sauce to make the dish extra special.

TOM'S ASPARAGUS AND MUSHROOM FRITTATA WITH HOMECHEF'S LIGHT PESTO

Serves 8 to 10

1½ pounds asparagus, trimmed and peeled
3 tablespoons extra virgin olive oil
3 tablespoons butter
1 medium red onion, finely chopped
8 ounces mushrooms, brushed clean and thickly sliced
12 eggs
½ cup water

fine sea salt and freshly ground pepper to taste
4 tablespoons finely chopped flat-leaf parsley
2 ounces Parmigiano-Reggiano, grated (about ½ cup)
HomeChef's Light Pesto
(see p. 217)

1. Blanch the asparagus for 2 minutes, drain, and cut into 2-inch pieces. Heat the olive oil and butter in a skillet, and sauté the onion and mushrooms for about 1 minute over medium heat. Add the asparagus, sauté an additional minute, and remove from the heat.
2. Put the eggs and water in a large bowl and beat until blended; stir in the onions, mushrooms, asparagus, salt, pepper, parsley, and Parmigiano.
3. Pour the egg mixture into a 12- or 14-inch ovenproof serving dish and bake in a preheated 375° oven about 20 minutes, until the eggs are set. Let stand 15 minutes. To serve, cut pie-shaped wedges, and spoon HomeChef's Light Pesto over each serving.

Make It Light: Eliminate three of the egg yolks; reduce the oil and butter to 3 tablespoons combined, and the cheese to 1 ounce (¼ cup).

Make It Ahead: You can complete steps 1 and 2 up to 2½ hours in advance. Put the frittata in the oven about 40 minutes before serving (step 3).

Variation:
Roasted Vegetable Frittata: Substitute 2 cups coarsely chopped roasted vegetables (p. 218) and 1 tablespoon chopped garlic for the onion, mushrooms and asparagus. Eliminate the butter, increase the olive oil to 5 tablespoons. Sauté the garlic in olive oil for 1 minute, add the vegetables and sauté 1 minute more, then proceed as for Tom's Asparagus Frittata, steps 2 and 3.

HOMECHEF'S LIGHT PESTO

Makes 1 cup

2 tablespoons extra virgin olive oil
2 cloves garlic
30 basil leaves
1 teaspoon fine sea salt
½ teaspoon freshly ground pepper

1 ounce toasted bread crumbs
(about ¼ cup)
1 ounce freshly grated
Parmigiano-Reggiano (about ¼ cup)
¼ cup water

Place the olive oil, garlic, basil, salt, and pepper in a food processor or blender and process to a fine paste. Add the bread crumbs and Parmigiano and process for 10 seconds more. With the machine running, add the water and process until the pesto is smooth and creamy.

Make It Ahead: Can be made up to 1 day in advance and refrigerated. Bring to room temperature before serving.

Grilled or roasted vegetables make a good side dish for almost any entrée, whether it's meat, poultry, or fish. If you are using the grill or oven to prepare the main course, you might as well take advantage of it and cook the vegetables at the same time. Another possibility is to prepare a medley of vegetables for a main course, or as part of a buffet (grilled and roasted vegetables both taste good hot or at room temperature). Just be sure to allow two hours for the vegetables to marinate prior to cooking them. Try one or two or all of these, and while you're at it, make enough so you have leftovers. Then tomorrow, you can make a frittata (p. 216) or some grilled vegetable sandwiches (make them on toasted French bread spread with a little goat cheese or cream cheese).

GRILLED OR ROASTED VEGETABLES

½ cup extra virgin olive oil
¼ cup balsamic vinegar
4 cloves garlic, finely chopped
1 teaspoon each sugar, fine sea salt,
   and finely ground black pepper

2 teaspoons chopped fresh oregano
4 tablespoons chopped fresh
   flat-leaf parsley
   vegetables of your choice
   (see suggestions below)

1. Combine the oil, vinegar, garlic, sugar, salt, and pepper in a large bowl. Place the vegetables in the bowl, and toss with the marinade. Marinate for 2 hours or more.
2. To grill, place the vegetables cut side up on a preheated grill, and brush with the marinade. Grill until soft, and nicely browned, about 15 minutes. You may turn them or not, as you wish, but be sure to baste them with the marinade. To roast, place the vegetables in a baking dish, brush with marinade, and roast about 30 minutes in a preheated 375° oven. Serve warm or at room temperature.

Suggested vegetables for grilling or roasting:
baby artichokes, trimmed, parboiled 10 minutes, and halved
asparagus, peeled
bell peppers, quartered and seeded
corn on the cob, blanched 1 minute
Japanese eggplants, halved lengthwise
garlic bulbs, unpeeled, top third cut off
large mushrooms, stems removed, left whole or cut in half
red onions, cut into 1-inch slices
small new potatoes, left whole or halved, parboiled 10 minutes
small tomatoes, halved
medium zucchini or other summer squash, halved lengthwise

VEGETABLE PREPARATION
TECHNIQUES

Following are brief notes on basic vegetable preparation. For more detailed explanations and photographs, refer to *The HomeChef* cookbook.

ARTICHOKES
Large artichokes. Cut off the stem at the base of the artichoke, and pull off all the tiny leaves near the bottom. Cut off the top inch of the artichoke and snip off the spiny tip of the remaining leaves with a pair of scissors. Swish in lukewarm water. Boil or steam until the lower leaves pull off easily and the bottom is soft (pierce it with a skewer to test). The leaves can be pulled off and used with dips and spreads. Remove the fuzzy choke at the center with a spoon; the bowl-shaped bottom can then be used as directed.

Artichoke bottoms. Cut off the stem and trim off all the leaves at the base of the artichoke as well as those above the bottom. Drop into boiling salted water that has lemon juice added. Lower the heat and simmer until tender, about 15 minutes, and cool in the cooking liquid. Remove the choke with a spoon. Can be stored in some of the cooking liquid until ready to use. (You can also prepare artichoke bottoms by cooking the whole artichoke first, then removing the leaves and choke. See above.)

Baby artichokes. Baby artichokes less than 1½ inches in diameter, are edible in their entirety, because the choke has not yet formed in them. To trim, cut off the stem, pull off all the tough outer leaves at the base, and cut about ¼ inch off the top. Swish in lukewarm water to clean, and use as directed. If baby artichokes are unavailable, artichoke bottoms can be substituted (see above).

ASPARAGUS
Asparagus should always be peeled because the outer peel will remain tough no matter how long it's cooked. First, snap off the tough root end of the asparagus where it naturally breaks when you bend it with your fingers. Then lay the asparagus down on a flat surface and peel the stalk to within 3 inches of the tip with a vegetable peeler.

BELL PEPPERS
Roasting and peeling. Place the pepper over a direct flame or under the broiler and char evenly, turning frequently. Place in a paper bag, and allow to cool. Peel away the charred outer skin with a paring knife (this is a messy job, best done at the sink). Cut it in half; cut away the stem and remove the seeds and membranes.

BROCCOLI
Select heads that are tightly closed and green or purple in color (yellow means the broccoli is old). Cut the broccoli florets off at the bottom, where they attach to the main stalk. Cut large florets in half or quarters. Slice away all the fibrous outer skin of the main stalk. The heart of the stalk is delicious and can be sliced and cooked along with the florets.

BRUSSELS SPROUTS

The heads of each sprout should be firm, tight, and bright green. Always select the smallest, as they are the best tasting. Store in the refrigerator for not more than 2 days after purchase. To prepare for cooking, trim the stem, and pull off any yellowed leaves. Cut an X in the stem of each sprout so that it will cook in the same time as the leaves.

EGGPLANT

The following technique should always be used before cooking regular eggplant as it removes excess moisture and eliminates bitterness: cut the eggplant according to the directions in your recipe and arrange on paper towels; sprinkle with coarse sea salt and let drain 1 hour. Brush off excess salt, pat dry with more paper towels, and proceed with your recipe. Japanese eggplant does not need to be salted.

GARLIC AND SHALLOTS

Choose firm bulbs that have not sprouted, and store in baskets or net bags, in a cool, dry, dark place. To peel garlic, remove the papery outer skin and separate the cloves. Cut off the tip ends, and hit each clove sharply with the side of a knife. This loosens the skin and causes it to pop off. To peel shallots, cut off the tops and bottoms of the shallot. With a small paring knife, peel away the first layer of flesh that is attached to the paperlike outer skin.

To prepare Roasted Garlic. Cut off the top quarter of a large head of garlic to expose the cloves, and place in a small ovenproof casserole. Drizzle with 3 tablespoons extra virgin olive oil, cover, and roast in a preheated 400° oven for approximately 45 minutes, or until the garlic feels soft to the touch. Separate the cloves, squeeze out the pulp, and use as directed in recipes.

LEEKS

Leeks have sand deep down in the bulb and must be cleaned carefully. Generally the dark green tops of the leeks are discarded as they are very bitter in flavor. Cut off the root and the upper dark green tops of the leek just above where the white part joins the green. Split the leaves lengthwise above the bulb once, and a second time at right angles to the first. Under running water, carefully clean the sand out of each section, checking each portion before going on to the next.

MUSHROOMS

Never soak fresh mushrooms in water when you clean them. They already have a high water content, and will absorb more if soaked. Ordinary cultivated mushrooms can be cleaned by gently brushing them with a mushroom brush. Wild mushrooms often have soil and sand imbedded in their "gills" and should be brushed gently under cool running water.

ONIONS

Choose firm onions that have not sprouted, and store in a cool, dry, dark place. Remove the papery outer skin before using. If the recipe calls for a whole onion, however, trim the root end narrowly so that it remains intact. This will keep the onion from falling apart as it cooks.

SPINACH

Cut off and discard the coarse stems. Swish the leaves in warm water (warm water is more effective in removing sand). Repeat, using cold water, and drain. Spinach cooks beautifully using only the water that clings to the leaves after washing. For salads, dry on paper towels or in a salad spinner.

SWISS CHARD

To prepare chard, cut the leaves from the stalks and string any large or tough stalks like celery. The stalks and leaves can be cooked separately, the leaves like spinach and the stalks like asparagus.

TOMATOES

Peeling. Dip the tomato in boiling water for 10 seconds, remove the stem, and slip off the skin. (Or refrigerate the tomato until needed, and slip the skin off just before using).

Seeding. Quarter the tomato, and scoop the seeds out with your fingers.

BOILING OR BLANCHING VEGETABLES

Bring water to a boil in a pot large enough to hold both vegetables and water to cover them. When water is boiling rapidly, (its surface covered with bubbles), add prepared vegetables to the rapidly boiling water for a brief period of time, (to bring out color and flavor, or to loosen skins for peeling), if you are blanching. If you wish to boil the vegetables until done, allow vegetables to boil for a longer period of time. Start checking for doneness with a wooden skewer after 30 or 40 seconds of cooking, depending upon the delicacy of the vegetable. When adequately cooked, drain, dry (when appropriate), and finish according to your recipe. The initial boiling of the vegetables may be done in advance and completed (sautéed, creamed, or puréed), several hours later. Be sure to undercook initially, to allow for any further cooking.

STEAMING VEGETABLES

Place a small amount of water in a saucepan, place pot over high heat, and bring water to a boil. Put the prepared vegetables in a steamer basket and place it over the boiling water. Cover the pot and steam until the vegetables reach their desired degree of doneness. For vegetables, steaming takes longer than boiling, and since the pan must be covered, steaming can discolor green vegetables and intensify the flavor of strong-tasting vegetables like cabbage, broccoli, and Brussels sprouts. Potatoes, carrots, mushrooms, beets, corn, and artichokes all steam beautifully.

GRILLING VEGETABLES

Vegetables grill very well, since the dry intense heat seals the outside of the vegetables, allowing the inner flesh to cook in its own juices. Always brush the outside skins or flesh with oil or marinade, and start the cooking over the highest heat. The vegetables can be moved away from the hottest part of the grill to finish cooking. To check doneness, poke with a skewer.

CHAPTER NINE

DESSERTS

In compiling this book, I sorted through all the recipes we have presented in our classes over the last few years. I was amazed to find the group that had the most recipes of all was desserts. That caused me to review our curriculum, and — you guessed it — I found out that we have more dessert classes than any other kind.

There are several obvious reasons why desserts are so popular. For one thing, most people have an irrepressible appetite for sweet things. Desserts are associated with happy times like birthdays and weddings; they also say I love you. And desserts are often given as a "reward," as in "Here is a cookie, it will make your hurt knee feel better," or "You can't have dessert until you finish your dinner," or "We are presenting you with this cake as a reward for your good service." So it's no wonder that desserts are high on everyone's list.

I would like to point out that there are many light, totally fat-free desserts, as well as some really rich ones, for the times when you feel like indulging yourself, or your friends and family. So, in the great dessert tradition, here is your reward — all the desserts voted best by all of us at HomeChef!

Note: For accuracy, dry ingredients in significant amounts are given first by weight, and then by cup (volume) measure. If you do not have a kitchen scale, use the cup measure.

FRUIT DESSERTS

When I plan meals, my preference is to have a richer first course or main course, and a very light dessert, and for a light dessert, you can't beat fresh fruits. The next two fruit desserts are perfect examples. Both are fat free, and wonderfully refreshing after a rich meal. The first is the simplest. You can use any kind of melon for it — cantaloupe is my favorite — but you must be sure the melon is ripe and sweet.

MELON WITH MARSALA
Serves 6

1 ripe melon, peeled, seeded, and
  sliced or cut into 1-inch cubes
2 ounces sugar (about ¼ cup)

½ cup Marsala
  fresh mint leaves for garnish

Melon slices should be arranged attractively on a platter; put melon cubes in a serving bowl. Sprinkle with sugar and Marsala, and garnish with mint leaves. Let stand 1 hour at room temperature before serving.

Make It Ahead: You can make this up to 8 hours in advance. Refrigerate and bring to room temperature 1 hour before serving.

This is a big recipe, but I urge you to make it all, even if it's more than you need for one meal. It keeps in the refrigerator for several days, and you will find it irresistible with granola for breakfast, or with yogurt for lunch. Macédoine is a French word for a dish of assorted fruits or vegetables, usually attractively sliced and marinated.

FRESH FRUIT MACÉDOINE WITH SERRANO CHILES
Serves 10 to 12

1 pineapple, peeled, cored, and cut
  into ¼-inch slices
2 ripe mangoes or papayas, peeled,
  pitted, and cut into ¼-inch slices
3 ripe kiwifruit, peeled and cut into
  ¼-inch slices
2 apples or pears, peeled, cored, and
  cut into ¼-inch slices
¾ cup seedless grapes, cut in half

2 oranges, peeled, cut into ¼-inch
  slices, seeds removed
1 cup strawberries, hulled and
  quartered lengthwise
2 serrano chiles, seeded and minced
7 ounces superfine sugar (about 1 cup)
  juice of 1 lime
½ cup Kirsch

In a large bowl, mix the prepared fruit and chiles together. Sprinkle with sugar, and toss with lime juice and Kirsch. Allow to macerate at least 2 hours before serving.

Make It Ahead: You can make this recipe up to 1 day in advance and refrigerate. Allow to stand at room temperature 1 hour before serving.

Recently I celebrated a very important birthday, and had a party for a large group of my closest women friends. This was our dessert, and it prompted one woman to say that it was the best party she'd been to since she was six!

SUMMER BERRIES IN A ROSE-FLAVORED CREAM

Serves 8

2½ cups milk
 2 roses in full bloom
 ½ teaspoon vanilla powder or extract
 4 ounces superfine sugar (about ½ cup)

6 egg yolks
1 pound fresh berries, cleaned
   and hulled

1. In a small saucepan, combine the milk, the petals from 1 rose, and the vanilla. Slowly bring to a boil, remove from the heat, cover, and let stand 1 hour. Strain out the rose petals.
2. Whisk the sugar and egg yolks together. Add it to the milk, and cook over medium heat, whisking constantly, until thickened, about 6 to 8 minutes. Remove from the heat, cool, and strain out any lumps.
3. To serve, spoon some of the rose-flavored cream into each serving dish, add a portion of berries, and scatter a few rose petals over each.

Make It Light: Use nonfat milk, and substitute 3 whole eggs for the egg yolks.

Make It Ahead: You can make the recipe through step 2 up to 3 hours in advance. When you are ready, proceed with step 3.

Take some fully ripe peaches, gently warm them to bring out their full flavor, then add a smooth buttery caramel sauce. I cannot imagine a more perfect combination. I usually make this an hour or so before dinner, and let it stand in the pan on the stove, until I'm ready to serve.

PEACHES IN CARAMEL SAUCE

Serves 8

8 tablespoons unsalted butter (4 ounces)
5 ounces superfine sugar (about ¾ cup)

½ cup Madeira
8 ripe peaches, peeled and halved

1. Melt the butter in a large skillet, add the sugar, and dissolve it over a low heat, stirring all the while. Add the Madeira and continue to stir until the sauce is smooth.
2. Add the peach halves, turning them over several times, spooning the syrup over them, allowing them to warm for 2 or 3 minutes. Can be served immediately, but will taste better if allowed to sit at least an hour.

Make It Light: Reduce the butter to 2 ounces (4 tablespoons).

Make It Ahead: You can make this up to 4 hours in advance. Allow the peaches to stand in the sauce until you are ready to serve, then rewarm them.

This dish brings back wonderful memories of alfresco dining one summer in Italy. The amaretti cookies that are stuffed into the peaches are crisp versions of what we call almond macaroons. Italian amaretti are available in Italian or gourmet food markets. If you cannot find them, substitute almond macaroons.

STUFFED BAKED PEACHES

Serves 6

3 ripe peaches, unpeeled, cut in half, and pitted
2 tablespoons unsalted butter
2 tablespoons sugar

3 amaretti, crushed
1 egg yolk
1 tablespoon Cognac
¼ cup each Marsala and water

Scoop out a little of the peach pulp from each peach half to enlarge the hollows. Chop the peach pulp finely and combine with the butter, sugar, amaretti, egg yolk, and Cognac. Stuff the peaches with this mixture, and arrange them in an open baking dish. Sprinkle each peach with Marsala and water, and pour the remainder into the bottom of the baking dish. Bake in a preheated 350° oven 30 minutes. Let stand at room temperature for about 30 minutes. Serve with some of the juices spooned over each peach.

Make It Light: Omit the butter and egg yolk.

Make It Ahead: You can make this dish up to 4 hours in advance. Serve at room temperature.

Here is a very pretty fruit dessert for the winter season. Poaching the pears in red wine turns them pink, which contrasts nicely with the warm, rich chocolate sauce.

PINK PEAR PURÉE WITH WARM CHOCOLATE SAUCE

Serves 8

2 cups red table wine
1 cup water
4 ounces sugar (about ½ cup)
3 pounds pears, peeled, cored, and quartered

4 tablespoons unsalted butter (2 ounces)
8 ounces semisweet chocolate
¼ cup heavy cream

1. Combine the wine, water, and sugar in a 6-quart saucepan, and bring to a boil. Add the pears and simmer gently until soft, about 5 to 6 minutes. Remove the pears and reduce the syrup over high heat until it measures 4 tablespoons. Purée the pears in a blender or food processor with 2 tablespoons of the butter and the reduced wine syrup. Transfer to a serving bowl.
2. In a small heavy saucepan or in the top of a double boiler, combine the remaining butter, chocolate, and cream. Stir over medium heat until the chocolate melts, 3 or 4 minutes. To serve, spoon the puréed pears into 8 dessert dishes, and top with warm chocolate sauce.

Make It Light: Omit the butter

Make It Ahead: You can poach and purée the pears up to 4 hours in advance (step 1). Make the sauce shortly before serving (step 2).

Another wintertime dessert, this one created by Rebecca Ets-Hokin, our cooking school director.

BRAISED VANILLA APPLES

Serves 8

6 large tart apples, cored, peeled, and quartered
1 vanilla bean, split in half

4 ounces sugar (about ½ cup)
¼ cup each water and rum

Place the apples and vanilla bean in a heavy sauté pan. Sprinkle the sugar on top, and add the water and the rum. Cook covered over low heat, shaking the pan occasionally, until the fruit is very soft, about 12 to 15 minutes. Transfer the apples to a serving platter and pour the syrup on top, removing the vanilla bean. Serve warm or at room temperature.

Make It Ahead: You can make the apples up to 4 hours in advance.

FROZEN DESSERTS

The French sorbet is the equivalent of our sherbet, the difference being that a sorbet does not contain any egg whites or milk. Essentially, it is a sweetened frozen fruit purée. Although they are made in an ice cream maker, sorbets are never firm like ice cream. They are refreshing, totally fat-free, and a great choice to finish a rich meal. You can use the Raspberry Sorbet as a master recipe, and substitute fruits and garnishes to suit yourself. I've suggested a number of variations to get you started.

RASPBERRY SORBET WITH BLUEBERRY GARNISH

Makes about 1 quart

6 **ounces sugar (about ¾ cup)**
¾ **cup water**
2 **pints fresh raspberries, puréed in the food processor or blender**

1 **tablespoon fresh lemon juice**
1 **pint fresh blueberries for garnish**

1. Combine the sugar and water in a saucepan, bring to a boil over medium-high heat. Boil for 30 seconds or until the syrup is clear. Remove from the heat and chill overnight.
2. Combine the chilled syrup, puréed raspberries, and lemon juice. Freeze in an ice cream maker following the manufacturer's instructions. Store the sorbet in a covered container in the freezer. Serve in stemmed dessert glasses, garnished with blueberries.

Make It Ahead: The sugar syrup needs to be made a day ahead. The sorbet itself is best made not more than 2 or 3 hours in advance, and kept frozen until served.

Variations:

Follow the directions in the main recipe above, substituting the following fruits for the raspberries and blueberries.

Mango Sorbet with Raspberries: 5 ripe mangoes, peeled and puréed; 1 pint fresh raspberries for garnish.

Kiwifruit Sorbet with Strawberries: 8 ripe kiwifruit, peeled and puréed, plus 1 tablespoon fresh lime juice in place of the lemon juice; 1 pint fresh strawberries, rinsed and sliced, for garnish.

Strawberry Sorbet with Blueberries: 2 pints fresh strawberries, hulled and puréed; 1 pint fresh blueberries for garnish.

Frappés are a kind of "instant" sorbet that does not require an ice cream freezer, and takes about 5 minutes to make, assuming you have some frozen fruit to begin with. If you store the frappé in the freezer, allow it to soften slightly and whisk it before serving. It should be very cold and fluffy.

SUMMER FRUIT FRAPPÉ
Serves 8 to 10

12 ounces frozen fruit (about 2 cups of berries, sliced peaches or bananas, etc.)
2 large egg whites, at room temperature

1 tablespoon fresh lemon juice
3 ounces sugar (about ½ cup)
1 tablespoon brandy

1. Chop the frozen fruit finely in a food processor or blender.
2. Transfer the finely chopped frozen fruit to a large bowl, or the bowl of your processor or electric mixer, and add the remaining ingredients. Whisk or beat the mixture until it is thick and fluffy, about 3 minutes in the food processor or 5 minutes in an electric mixer. Serve immediately or freeze until firm. If frozen, transfer to the regular section of the refrigerator 30 minutes before serving. Whisk and serve.

Make It Ahead: Best served right after it is made, but can be prepared and frozen up to 6 hours in advance. Transfer to the regular section of the refrigerator 30 minutes before serving. Whisk and serve.

Everyone loves ice cream, and our students are no exception. They voted on their five favorite flavors, then I selected the one recipe to go in this book. Since I love cinnamon, it wasn't too hard to make a choice. This is rich and sweet — everything one expects from a good homemade ice cream.

CINNAMON ICE CREAM
Makes 1 quart

½ vanilla bean, split lengthwise
4 ounces sugar (about ½ cup)
2½ cups heavy cream
½ teaspoon ground cinnamon

2 cinnamon sticks (about 8 inches altogether)
5 egg yolks

1. In a food processor or blender, process the vanilla bean and sugar until finely blended. Transfer the vanilla-sugar to a heavy saucepan, and add the cream, ground cinnamon, and cinnamon sticks. Heat slowly to a low simmer, and let simmer for 2 minutes. Remove from the heat, cover, and let steep for 1 hour. Remove cinnamon sticks.
2. Whisk egg yolks together and slowly whisk into the infused cream. Return the pot to a medium heat and cook, stirring, until slightly thickened, about 2 or 3 minutes. Cool slightly, and refrigerate for 2 hours. Freeze in an ice cream maker following the manufacturer's instructions. Store the ice cream in a covered container in the freezer. Serve in stemmed dessert glasses.

Make It Light: Substitute 2½ cups whole milk for the cream and 3 whole eggs for the egg yolks.

Make It Ahead: This ice cream is best made not more than 8 hours in advance. Keep frozen until served. At a minimum, allow 1 hour for the cinnamon to steep, 2 hours to chill.

PUDDINGS, CUSTARDS, AND CREAMS

A dish from my childhood, and a great way to use up those bananas that are just about to go beyond ripe.

BANANA CREAM PUDDING

Serves 8

4 very ripe bananas
3 cups milk
3 tablespoons cornstarch
3 ounces sugar (about ½ cup)

⅛ teaspoon each fine sea salt and freshly ground nutmeg
4 eggs, lightly beaten
1 tablespoon vanilla powder or extract

1. Mash one banana in a saucepan and combine with the milk. Bring to a boil, cover, and remove from the heat.
2. In another saucepan, over low heat, combine the cornstarch, sugar, salt, nutmeg, eggs, and vanilla, and, using a wire whisk, gradually stir in the hot milk and banana mixture. Cook, stirring, until the pudding thickens, about 3 or 4 minutes.
3. Slice the remaining 3 bananas into 8 serving dishes. Spoon the pudding over the bananas. This can be served warm or chilled.

Make It Light: Use nonfat milk and substitute 2 whole eggs and 2 egg whites for the 4 eggs.

Make It Ahead: You can make this recipe up to 1 day in advance. Cover and refrigerate until serving.

Clafouti is a simple dessert made during the short cherry season in France. Essentially, it is a pancake batter that is poured over pitted cherries, then baked. It looks a little like a large rectangular tart without a crust, and is usually served warm, topped with powdered sugar. After the cherry season, substitute any ripe fruit in your *clafouti*. Ideally, it should be made in an attractive dish that can go from the oven to the table.

CLAFOUTI
Serves 8 to 10

1 tablespoon unsalted butter, melted
6 ounces granulated sugar (about ¾ cup)
2 pounds fresh cherries, pitted
6 eggs
5 ounces all-purpose flour (about 1 cup)

1 tablespoon vanilla powder
   or extract
½ teaspoon fine sea salt
4 cups half-and-half
   confectioners' sugar for garnish

1. Brush the melted butter onto the sides and bottom of a 12-inch rectangular or oval baking dish. Sprinkle with 2 ounces (¼ cup) granulated sugar, and spread the pitted cherries over the bottom of the prepared dish.

2. Combine the eggs, flour, vanilla, salt, and half-and-half in a mixing bowl, whisk 1 minute, then slowly whisk in the remaining 4 ounces (½ cup) granulated sugar. Pour this batter over the cherries and bake 30 to 40 minutes in a preheated 375° oven, until puffy and brown. Dust with confectioners' sugar, and serve warm or at room temperature.

Make It Light: Substitute 4 cups nonfat milk for the half-and-half, and eliminate 3 of the egg yolks.

Make It Ahead: You can make this dish up to 3 hours in advance of serving.

Without question, *Crème Brûlée,* with its creamy, smooth richness, and crisp, hard, caramel crust, is the ultimate custard. Literally translated, *crème brûlée* means "burnt custard." Many people think of this as a French dessert, but according to some, it is actually Creole. If calories or cholesterol are a concern, try the "Make-It-Light" version.

CRÈME BRÛLÉE
Serves 8 to 10

2 cups crème fraîche
2 cups heavy cream
5 ounces granulated sugar
   (a scant ¾ cup)

8 egg yolks
1 tablespoon vanilla powder or extract
5 ounces light brown sugar
   (about 1 cup)

1. Combine the crème fraîche and whipping cream in a saucepan and bring just to a boil; remove from the heat. In a small bowl, whisk the granulated sugar and egg yolks together until light in color. Return the cream to the burner, and over low heat stir in the sugar-egg yolk mixture. Continue to cook, stirring, until thickened just enough to coat a wooden spoon with a light, creamy layer, about 5 or 6 minutes. Stir in the vanilla and pour through a coarse strainer into a 12-inch rectangular or oval ovenproof serving dish and chill overnight.
2. Sprinkle the brown sugar evenly over the custard so that it is completely covered (a coarse sieve may help). Place the dish under a preheated broiler to caramelize the sugar, about 3 or 4 minutes, watching carefully to prevent burning. Serve immediately or return the custard to the refrigerator to chill 1 hour before serving.

Make It Light: Substitute 2 cups Yogurt Cheese made with vanilla yogurt (p. 14) for the crème fraîche, 2 cups regular milk for the heavy cream. Substitute 4 whole eggs plus 2 egg yolks for the 8 yolks called for in the recipe.

Coeur à la Crème, which means "heart of cream" in French, is a wonderful way to say "I love you" to your guests. You will need a special heart-shaped basket or porcelain *coeur à la crème* mold to make this dessert: it has holes in the bottom to allow the whey to drain from the cheese. Directions are given for making one large mold, but you could use individual *coeur à la crème* molds, too, if you prefer. All are available in gourmet kitchen stores.

COEUR À LA CRÈME

Serves 8 to 10

8 ounces cottage cheese
8 ounces cream cheese
1 cup crème fraîche

½ teaspoon fine sea salt
2 tablespoons confectioners' sugar
1 pound strawberries, rinsed and sliced

Put all ingredients except the strawberries in a bowl and beat until smooth and creamy (an electric mixer works best). Using a large piece of cheesecloth, line a heart-shaped basket or *coeur à la crème* mold with the cheesecloth, extending the extra cloth past the edges of the mold, and fill with the cheese mixture. Fold the excess cloth back over the cheese, and set the basket or mold on a plate in the refrigerator for 3 days to drain off the whey. When ready to serve, unmold the heart onto a serving dish, and remove the cheesecloth. Garnish with strawberries.

Make It Light: Use nonfat cottage cheese for the cottage cheese, and 3 cups of Yogurt Cheese made with vanilla-flavored yogurt (p. 14) for the cream cheese and crème fraîche.

Make It Ahead: You need to make this 3 days in advance of serving.

CAKES, BARS, AND COOKIES

This wonderful cake appeared in my first cookbook, *The San Francisco Dinner Party Cookbook,* which is out of print. I've included it here because it's just too good to be "out of print."

CHOCOLATE-CHESTNUT CAKE
WITH CHOCOLATE CREAM

Serves 8 to 10

3 ounces bittersweet chocolate
4 tablespoons water
4 eggs, separated
4 ounces sugar (about ½ cup)

8 ounces canned chestnut purée
2 ounces cake flour (about ½ cup)
Chocolate Cream (see recipe below)

1. Put the chocolate and water in a heavy saucepan, or in the top of a double boiler, over low heat. When the chocolate has melted, remove from the heat and set aside to cool. Whisk the egg whites until soft peaks form and set aside.
2. In a mixing bowl, whisk the egg yolks and sugar together until thickened (use an electric mixer if you want). Add the melted chocolate, puréed chestnuts, and flour, and mix well. Carefully fold in the whisked egg whites.
3. Grease and flour the sides of two 8-inch cake pans and line the bottoms with parchment paper. Pour the batter into the pans, and bake for 40 minutes, in a preheated 350° oven. Allow cakes to cool in the pan about 10 minutes before unmolding onto a cake rack.
4. When the cakes are completely cooled, spread the Chocolate Cream between the two layers and over the top.

Make It Ahead: You can make this cake up to 8 hours in advance; refrigerate, and let stand at room temperature 1 hour before serving.

CHOCOLATE CREAM

3 ounces bittersweet chocolate
3 tablespoons water
2 egg yolks

2 tablespoons confectioners' sugar
1 tablespoon dark rum
1 cup crème fraîche, whipped

1. Put the chocolate and water in a heavy saucepan, or in the top of a double boiler over low heat. When the chocolate has melted, remove from the heat and cool slightly.
2. In a mixing bowl, combine the melted chocolate, egg yolks, confectioners' sugar, and rum. Whisk until fluffy and smooth. Fold in the whipped crème fraîche.

Originally, this cake was really rich and loaded with calories (it contained a half pound of butter, and a half pound of chocolate). I streamlined it drastically for our Light Cooking Basics class. It has been a big success, and when you taste it, I don't think you will miss all those calories at all.

HOMECHEF'S
LIGHT CHOCOLATE ESPRESSO DECADENCE
Serves 12

4 ounces pitted prunes (about ¾ cup)
1 cup brandy
7 ounces sugar (about 1 cup)
1 cup nonfat milk
6 tablespoons rice bran oil
1 tablespoon raspberry wine vinegar
2 teaspoons vanilla extract
6 ounces unbleached white flour
   (about 1¼ cups)

2 ounces unsweetened cocoa
   (about ⅓ cup)
1 tablespoon espresso powder
1 teaspoon baking soda
3 ounces bittersweet chocolate, melted
   candied violets and roses for garnish

1. Put the prunes and brandy in a small saucepan, cover, and warm over very low heat for 30 minutes, until the prunes are very soft. Cool and purée prunes and brandy in a blender or food processor until smooth.

2. Combine the puréed prunes, sugar, milk, oil, vinegar, and vanilla in a mixing bowl. Sift together the flour, cocoa, espresso powder, and baking soda, and add this to the prune mixture, blending until smooth.

3. Grease the sides of a 9- or 10-inch cake pan and line the bottom with parchment paper. Pour the batter into the pan, and bake in a preheated 350° oven for 30 to 40 minutes, or until the top of the cake feels firm to the touch. Allow to cool in the pan 10 minutes, then turn out to cool on a rack.

4. When cool, drizzle the melted chocolate randomly on top of the cake and decorate with candied violets and roses.

Make It Ahead: You can make this cake up to 1 day in advance. Keep covered until ready to serve.

Rebecca created this rich, rich dessert for a class called A Romantic Valentine's Dinner for Two. She baked it in individual heart molds, but you can use ramekins just as well. Don't overbake these little cakes and they will truly melt in your mouth.

MELTED CHOCOLATE CAKES

Serves 6

6 ounces semisweet chocolate
6 ounces unsalted butter
3 whole eggs plus 3 egg yolks
3 ounces granulated sugar (about ⅓ cup)

5 tablespoons flour
2 teaspoons Grand Marnier
  zest of 1 orange, finely chopped
  confectioners' sugar for garnish

1. Melt the chocolate and butter together in a heavy saucepan or in the top of a double boiler over low heat. Remove from the heat and set aside to cool. In a large bowl, beat the eggs, extra yolks, and granulated sugar together until soft peaks form. Sift in the flour, and fold it into the eggs.
2. Combine the melted chocolate, butter, Grand Marnier, and orange zest in a small bowl, and fold in about a cup of the flour-egg mixture. Return all to the larger bowl of batter and fold to combine.
3. Butter and flour six 4- or 5-inch individual heart-shaped molds or ramekins, and pour in the batter. Bake in a preheated 350° oven for 15 minutes. Allow to stand 5 minutes before unmolding; dust with confectioners' sugar, and serve warm.

Make It Ahead: You can have the batter mixed and poured into the molds up to 2 hours in advance. Put them in the oven about 20 minutes before you plan to serve them.

In Italian, *tiramisù* means "pick me up," which is an appropriate name for this very popular dessert. It is essentially a "compounded" confection made up of ladyfingers, a Marsala-flavored custard called *zabaglione,* and mascarpone, a rich fresh cream cheese. It's on the menu in many fine restaurants, so naturally, our students want to know how to make it at home. Here is our quick-and-easy version, guaranteed to lift everyone's spirit a little.

TIRAMISÙ
Serves 10 to 12

6 **egg yolks**
4 **ounces superfine sugar (about ½ cup)**
¾ **cup Marsala**
¼ **cup espresso coffee, cooled**
1 **pound mascarpone cheese**
2 **egg whites, whisked until soft peaks form**

24 **ladyfingers (or two 9-inch sponge cakes or pound cakes)**
¾ **cup rum**
3 **ounces unsweetened cocoa powder (about ½ cup)**
bittersweet chocolate shavings for garnish

1. In the top of a double boiler, over a medium heat, whisk the egg yolks and sugar until light colored. Slowly add the Marsala, whisking continuously, and keep whisking until the zabaglione thickens. Cool completely.
2. Beat espresso and mascarpone together until smooth, and fold into the zabaglione. Finally, fold in the whisked egg whites and set aside.
3. Line the bottom of a 10 × 14-inch serving dish with half the ladyfingers (if you are using cakes, line it with a layer of ½-inch-thick slices of cake). Sprinkle with the rum, spread with half the mascarpone mixture, and sprinkle with half the cocoa powder. Repeat the process with the remaining ladyfingers (or cake), mascarpone, and cocoa. Cover and refrigerate for 2 hours before serving. Garnish with chocolate shavings.

Make It Ahead: You can make this up to 6 hours in advance (allow a minimum of 2 hours for the *Tiramisù* to chill).

This is the same cheesecake recipe I used years ago in the very first HomeChef classes ever. I haven't made any changes in it at all, and people seem to love it just as it is. I can't imagine a richer more satisfying dessert — just remember, a small portion goes a long way.

HOMECHEF'S RICH CREAM CHEESECAKE

Serves 10 to 12

7 ounces graham cracker crumbs (about 1¼ cups)	1 teaspoon finely chopped lemon zest
13 ounces sugar (about 1 ¾ cups)	3 tablespoons fresh lemon juice
1 teaspoon ground cinnamon	2 pounds cream cheese
¼ cup melted butter	2 teaspoons vanilla powder or extract
	4 eggs, lightly beaten

1. In a bowl, mix the crumbs with 1 tablespoon sugar and the cinnamon. Stir in the melted butter and combine well. Press the mixture onto the bottom and sides of a 9-inch springform pan. Chill 1 hour.

2. Combine the lemon zest and juice and set aside. Using an electric mixer, beat the cheese until it is smooth. Add the vanilla and the remaining sugar and beat well. Add the eggs and mix gently. Stir in the lemon zest and juice.

3. Spoon the batter into the graham cracker shell and bake in a preheated 350° oven 45 minutes. Cool and refrigerate until well chilled, about 8 hours. Unmold before serving.

Make It Light: See HomeChef's Light and Easy Cheesecake (recipe follows).

Make It Ahead: You can make this cheesecake up to 1 day ahead and refrigerate. If you make it the same day, allow a minimum of 9 hours — 1 hour for baking, and 8 hours for chilling.

About five or six years ago, our students began asking for a lower fat version of our rich cheesecake. I created one by substituting Yogurt Cheese for the cream cheese in the rich version. Both are very good, and best of all, now you have a choice!

HOMECHEF'S LIGHT AND EASY CHEESECAKE
Serves 10 to 12

3 cups Yogurt Cheese (p. 14), made with vanilla-flavored low-fat or nonfat yogurt

3 ounces superfine sugar (about ⅓ cup)

3 tablespoons cornstarch

1 tablespoon vanilla powder or extract

1 teaspoon finely grated lemon zest, chopped

3 eggs, lightly beaten

1. In a large mixing bowl, combine the Yogurt Cheese, sugar, cornstarch, vanilla, and lemon zest; mix gently until blended, then stir in the eggs.
2. Pour into a lightly greased 9-inch springform pan, and bake in a preheated 325° oven until the center is set, approximately 45 minutes. Cool and refrigerate until completely chilled through, about 6 hours. Unmold before cutting and serving.

Make It Ahead: You can make this cheesecake up to 1 day ahead and refrigerate. If you make it the same day, allow a minimum of about 7 hours — 45 minutes to bake, and about 6 hours to chill.

This recipe comes from one of our instructors, Amy Sanders. These rich nut bars are featured before the Christmas holidays every year in a class we call Festive Cakes and Bars.

PECAN BARS

Makes about 30 bars

1¾ cups unsalted butter (14 ounces)
10 ounces unbleached white flour
      (about 2 cups)
2½ ounces confectioners' sugar
      (about ½ cup)
⅛ teaspoon fine sea salt

4 ounces brown sugar (½ cup,
      packed, plus 2 tablespoons)
4 ounces honey (6 tablespoons)
3 tablespoons crème fraîche
8 ounces pecans (about 1½ cups), toasted

1. Chill 8 ounces (1 cup) of the butter, and cut into 8 pieces. Combine flour, sugar, and salt in a food processor or electric mixer. Add the chilled butter and process until mixture resembles coarse meal (if by hand, cut the butter in with a pastry blender or two knives). Lightly grease the sides of a 9 × 12 × 2-inch pan and line the bottom with parchment paper. Press the mixture evenly into the pan and bake in a preheated 350° oven 20 minutes.
2. Meanwhile, melt and cool the remaining butter. Combine the melted butter, brown sugar, honey, and crème fraîche. Stir in the pecans.
3. When the pastry has baked 20 minutes, remove it from the oven, and spread the pecan mixture evenly over it. Bake an additional 25 minutes. Cool completely, and cut into diamonds or squares.

Make It Ahead: Can be made up to 1 day in advance.

Everyone loves these crispy, twice-baked Italian cookies. They are surprisingly easy to make, and without exception, our students always tell me they like these better than the ones that come in fancy packages at gourmet shops.

BISCOTTI
Makes about 3 dozen

8 tablespoons unsalted butter (4 ounces)

7 ounces sugar (about 1 cup)

2 teaspoons almond extract (or vanilla extract or powder)

3 large eggs, lightly beaten

10 ounces flour (about 2 cups)

½ teaspoon fine sea salt

2 teaspoons baking powder

5 ounces hazelnuts (about 1 cup), toasted and left whole or very coarsely chopped

1. In a mixing bowl, cream the butter until it is light (you can use an electric mixer if you like). Gradually beat in the sugar and extract (or powder), and then beat in the eggs. Stir in the flour, salt, and baking powder. Mix in the nuts thoroughly.

2. Line two baking sheets with parchment paper. Spoon a "loaf" of batter about 3 inches wide and 12 inches long onto each sheet; bake in a preheated 375° oven for 20 minutes, to a pale golden color (they should still be soft). Transfer from the pan to a rack and cool about 30 minutes. Cut each loaf into diagonal slices about ½ to ¾ inches thick. Arrange the slices flat on the baking sheets, and bake at 375° an additional 15 minutes or until lightly toasted. Cool completely, and store in airtight containers.

Make It Ahead: You can store these biscotti in airtight containers for up to a week.

I always like to take these moist, cakelike brownies along on picnics, but of course they're good for just about any occasion you can think of.

BLACK AND WHITE DOUBLE FUDGE BROWNIES
Makes about 30

5 ounces bittersweet chocolate
1 cup unsalted butter (8 ounces)
3 large eggs
7 ounces sugar (about 1 cup)
8 ounces unbleached white flour
   (about 1½ cups)

5 ounces white chocolate chips
   (about 1 cup)
5 ounces walnuts, toasted in a
   preheated 300° oven for 5 minutes
   (1 cup)

1. Melt the bittersweet chocolate and butter together in a small saucepan or in the top of a double boiler over very low heat, then remove from the heat and cool slightly.
2. Whisk the eggs and sugar together in a mixing bowl until frothy. Add the melted chocolate and butter and blend well. Add the flour and stir until mixed. Fold in the white chocolate chips and walnuts.
3. Line a 9 × 13-inch baking pan with parchment paper. Spread the batter in the pan, and bake in a preheated 350° oven 25 to 30 minutes, until the edges pull away from the pan. Allow to cool, then turn out and cut.

Make It Ahead: Will keep for up to 3 days. Cool completely and store in airtight containers.

I will never forget these cookies, because my grandmother *always* had them on hand. I think the recipe must be a standard one of the thirties or forties, put out by a company manufacturing peanut butter. However, it *still* works, and they still taste very wonderful to me.

GRANDMA ADA'S PEANUT BUTTER COOKIES
Makes about 3 dozen cookies

¾ cup creamy peanut butter
4 tablespoons each unsalted butter
   and solid vegetable shortening
9 ounces light brown sugar
   (1¼ cups firmly packed)

3 tablespoons milk
1 tablespoon vanilla extract
1 egg
8½ ounces flour (about 1¾ cups)
¾ teaspoon each salt and baking soda

1. Combine peanut butter, butter, vegetable shortening, brown sugar, milk, and vanilla in a large bowl, and beat until well blended (use an electric mixer if you like). Beat in the egg.
2. Combine the flour, salt, and baking soda (sifting is not necessary); add to the peanut butter mixture, and mix until blended. Drop by teaspoonfuls 2 inches apart onto an ungreased baking sheet. Flatten slightly in a crisscross pattern with the tines of a fork. Bake in a preheated 375° oven for 7 or 8 minutes, until just browned.

Make It Ahead: These cookies will keep for a week. Cool completely and pack in an airtight container.

COBBLERS, CRISPS, AND PIES

A cobbler is a baked fruit dessert with a rich biscuit topping, a perfect balance of sweetness and tartness. Since you will be serving this from the baking dish, consider the dish as an ingredient and use one that is attractive enough to bring to the table. Try substituting other fruits and berries for the raspberries and peaches in this recipe.

RASPBERRY-PEACH COBBLER

Serves 8 to 10

4 cups raspberries

2 pounds peaches, peeled, pitted, and cut into ½-inch slices

3 ounces sugar (about ½ cup) or more to taste

zest of 1 lemon, finely chopped

2 tablespoons fresh lemon juice

3 tablespoons unsalted butter

Biscuit Dough (recipe follows)

confectioners' sugar

1. In a 2½- or 3-quart baking dish, combine raspberries and peaches with the sugar. Sprinkle with lemon zest and lemon juice, and dot with butter.

2. Roll the dough out to ¼-inch thickness, in the shape of the baking dish. Trim slightly smaller than the dish, and crimp edges with your fingers. Lay the dough over the fruit so the edges do not quite touch the sides of the dish. Cut several steam vents in dough, at least ¼ inch wide and deep enough to expose fruit. (Or the dough can be rolled out and cut into 10 or 12 diamonds, rounds, or squares, and evenly arranged on top of the fruit. This way, each person gets a neat serving.)

3. Bake in a preheated 400° oven for 30 minutes, or until the crust is browned and fruit is tender. Allow to cool 30 minutes, then dust with confectioners' sugar and serve warm.

Make It Light: Omit the butter.

Make It Ahead: You can assemble the cobbler (steps 1 and 2) up to 3 hours in advance. Put it in the oven about an hour before you plan to serve it (step 3).

BISCUIT DOUGH

10 ounces unbleached white flour
     (about 2 cups)
 1 teaspoon fine sea salt
 1 tablespoon each baking powder
     and sugar

 4 tablespoons unsalted butter,
     chilled (2 ounces)
 1 cup heavy cream

Combine flour, salt, baking powder, and sugar in the bowl of a food processor or electric mixer. Add the butter and process 5 seconds, until the mixture is crumbly; add the cream and process until dough holds together in a ball, about 20 seconds more. You can also make the dough by hand, using a fork or pastry blender, cutting the butter into the dry ingredients until the mixture is crumbly, then quickly stirring in the cream to form a dough. Do not overwork mixture. The dough can be used immediately or wrapped in plastic and refrigerated.

Make It Light: Substitute ½ cup water and ½ cup cream for the 1 cup cream.

Make It Ahead: You can make the dough up to 1 day in advance. Wrap it in plastic wrap and refrigerate. Remove from refrigerator 30 minutes before rolling out.

Crisps — or crumbles, as they are sometimes called — are similar to cobblers, but they have a lighter, crunchier topping instead of a biscuit topping. Choose any fruit you wish — apples, pears, peaches, nectarines, plums, cherries, and all kinds of berries work well. The only criteria is that they be perfectly ripe. For a richer dessert, serve the crisp with ice cream or whipped cream.

FRESH FRUIT CRISP

Serves 8 or 10

2 pounds ripe fruit (see above)
5 ounces brown sugar (about ¾ cup
    firmly packed)
1 tablespoon fresh lemon juice
3 ounces rolled oats (about 1 cup)

2 ounces unbleached white flour
    (about ½ cup)
4 tablespoons unsalted butter,
    melted (2 ounces)
½ teaspoon fine sea salt

1. Wash and prepare the fruit as necessary (peel, core, pit, etc.). Large fruit should be quartered or thickly sliced, but don't cut it up too small. Combine the fruit with half the sugar and arrange over the bottom of a lightly greased shallow baking dish. Sprinkle with lemon juice.
2. In a small bowl, combine the remaining sugar, oats, flour, butter, and salt. Mix until crumbly and spread over the fruit.
3. Bake in a preheated 375° oven for 30 minutes, or until fruit is tender and the topping is crisp. Cool 30 minutes, and serve.

Make It Light: Reduce the amount of butter to 2 tablespoons.

Make It Ahead: You can assemble the crisp (steps 1 and 2) up to 3 hours in advance. Put it in the oven about an hour before you plan to serve it (step 3).

An old-fashioned American pie, especially good when the weather turns hot.

FRESH STRAWBERRY PIE

Serves 8 to 10

3 pints fresh strawberries, hulled, rinsed, and dried
7 ounces granulated sugar (about 1 cup)
3 tablespoons cornstarch
½ cup water
1 tablespoon unsalted butter
1 prebaked 10- or 11-inch pie shell (p. 251)
1 cup heavy whipping cream, whipped, for garnish

1. Select a few perfect berries for garnish; then crush enough berries to fill a one-cup measure. Cut the remainder in half and set aside.
2. Combine the sugar, cornstarch, water, and the crushed berries in a small saucepan. Cook over medium heat, stirring frequently, until the mixture comes to a boil. Reduce heat to low and continue cooking, stirring constantly, until thickened and clear (about 2 minutes). Remove from the heat and stir in the butter until melted. Allow the mixture to cool.
3. Arrange the halved berries cut side down in the baked pie shell and pour the cooled mixture over them. Gently shake the pie plate so the mixture seeps down around the berries. Chill the pie several hours. Garnish with whipped cream and the reserved whole berries just before serving.

Make It Light: Omit the whipped cream garnish.

Make It Ahead: You can make this up to 4 hours in advance and refrigerate. Add garnish before serving.

This is one of the richest and best pies I have ever tasted. It's a regular part of our Cooking with Chocolate class.

CHOCOLATE PIE

Serves 8 to 10

5 ounces walnuts (about 1 cup), toasted and finely chopped
5 ounces superfine sugar (about ¾ cup)
1 ounce unsweetened cocoa powder (about ¼ cup)
5 eggs, separated

1 teaspoon vanilla powder or extract
2 tablespoons chopped orange zest,
¾ cup unsalted butter (6 ounces), melted and cooled
1 unbaked 10-inch pie shell (p. 251)

1. Combine walnuts, sugar, and cocoa in a large bowl and mix well. Add the egg yolks, vanilla, orange zest, and melted butter, and beat until thick and smooth.
2. Whisk the egg whites to soft peaks and fold into the chocolate mixture. Spoon filling into pie shell, and bake 40 minutes in a preheated 375° oven. Allow to cool 20 minutes, then chill several hours before serving.

Make It Ahead: You can make this pie up to 6 hours in advance; refrigerate until serving.

This is delicious and patriotic all at the same time, and a lot of fun to serve!

FOURTH OF JULY CELEBRATION TART

Serves 8

1 pint raspberries, rinsed and dried
1 pint blueberries, rinsed and dried
1 pint strawberries rinsed, dried, and sliced

1 prebaked 10-inch tart or pie shell (p. 251)
½ cup clear wine or fruit jelly
1 tablespoon water
1 quart vanilla ice cream

Arrange the berries in the tart shell in concentric circles, alternating the colors. Combine the jelly with the water, warming it enough so it can be spread easily; brush it over the berries. Serve with scoops of vanilla ice cream.

Make It Light: Omit the ice cream.

Make It Ahead: You can make this tart up to 4 hours in advance. Do not refrigerate.

Tarte Tatin is a classic French pastry that is enjoying a renewed popularity, at least among our students. According to the historians, this upside down apple pie was created when the two Tatin sisters baked their father's favorite caramel-topped apple pie and accidentally dropped it upside down on the floor. The sisters scooped it up with a baker's paddle, then slid it onto a serving plate with the apples and caramel now on the bottom, and the pastry on top. The result was a huge success, and the tart is made that way to this day, without being dropped, of course!

TARTE TATIN
Serves 8

7 ounces sugar (about 1 cup)
3 tablespoons water
3 pounds tart apples (about 6), peeled, cored, and cut into 8 pieces each

4 tablespoons unsalted butter (2 ounces)
½ recipe HomeChef's Basic Pastry Dough (p. 251)

1. Combine half the sugar and the water in a small skillet or saucepan, and cook over high heat until the sugar turns to a golden caramel. Pour the caramel into the bottom of a 9- or 10-inch cake pan, tilting the pan so that the caramel coats the bottom.
2. Lay the pieces of apple over the caramel, sprinkle with the remaining sugar, and dot with butter.
3. Roll out the pastry about ¼ inch thick, and about 2 inches larger than the pan all around. Lay the pastry on top of the apples, and tuck the extra pastry down around the inside of the pan. Prick the pastry in several places with a fork.
4. Bake in a preheated 375° oven, about 45 minutes — until crust is golden brown. Let cool about 30 minutes, then turn it out onto a serving platter, so that the crust forms the base, with the caramelized apples on top. Serve warm.

Make It Light: Reduce the butter to 2 tablespoons.

Make It Ahead: You can make this pie up to 4 hours in advance through step 3, and refrigerate. Put the pie in the oven about 1½ hours before serving (step 4).

This basic pastry dough can be used in any recipe that calls for either an *unbaked* or *prebaked* pie or tart shell. The recipe yields about 1 pound of dough, enough for an 9-, 10-, or 11-inch pie or tart shell. Any unused dough can be wrapped well and stored in the freezer for up to 1 month. Directions are given for making the dough by hand, but you can use a food processor or electric mixer, as well.

HOMECHEF'S BASIC PASTRY DOUGH

8 ounces unbleached white flour
  (1½ cups)
½ teaspoon salt
10 tablespoons unsalted butter
  (5 ounces), chilled

⅛ teaspoon vinegar or fresh
  lemon juice
4 to 5 tablespoons ice water

1. Combine the flour and salt. Cut the butter into 8 pieces; using a pastry blender or two knives, work the butter into the flour until the mixture is crumbly.
2. Mixing the dough lightly, add the vinegar or lemon juice, and then add the water gradually (you may not need it all or you may need a little more), until the dough gathers together into a smooth ball.
3. Flatten the dough, sprinkle with a little flour, wrap in plastic, and allow to rest in the refrigerator for at least 1 hour (or up to 8 hours) before rolling out.
4. On a lightly floured surface, roll the dough out into a circle slightly larger than the pie or tart pan. Roll the pastry around the rolling pin and unroll the pastry into the pie or tart pan. With the knuckles of your fingers, gently ease the pastry into the mold, allowing for shrinkage. If this is for a tart, roll the pin over the edges of the tin to cut off excess pastry. For a pie, trim the edge with a paring knife, and decorate the rim of the pastry by gently pressing it with the tines of the fork. Chill 30 minutes before filling and baking.

To prebake the pie or tart shell, roll out the dough and fit it into the pan as described above. Line the dough with parchment paper, and fill to the brim with pie weights. (You can use rice or beans, instead, but the shell will retain its shape best with ceramic or metal pie weights, available in gourmet kitchen stores.) Bake in a preheated 375° oven about 20 minutes, or until the edges begin to brown. Remove from the oven, take out the weights and parchment, and return to the oven for an additional 5 minutes to brown the bottom crust. Transfer to a rack and cool.

GLOSSARY

al dente An Italian phrase used to describe pasta cooked just enough to offer a slight resistance when bitten into (literally, "to the teeth"). Pasta that is cooked al dente is neither undercooked nor mushy.

gratin A preparation in which the food is sprinkled with bread crumbs and/or grated cheese and baked or broiled until brown. Also used to describe the oven-proof dish used to make a gratin.

bain-marie See **water bath.**

basmati rice An aromatic long-grained rice from South Asia. If unavailable, substitute with long-grain white rice.

baste To brush or spoon a sauce, pan juices, or other liquid over foods during cooking.

bisque A thick, creamy soup, classically made with shellfish, but sometimes made of puréed vegetables or meats.

blanch To plunge briefly into boiling water, to set the color and flavor of vegetables, or to loosen the skin of tomatoes or peaches, or to remove excess salt, as from bacon. Foods that have been blanched are usually cooked a second time until done. Also known as parboiling or preboiling.

bouquet garni A small packet of fresh or dried herbs (parsley, celery, bay leaves, cloves, etc.), typically wrapped in cheesecloth and tied with string to facilitate its removal. The bundle is added to soups or braised dishes while they are cooking, then removed and discarded before serving.

braise To cook slowly in a small amount of liquid in a covered casserole or pot. This method is often used with tougher cuts of meat or poultry. Also known as stewing.

caramelize To heat sugar until it turns a pale brown caramel color.

clarified butter Butter that has been made clear by heating it, then separating out and discarding the milk solids.

egg wash A mixture of egg and water or milk, brushed on pastry to glaze it.

macerate To place food, usually fruit in a liquid in order that the fruit absorb certain flavors.

parboil See **blanch**

preboil See **blanch**

poach To cook gently in liquid, keeping the liquid below the boiling point.

rice bran oil An unsaturated oil, derived from the bran of brown rice. It is an all-purpose cooking oil with a light, delicate taste, ideal for baking or sautéing.

reduce To boil a liquid, such as a sauce or stock, to thicken it and/or concentrate the flavors.

superfine sugar A very fine granulated sugar which dissolves so quickly that it is sometimes called instant sugar. Available in boxes in most grocery stores.

sauté A French term meaning to cook very rapidly in an open skillet. The equivalent American term is pan-fry.

stir-fry To cook rapidly over high fire with a small amount of oil, stirring all the while. Typically done with food that has been cut into small pieces. A basic method in Asian cooking.

water bath   A pan of hot water in which smaller containers of food are set then placed in the oven to bake. The hot water distributes the heat evenly, and produces steam, which keeps the food from drying out. This method is often used in making custards, soufflé puddings, and pâtés or terrines. The water in the bath should come about halfway up the sides of the inner container. If you need to add water during the cooking, it should be hot.

whey   A clear liquid that separates from milk products such as yogurt or some fresh cheeses, when they are drained.

zest   The outer, colored part of citrus fruits. It is usually grated and chopped, then used as a flavoring ingredient.

INDEX

NOTES

NOTES

NOTES

NOTES

NOTES

NOTES

NOTES

NOTES

NOTES

NOTES

NOTES

NOTES